Quantitative Methods for Financial Analysis

SECOND EDITION

Edited by

Stephen J. Brown, Ph.D.

Mark P. Kritzman, CFA

Sponsored by
The Institute of
Chartered Financial Analysts

DOW JONES–IRWIN
Homewood, Illinois 60430

Project editor: Karen J. Murphy
Production manager: Bette K. Ittersagen
Compositor: Arcata Graphics/Kingsport
Typeface: 11/13 Times Roman
Printer: R. R. Donnelley & Sons Company

Library of Congress Cataloging-in-Publication Data

Quantitative methods for financial analysis/edited by Stephen J.
  Brown, Mark P. Kritzman; sponsored by the Institute of Chartered
  Financial Analysts.—2nd ed.
      p.   cm.
    ISBN 1-55623-282-9.—ISBN 1-55623-306-X (pbk.)
      1. Investments—Decision making—Mathematics.   2. Investments—
  —Decision making—Statistical models.   I. Brown, Stephen J.
  II. Kritzman, Mark P.   III. Institute of Chartered Financial
  Analysts.
  HG4515.3.Q36   1990
  332.6'01'51—dc20

                                                    89–23271
                                                    CIP

Printed in the United States of America

1 2 3 4 5 6 7 8 9 0 DO 6 5 4 3 2 1 0 9

Quantitative Methods for Financial Analysis

BIOGRAPHIES

Christopher B. Barry is Professor of Finance and holder of the Robert and Maria Lowdon Chair in Business Administration at Texas Christian University. Previously he was chairman of the Finance Department at Southern Methodist University and was the founding director of SMU's Center for the Study of Financial Institutions and Markets. He teaches and conducts research in the fields of investments, portfolio theory, and corporate finance. He holds a B.S. degree from Georgia Tech and a D.B.A. from Indiana University. He has previously been on the faculties of the University of Texas at Austin and the University of Florida. His research in finance has been published in *Journal of Finance, Journal of Financial Economics, Journal of Financial and Quantitative Analysis, Journal of Portfolio Management,* and other journals.

Stephen Brown is Yamaichi Faculty Fellow and Professor of Finance at the Leonard N. Stern School of Business (Graduate Division), New York University. He graduated from Monash University in Australia and studied at the University of Chicago, earning an M.B.A. in 1974 and a Ph.D in 1976. Following successive appointments as a member of the technical staff at Bell Laboratories and associate professor at Yale University he joined the faculty of New York University in 1986. He is vice president of the Western Finance Association, currently serves on the Board of Directors of the American Finance Association, and is an editor of *Review of Financial Studies,* published

v

by Oxford University Press. He has published numerous articles and three books on finance and economics-related areas. He has been retained as a consultant on investment issues both in the United States and Japan and has served as an expert witness for the U.S. Department of Justice.

Andrew H. Chen is a Distinguished Professor of Finance in the Edwin L. Cox School of Business at Southern Methodist University. He received an M.A. in economics and a Ph.D. in finance from the University of California, Berkeley. He previously taught at the State University of New York at Buffalo; the University of California, Berkeley; and Ohio State University. He is editor of *Research in Finance*, published by JAI Press, and is currently associate editor of *Journal of Money, Credit, and Banking* and *The Financial Review*. He is a former associate editor of *Journal of Financial and Quantitative Analysis, Management Science*, and *Journal of Economics and Business*. His articles have been published in books and journals, including *Journal of Financial Economics, Journal of Financial and Quantitative Analysis*, and *Journal of Futures Markets*.

Margaret A. Corwin is Managing Director of the products division of Ibbotson Associates in Chicago. Formerly she was the financial vice president for Abbot Contractors and prior to that was senior research associate for the American Planning Association. She holds a CPA from the University of Illinois and master's degrees from both the University of Chiago and Loyola University.

H. Russell Fogler is a partner in the equity management firm of Aronson and Fogler. Previously he was a professor of management science at the University of Florida and an academic consultant to the Frank Russell Company on performance measurement, asset allocation, and optimization. He has authored several books and published over 25 articles in journals such as *Journal of Finance, Journal of Portfolio Management, Journal of Financial and Quantitative Analysis, Management Science, Decision Sciences*, and *Accounting Review*. He has been an associate editor of *Financial Management* and is currently on the editorial board of *Journal of Portfolio Management*.

Susan Hudson-Wilson, CFA, is a Vice President of John Hancock Properties, Inc., in Boston. Prior to that she was regional director, real estate, in the Investment Division at UNUM Life Corporation, Portland, Maine. At Union Mutual she developed the Real Estate Market Index and its portfolio implications and applications. Prior to joining Union Mutual, she was a senior economist at Data Resources in Lexington, Massachusetts, where she constructed and managed various econometric forecasting models. She graduated from the University of Vermont in 1976 with a B.A. in economics and received her M.A. in economics in 1982 from Boston University.

Roger G. Ibbotson is Professor in the Practice of Finance, Yale School of Management, and is also president of Ibbotson Associates, an investment consulting firm in Chicago and New Haven. He is coauthor (with Rex Sinquefield) of *Stocks, Bonds, Bills, and Inflation,* coauthor (with Gary Brinson) of *Investment Markets: Gaining the Performance Advantage,* and coauthor (with Thomas S. Coleman and Lawrence Fisher) of *U.S. Treasury Yield Curves: 1926–1988.* He has also written numerous scholarly articles. He previously taught at the University of Chicago, where he was executive director of the Center for Research in Security Prices. He received a B.S. from Purdue University, an M.B.A. from Indiana University, and a Ph.D. from the University of Chicago.

Mark P. Kritzman, CFA, is a partner of Windham Capital Management, an investment advisory firm located in New York City. Prior to cofounding WCM he was a general partner of New Amsterdam Partners and, before that, a vice president in the Investment Management Group at Bankers Trust Company. He also held investment positions at AT&T and The Equitable Life Assurance Society. He is a past president of the Investment Technology Association, a member of the Prize Committee of The Institute for Quantitative Research in Finance, a member of the Candidate Curriculum Committee of The Institute of Chartered Financial Analysts, and a member of the Review Board of the ICFA's Research Foundation. He has published numerous articles on the application of financial theory to investment management. He holds a B.S. degree in economics from St. John's University and an M.B.A. from New York University.

Since the publication of the first edition of *Quantitative Methods for Financial Analysis* in 1986, this book has been studied extensively by thousands of CFA candidates, financial practitioners, and professors and students of finance. Consequently we have been the beneficiary of numerous criticisms and suggestions. We have taken all of these comments seriously and have made an effort to address them in this revision.

Most of the changes reflect elaboration and elucidation of various notions. However, at the suggestion of many readers, we have included additional material. In particular we have added a discussion of classification techniques such as cluster analysis in the chapter on the introduction to quantitative methods. Also we have expanded the chapter on derivative securities to include a discussion of financial futures. In the chapter on asset allocation we have added a discussion of currency risk and tactical asset allocation; and based on many of the insights from André Perold and William Sharpe's paper entitled "Dynamic Strategies for Asset Allocation" we have attempted to convey the essence of dynamic strategies within the framework of payoff diagrams. We have also included sample problems and questions at the end of each of the chapters. Finally, we have added an appendix and a glossary of terms. The Appendix presents a primer on statistical concepts for those who require such a review. It contains a cumulative normal distribution table and a guide for its use, as well as a numerical approximation procedure that can easily be used in spreadsheet software. In addition it includes an introduction and motivation for the use of logarithms in financial analysis.

Despite these revisions the purpose and focus of the book remain the same: to review the use of quantitative methods in the context of the investment decision-making process.

- The mathematics of valuation can help determine the value of an investment, based upon what is known about the potential cash flow resulting from the investment.
- Statistics and data analysis can be used to simplify and refine the information relating to future cash flows.
- These techniques can also be used to allow the analyst to account for the uncertainty of future cash flows, the risk inherent in the investment process.

As with the first edition, our approach is to emphasize the limitations of quantitative methods as well as their merits and to underscore the need to combine them with sound practical judgment.

Chapter One introduces the quantitative methods commonly used in financial analysis. Most of the procedures described in this chapter are readily amenable to spreadsheet software; hence we focus on the intuition of these procedures with limited mathematical development.

The remaining chapters demonstrate how the procedures presented in Chapter One can be applied in a variety of specialized areas of financial analysis. Chapters Two, Three, and Four cover, respectively, the application of quantitative methods to equity, fixed income, and real estate analysis. Chapter Five covers quantitative methods within the context of derivative securities analysis, while Chapter Six and Chapter Seven deal with asset allocation and performance measurement, respectively.

We hope the reader will appreciate the commonality of the quantitative concepts used in specialized areas of financial analysis. It should be of some comfort to the financial analysts that seemingly disparate areas of specialization have a basic unity in terms of the underlying quantitative concepts. This unity implies that the financial analyst who understands a few basic quantitative principles will be able to recognize and use the appropriate quantitative methods to solve new and unfamiliar problems.

Stephen J. Brown
Mark P. Kritzman

CONTENTS

Introduction to Quantitative Methods

Stephen J. Brown

This chapter introduces quantitative methods and shows some of the ways in which they can be applied in the context of the investment decision-making process. Mathematics of Valuation covers the set of techniques that can be used to relate future cash flows to current value and to measure the return on alternative investments. The next section, Statistics and Data Analysis, introduces the statistical procedures that can be used to characterize and simplify the available information. Finally, Uncertainty and Valuation addresses procedures for measuring the impact of uncertainty on the valuation process. Subsequent chapters will show how these procedures are actually used in the analysis of equity, fixed income, real estate, and derivative securities and how they are applied in asset allocation and performance measurement.

MATHEMATICS OF VALUATION

Present Value

All investments can be characterized by the cash flows they generate. These cash flows represent cash received by the investor as a result of the decision to invest, including income received over the holding period of the investment

1

as well as the cash received from the ultimate sale or disposal of the asset, after all taxes are paid. Valuation, then, is simply a problem of comparing alternative cash flows.

Present value answers the question "How much money must I set aside in a comparable investment of similar risk to *duplicate exactly* the cash flows of this investment?" The following example illustrates the concept of present value.

Example: You are solicited to participate in an Oklahoma oil venture that you are told will be worth $1.6 million one year from today, after the well is drilled. One thousand shares are to be offered at $1,000 a share, and the shareholders will share equally in the proceeds from the drilling.

The apparent simplicity of this example is deceptive. Assume that all tax implications are accounted for and that the commitment must be made today. Is the $1.6 million estimated value one year from now a reliable estimate? We will assume that it is, for now. If similar investments of a comparable risk earn 20 percent per year after taxes, what are 100 shares of this oil venture worth?

If the investor were to invest $133,333 in the alternative investment, he or she would expect to receive $160,000 at the end of the year:

$$\$133{,}333 \times (1 + .20) = \$160{,}000$$

Alternatively $133,333 could be thought of as the maximum amount the investor could borrow against the $160,000 that represents the future value of the oil venture if investments of a similar risk require a 20 percent return:

$$\text{Maximum} = \frac{\$160{,}000}{1 + .20} = \$133{,}333$$

In this sense, the oil participation is worth $133,333. At $100,000 the oil participation is "undervalued" to the extent that the investor could borrow $133,333 and invest $100,000 in the oil venture, leaving the investor better off by $33,333. This amount represents the extent to which the oil venture is undervalued and is, in a sense, the arbitrage profit to the investor for financing the venture. The extent of this undervaluation is referred to as the *net present value* of the venture. In other words the net present value is the present value of the cash received from the venture minus the initial investment.

Would it be worthwhile to receive the proceeds from the oil venture in two annual installments of $80,000 each, for a total of $160,000? The first installment, due a year from today, can be matched by $66,667 now invested at 20 percent interest. If money invested for two years requires a return of 20 percent per year as well, then $55,555 invested for two years will match the second installment that represents the balance of the proceeds:

$$\$55,555 \times (1 + .20)^2 = \$80,000$$

or

$$\$55,555 = \frac{\$80,000}{(1 + .20)^2}$$

In other words the present value of the two-installment plan is the sum of $66,667 and $55,555, or $122,222:

$$\text{Present value} = \frac{\$80,000}{1 + .20} + \frac{\$80,000}{(1 + .20)^2} = \$122,222$$

This amount is less than the value of the $133,333 single-installment plan. Typically, investments that commit funds for two or more years require a return somewhat in excess of the one-year return. In this case the value of the installment plan is even less.

This example suggests the most basic formula in financial mathematics: the present value formula. Let us denote by symbols the cash flow of the investment one period from now as C_1, the cash flow two periods from now as C_2, that of three periods from now as C_3, and so on. We will also represent the return on alternative investments, or *discount rate*, for one period as r_1, the two-period return as r_2 per period, and the three-period return as r_3 per period. The present value formula is

$$\text{Present value} = \frac{C_1}{1 + r_1} + \frac{C_2}{(1 + r_2)^2} + \frac{C_3}{(1 + r_3)^3} + \cdots$$

where

$C_1, C_2, C_3 = $ Cash flows for periods 1, 2, and 3.
$r_1, r_2, r_3 = $ Rates of return for periods 1, 2, and 3.

This formula is completely general and can be applied to a wide range of investment problems. It appears complex yet is actually quite straightforward to apply, given access to personal computers with spreadsheet software.

While present value discounts all cash flows of the investment to the present, the analogous concept of *future value* brings the cash flows to the ending holding period of the investment. The measure of future value assumes all cash flows from the venture are reinvested in similar-risk ventures for the duration of the holding period. At that point the resulting cumulative cash value is compared to what would have been obtained had the original investment been made elsewhere.

In the oil participation the future value of the cash flows is simply $160,000, the value of the venture at the end of the year. This may be compared to $120,000, which is the amount that would have been obtained had the money been invested elsewhere. Thus the project is undervalued to the extent of $40,000 in terms of dollars next year or $33,333 in terms of dollars today:

$$\frac{\$40,000}{1 + .20} = \$33,333$$

This answer is the same as before.

Future value is often used in the context of evaluating money managers, where the question is asked, "To what value would a dollar have grown if given to this particular manager to manage?" For more general valuation problems it is less useful, since the holding periods of different investments are rarely comparable.

Much of the apparent complexity of financial mathematics arises from the use of shortcut versions of the present value formula. Such shortcuts generally antedate the ready availability of spreadsheet software and use simplifying assumptions to make the calculations easier. One such simplified assumption is that the interest rate is not affected by the period of the investment.[1] Each formula we shall discuss is in fact a special case of the present value formula. However because these special cases *appear* so very different, they have in many cases taken on a life of their own.

Perpetuity Formula.   The first special case is known as the *perpetuity formula*. It is sometimes convenient to make the simplified assumption that a particular investment will generate forever a steady cash flow.

---

[1] The way interest rates vary as a function of the period of the investment is called the *yield curve;* the assumption that all interest rates are the same is referred to as a *flat yield curve.*

> *Example:* Sure Thing Energy Associates Limited is expected to pay an annual dividend of $10 per share for the foreseeable future. How much is a share of Sure Thing worth today?

If the required return on equivalent investments is 20 percent regardless of the period of the investment, then $50 invested at that rate will also generate $10 annually for the foreseeable future:

$$\$50 \times .20 = \$10$$

or

$$\$50 = \frac{\$10}{.20}$$

Thus the present value of the dividends of Sure Thing is $50, and that is as much as one would pay for a share of Sure Thing. The perpetuity formula is

$$\text{Present value} = \frac{C}{r}$$

where

C = (Constant) cash flow received at the end of each period.
r = (Constant) rate of return.

This formula is actually a special case of the earlier formula where there are an infinite number of cash flows (C_1, C_2, C_3, and so on) that are all the same and equal to C and where all rates of return (r_1, r_2, r_3, and all other rates of return) are equal to each other. The assumption that the investor will receive a given cash flow forever may seem a little extreme. Fortunately it does little damage where cash flows are expected to persist for a long period of time (though not forever) and where the required rate of return is high. It is frequently used to value real estate investments and preferred stock issues that satisfy these conditions and where the simplicity of the formula recommends it to analysts.

The formula requires some modification where the cash flows increase over time. Suppose in the above example the dividends of Sure Thing were expected to grow at the rate of 5 percent per annum: $10 next year, $10.50 the following year, and so on. If one thinks about the amount of money that must be set aside at 20 percent to match this investment, then $50 would match *this* year's dividend but would be $.50 short for the next dividend. However, $66.67 at 20 percent would yield $10 *plus* a 5 percent growth in the principal amount of $66.67, sufficient to pay out $10.50 next year and further increments in the following years. In other words,

$$\$66.67 \times .20 = \$10 + (\$66.67 \times .05)$$

Next year the principal will equal $70, which is 5 percent greater than $66.67. At that time,

$$\$70 \times .20 = \$10.50 + (\$70 \times .05)$$

For this reason $66.67 is the present value of the growing perpetuity. This amount must be set aside at 20 percent interest to match exactly the cash flows of the investment; it represents the maximum one would pay to acquire the sequence of growing dividends. In other words,

$$\$66.67 \times (.20 - .05) = \$10$$

or

$$\$66.67 = \frac{\$10}{.20 - .05}$$

and $66.67 is the maximum one would pay for a share of Sure Thing. In this particular application the formula for the present value of a growing perpetuity is

$$\text{Present value} = \frac{C}{r - g}$$

where

C = Cash flow next period.
g = Rate of growth of cash flows.
r = (Constant) rate of return.

This formula is often referred to as the *dividend discount model,* or *dividend growth model,* where C is the next dividend, r is the required return by investors, and g is the expected rate of growth of future dividends. This stock valuation model is the most popular and appears in many guises (for example, if value and the initial dividend payment are each divided by the earnings of the firm and the formula is rearranged in terms of accounting identities, we have what is known as the *price-earnings ratio model*). After some tedious algebra, it is possible to see that this formula is also a special case of the original present value formula.

Annuity Formula. Another formula that is very commonly used in analysis is the *annuity formula*.

Example: Oiler Bank and Trust (OBT) has a note backed by an equipment lien that obliges Sure Thing to pay OBT 10 annual installments of $10,000, with the next payment due one year from today. How much is the note worth to OBT?

Assume again that the required return is 20 percent. The Sure Thing note could be thought of as two agreements:

1. An agreement by Sure Thing to make annual payments to OBT in perpetuity. Such an agreement would be worth $50,000 to OBT:

$$\frac{\$10,000}{.20} = \$50,000$$

2. An agreement by OBT to return the note to Sure Thing 10 years from now. This action would cost OBT $50,000 at that time (the value in 10 years' time of the continuing perpetuity) or $8,075 today:

$$\frac{\$50,000}{(1 + .20)^{10}} = \$8,075$$

Thus the note is worth $41,925 today, or $50,000 less $8,075.

An annuity that promises a fixed amount on a periodic basis for a finite period of time is simply the difference between a perpetuity and an appropriately discounted perpetuity. The formula follows:

$$\text{Present value} = C \times \left[\frac{1}{r} - \left(\frac{1}{r} \times \frac{1}{(1 + r)^N}\right)\right]$$

where

C = (Constant) cash flow per period starting next period.
N = Number of periodic payments.
r = (Constant) rate of return.

To see how this formula is applied, consider the two-installment example considered earlier, where $80,000 is received next year and the balance of $80,000 is received two years from today. The sum of $80,000 represents the fixed payment C, and $N = 2$ (two payments). Present value then is

$$\text{Present value} = \$80{,}000 \times \left[\frac{1}{.20} - \left(\frac{1}{.20} \times \frac{1}{(1 + .20)^2}\right)\right]$$

$$= \$80{,}000 \times \left[5 - \left(5 \times \frac{1}{1.44}\right)\right]$$

$$= \$80{,}000 \times 1.5278 = \$122{,}222$$

This amount is the same as derived earlier and illustrates that the annuity formula is also a special case of the more general present value formula.

A Caution.   The perpetuity, growing perpetuity, and annuity formulas are tools that can simplify present value arithmetic. But like all tools they must be handled with great care. Because the formulas assume interest rates to be invariant to the term of the investment, analysts implicitly assume yield curves are level, or "flat," when they employ them. This assumption can be particularly hazardous in bond analysis. The dividend discount model sometimes assumes dividends will grow at a constant, known rate into the future. If analysis were to show, for example, that the current growth of IBM was greater than that of the economy as a whole, uncritical application of this growth rate into the formula is tantamount to assuming that IBM will eventually swallow up the entirety of the U.S. economy. Furthermore, if IBM dividends were expected to grow at a rate equal to the rate of return, the formula would suggest IBM stock would have an infinite value. While it is possible to "jury-rig" the formulas to allow for some changes in interest rates with term to maturity and for different growth rates over the life of the investment, it is conceptually simpler to compute the present values directly, using the general formula in the context of spreadsheet or other computer software products.

Rate of Return Measurements

It is very common to compare investments according to their *rates of return*. In a single-period example, as noted in the oil participation case, the return is easily computed. Suppose the oil participation share is worth only $1,280 at year-end, where the remaining $320 represents an end-of-year distribution to shareholders. The annual rate of return measure is

$$\text{Rate of return} = \frac{\$320 + \$1{,}280 - \$1{,}000}{\$1{,}000} = .60$$

The formula is

$$\text{Rate of return} = \frac{\text{Income} + \text{Current value} - \text{Value last period}}{\text{Value last period}}$$

This return measure is sometimes called a *total return* measure since it includes yield from current income as well as yield from capital appreciation (current value − value last period). The distinction between income and capital gains is not usually important for nontaxable pension funds[2] but is crucial for trust funds that draw a distinction between income and principal beneficiaries, for endowment funds where spending rules depend on the return measure, and for taxable investors whose income and realized capital gains are taxed at different rates.

Suppose the oil venture is to last two years and will be worth $1.6 million at that time:

	Value per Share	Income per Share
At start of venture	$1,000	$ 0.00
After one year	1,280	320.00
After two years	1,600	0.00

The total return for the first year is 60 percent and that for the second is 25 percent:

$$\text{Second-year return} = \frac{\$1,600 - \$1,280}{\$1,280} = .25$$

There are several approaches to obtaining a single return measure for this investment.

Arithmetic Return.   The average of successive returns is termed the *arithmetic return*. In the example the average of 60 percent and 25 percent is 42.5 percent:

$$\frac{.60 + .25}{2} = .425$$

The general formula for the arithmetic return is

$$\text{Arithmetic return} = \frac{R_1 + R_2 + R_3 + \cdots + R_N}{N}$$

---

[2]Some argue that assets are priced after consideration of taxes; hence tax-exempt investors should prefer investments with a high income component.

where

$R_1, R_2, R_3, \cdots R_N$ = Returns for periods 1, 2, 3, through N.
N = Number of periods.

The 42.5 percent number attempts to measure the "typical" annual return on investments of this type. It does not, however, measure the realized return to the investor over the holding period of the investment.

Geometric Return. The *geometric rate of return* is the compounded value of successive returns (usually) expressed on an annual basis. In the oil venture, 100 shares of the venture are purchased at $1,000 per share. At year-end the shares are worth $128,000 in total, and the investor receives $32,000 in income. If this income is used to purchase 25 additional shares at $1,280 a share, worth a total of $32,000, the total investment is worth $200,000 (125 × $1,600) two years from today. In other words the original investment has doubled in value. This doubling in value can be computed directly as

$$(1 + .60) \times (1 + .25) = 2.00$$

This 100 percent return represents a two-year return. To *annualize* this number consider what rate of return compounded twice doubles the value of the original investment:

$$(1 + .4142)^2 = (1 + .60) \times (1 + .25)$$

Thus the geometric return is 41.42 percent. Using most pocket calculators it can easily be computed:

Geometric return = $[(1 + .60) \times (1 + .25)]^{1/2} - 1 = .4142$

Returns are often computed on a quarterly, monthly, or even daily basis. *Annualization*, taking the compound growth to the power of the reciprocal of the number of years under consideration, is a procedure for bringing these different return measures to a comparable basis.

The general formula for the geometric return is

Geometric return = $[(1 + R_1) \times (1 + R_2)$
$\times (1 + R_3) \times \cdots \times (1 + R_N)]^{1/M} - 1$

where

$R_1, R_2, R_3, \ldots R_N$ = Rates of return for periods 1, 2, 3, through N.
N = Number of periods.
M = Number of years that comprise N periods.

TABLE 1–1
Total Annual Returns by Investment Class, 1926–1984

	Arithmetic Return	Geometric Return	Standard Deviation*
Small stocks	18.2%	12.4%	36.3%
Common stocks	11.7	9.5	21.2
Long-term corporate bonds	4.6	4.4	7.6

*This measure is explained on page 23.

SOURCE OF DATA: Ibbotson Associates, *Stocks, Bonds, Bills and Inflation: 1985 Yearbook* (Chicago: Ibbotson Associates, Capital Management Research Center, 1986), pp. 94–99.

Note that the 41.42 percent geometric return measure is less than the 42.5 percent arithmetic return. This will always be the case, and the measures differ more the greater the variability of returns.

Example: You expect Sure Thing preferred stocks to have a return of minus 50 percent next year but to double in value the following year. In other words $1.00 invested today in Sure Thing would be worth $.50 a year from today and $1.00 the subsequent year. What is the holding period return on this investment?

Even though the arithmetic return is 25 percent (average of − .50 and 1.00), in two years the investment will be worth no more than its value today. Hence the geometric return is zero:

$$\text{Geometric return} = [(1 + -.5) \times (1 + 1)]^{1/2} - 1 = 0.0$$

This example demonstrates that when there are reports of extraordinary returns associated with investments for which the returns are highly variable, one should carefully check the method by which returns are computed.[3]

To give some idea of the difference between the methods of computing returns, Table 1–1 shows arithmetic and geometric return measures for broad classes of investments. Small stocks, whose returns are highly variable, have a much higher arithmetic than geometric return, as we would expect.

---

[3]Typically, the arithmetic average is used with cross-sectional data while the geometric average is used with time-series data.

Internal Rate of Return. The *internal rate of return* answers the question "At what (constant) rate of return would the present value of the future cash flows of the investment exactly equal the current value of the investment?" Suppose, as before, a share of the oil venture is worth $1,000 today but will yield $320 next year and be sold for $1,600 the following year. The internal rate of return is that return r for which

$$\$1,000 = \frac{\$320}{1+r} + \frac{\$1,600}{(1+r)^2}$$

It implies a return r of 43.5 percent. This number can be obtained by a process of trial and error, which has been automated in a number of financial calculators and spreadsheet software products. Where the investment under consideration is a bond this internal rate of return is referred to as the *yield to maturity* of the bond.

The 43.5 percent number is greater than either the arithmetic or geometric rates of return for this example because the internal rate of return calculation implicitly assumes a flat yield curve; money can be invested *and reinvested* in the oil venture to yield a 43.5 percent return. Evidently the assumption was not valid in this example; after the first year, income can be invested to yield only 25 percent. The internal rate of return, interpreted as a yield to maturity, is a fundamental tool of bond analysis. This yield curve insight suggests caution in interpreting the measure where short rates differ substantially from long rates and particularly where the yield curve is thought not to be stable.

Time-Weighted versus Dollar-Weighted Rates of Return. An application where the difference between geometric and internal rates of return is of some importance is in the context of money manager performance measurement.

Example: Oilpro Securities Inc. and OilQuest are two money managers for the XYZ pension fund. They were both given $200,000 to manage; Oilpro was given the money as a lump sum whereas OilQuest, being new to the business, was given the money in two annual installments of $100,000 each. Both managers invested 100 percent of the assets in the same oil venture, which experienced a 60 percent return in the first year and 25 percent in the second. How do their respective performances compare?

One common performance measure, called the *dollar-weighted rate of return,* is nothing more than the internal rate of return of the fund under management. The fund gave to Oilpro $200,000, which grew to $400,000 at the end of two years. The dollar-weighted return is that return r for which

$$\$200,000 = \frac{\$400,000}{(1 + r)^2}$$

It implies a dollar-weighted return of 41.42 percent. On the other hand, OilQuest was given $100,000 initially and $100,000 after a year, which, given the 60 percent return in the first year and the 25 percent return in the second year, implied that the first part of the fund grew to $200,000 while the second part grew to $125,000, totaling $325,000, after two years. The dollar-weighted return for OilQuest is thus the return r for which

$$\$100,000 = \frac{-\$100,000}{(1 + r)} + \frac{\$325,000}{(1 + r)^2}$$

The result is a dollar-weighted return of 37.08 percent.

The investment policies of the two managers were identical, yet Oilpro would appear the better manager by more than four percentage points per year! Yes, the fund was more valuable after two years left with that manager, but that is totally an artifact of the way in which the two managers were funded. The geometric return—in this context the *time-weighted rate of return*—does not suffer from this drawback and gives a 41.42 percent return to each manager regardless of the way in which the managers were funded. The comparison between the two measures becomes more difficult in the context where the money manager is funded and is required to make disbursements within a given reporting period. The concept of continuously compounded return assists us in this regard.

Continuously Compounded Return. The exact timing of cash flows is crucial in evaluating the performance of money managers. A manager who does not reinvest the proceeds from the sale of securities or the income from investments in a timely fashion would be guilty of mismanagement of the fund assets. Up to this point in the discussion it has been assumed that cash flows occur on a regular basis, at the end of every month or year for the holding period of the investment. This assumption, of course, is unrealistic. In any investment program, cash flows occur on an irregular basis throughout the year. The return that represents an appropriate basis of comparison is one that reflects the continuous reinvestment of these cash flows. Such a return is referred to as a *continuously compounded return.*

Suppose a particular investment is expected to earn an income equal to 10 percent of its current value over the course of the coming year. If the income comes in the form of a lump-sum payment at year-end the return on the investment would be 10 percent. If the income comes in the form of two equal installments, one in the middle of the year and one at year-end, the investment should earn more than 10 percent since a 10 percent return would assume that the interim installment was not reinvested.

If the interim income were reinvested in ventures earning a similar return, the annual return would be 5 percent compounded twice, or 10.25 percent. If on the other hand the income were to come on a daily basis, the annual return would be given by $\frac{1}{365}$ of 10 percent compounded 365 times, or 10.52 percent. The 10.52 percent annual return represents the maximum return measured on an annual basis from an investment yielding 10 percent when continuously compounded. In other words a 10.52 percent annually compounded return corresponds to a 10 percent continuously compounded return.[4]

Example: Oilpro placed an additional $100,000 in a short-term interest fund for seven months. This fund yielded a 10 percent return, continuously compounded, for the period in question. How much was Oilpro's investment worth at the time the funds were withdrawn?

As noted above, a dollar growing at 10 percent continuously compounded would equal $1.1052 at year-end. However, in this case the investment is only for seven months, or $\frac{7}{12}$ of a year. One way to compute the future value of the investment would be to take the 365th fraction of 10 percent compounded for $\frac{7}{12}$ of 365 days, or 213 days. A simpler approach is to convert the continuously compounded rate to the equivalent annually compounded rate of 10.52 percent and compound this value for the appropriate fraction of the year:

$$\$100,000 \times (1 + .10/365)^{213} = \$100,000 \times (1 + .1052)^{7/12} = \$106,008$$

---

[4]The calculations that convert a particular continuously compounded rate to an equivalent annually compounded rate would appear a little cumbersome were it not for a convenient mathematical result. As we saw, $1.00 would grow to $1.1052 at a continuously compounded rate of 10 percent. The amount $1.1052 happens to equal $1.00 \times 2.718282^{.10}$, where 2.718282 is the mathematical constant e, giving rise to the formula

Annually compounded rate = $2.718282^{\text{Continuously compounded rate}} - 1.00$

Thus Oilpro ought to have been able to withdraw $106,008 from the short-term interest fund at the end of seven months.

The point of this example is to show that where rates of return can be considered continuously compounded, the future value (and present value) formula applies in the context of cash flows that occur throughout the year.

STATISTICS AND DATA ANALYSIS

Relationship to the Theory of Value

The advent of spreadsheet software has focused attention on the central question of analysis: where do the numbers come from? Earlier in this chapter we showed how to derive measures of value, given information about future cash flows. Statistical methods process the available information into a form useful to the valuation process.

In the oil venture example the beginning $1.6 million number was taken as given. Is this a reasonable figure? Does it conform to what is known about the oil exploration business? The methods of statistics are obviously useful in this context, and we shall consider a variety of ways of processing the available data to derive simple summary measures of this data. In that example it appeared that only the opinion of the promoter supported the number. The interests of the promoter obviously differ from those of the investor, and statistical methods can be used to examine whether the number is unduly optimistic in light of prior claims by the promoter. Finally, the venture is quite risky. What effect can or should recognition of this risk have on the valuation process? Again statistical methods are useful in this context.

Statistical methods are crucial to the valuation process. Their usefulness falls under three headings:

- Reduction of large quantities of data into simple summary measures that describe the data and the relationships among the data.
- Statistical examination of hypotheses on which the valuation is based.
- Quantitative measurement of risk.

The remainder of this section will examine the first two issues, while the third will be studied in the next section.

Descriptive Statistics

The central task of descriptive statistics is to reduce a large amount of information into a comprehensible form. Statisticians use the term *measure of central tendency* to describe a single number that represents many numbers.

The $1.6 million number could be said to be a measure of central tendency that reflects the recent history of returns to oil ventures; alternatively it could be thought of as representing the entire range of possible financial outcomes to this venture. It is evidently somewhat meaningless without some indication of how actual outcomes may differ from $1.6 million. Statisticians use the term *measure of dispersion* to describe the extent to which the actual numbers may differ from the measure of central tendency.

Measures of Central Tendency. The most familiar measure of central tendency is the *simple average*. Suppose that the $1.6 million number was based on an economic model that used data for 50 recent drillings to form some estimate of the cost of the project. These data are provided as Table 1–2.

TABLE 1–2
Oil Venture: Drilling Costs

Well Number	Cost	Well Number	Cost
1	$473,760	26	$216,924
2	230,198	27	225,957
3	241,897	28	245,592
4	219,475	29	221,158
5	222,832	30	241,640
6	211,014	31	201,033
7	210,757	32	196,914
8	357,842	33	224,182
9	221,924	34	200,587
10	216,699	35	239,048
11	198,449	36	379,388
12	218,222	37	212,348
13	386,870	38	301,041
14	289,839	39	263,423
15	199,965	40	314,995
16	228,909	41	298,102
17	477,595	42	198,707
18	567,581	43	195,289
19	225,357	44	229,207
20	207,746	45	239,331
21	244,585	46	202,135
22	255,646	47	205,490
23	215,328	48	316,954
24	199,988	49	221,764
25	282,001	50	242,804

The average cost was $256,770, which would appear to be a reasonable estimate for these purposes. The simple average obtained by adding up the data and dividing by the number of items is referred to by statisticians as the *sample mean*. This does not mean that this particular oil venture will cost $256,770. In fact a number of recent oil wells cost considerably more. Number 18 cost over $500,000. Furthermore over half the wells in the study cost less than $256,770. What is going on here?

Table 1–3 shows the data presented in Table 1–2 ranked in order of the size of the cost of each well. Almost three quarters of the wells cost less than the average of $256,770. The abnormally high costs of wells 1, 17, and 18 seem to have caused the average to be higher than the cost of most of the wells. Thus it could be argued that the average is not a reasonable single number to characterize the cost of this venture.

TABLE 1–3
Oil Venture: Drilling Costs Ranked by Cost

Well Number	Cost	Well Number	Cost
43	$195,289	27	$225,957
32	196,914	16	228,909
11	198,499	44	229,207
42	198,707	2	230,198
15	199,965	35	239,048
24	199,988	45	239,331
34	200,587	30	241,640
31	201,033	3	241,897
46	202,135	50	242,804
47	205,490	21	244,585
20	207,746	28	245,592
7	210,757	22	255,646
6	211,014	39	263,423
37	212,348	25	282,001
23	215,328	14	289,839
10	216,699	41	298,102
26	216,924	38	301,041
12	218,222	40	314,995
4	219,475	48	316,954
29	221,158	8	357,842
49	221,764	36	379,388
9	221,924	13	386,870
5	222,832	1	473,760
33	224,182	17	477,595
19	225,357	18	567,581

Another measure of central tendency is the *median*, a number chosen such that half of the data are above it and the remaining data are below it. In this example the median is $225,657, halfway between the cost of wells 19 and 27. The costs of wells 1, 17, and 18 are said to be *outliers* in the sense that they are extreme relative to the others. If we argue that these values are not representative of the true cost of drilling a well, then they should not have significant impact on the measure of central tendency. The median has the property that it is not affected by the magnitude of outliers.

Still another measure of central tendency useful in certain applications is the most common value of the data, otherwise referred to as the *mode*. In the above example it would appear that there is no "common value" and each cost is different. However, if we classify costs into ranges of $50,000 and count the number of wells that fall into each cost classification, a pattern emerges.

A *histogram* is a graphical representation of such a classification of data. The histogram for the data contained in Table 1–2 is given as Figure 1–1. This histogram indicates that there are 6 wells that cost between $150,000 and $200,000, 30 that cost between $200,000 and $250,000, 5 that cost between $250,000 and $300,000, and so forth. The *modal range* is $200,000 to $250,000. A reasonable value for the central tendency would lie in this range; the mode would be given by a weighted average of the midpoints of the adjacent ranges:

$$\text{Mode} = \frac{(6 \times \$175,000) + (30 \times \$225,000) + (5 \times \$275,000)}{6 + 30 + 5}$$

$$= \$223,780$$

The mode is perhaps the most intuitive of the measures of central tendency. Ultimately it is also the least satisfactory. There are two major problems with this measure:

1. The mode is sensitive to the precise classification chosen. Suppose the data were broken into ranges of $20,000. Thirteen wells cost between $200,000 and $220,000, and 12 cost between $220,000 and $240,000. By this classification the mode lies between $200,000 and $220,000.

2. Even given the classification of the data, the mode is not unambiguous. Suppose that instead of 1 there were 30 wells that cost between $550,000 and $600,000. In this case the mode is ambiguous, and the distribution of the data is said to be *bimodal*. While evidently a problem for the mode, if this were the case it would also be a problem for the mean and median, both of which would then be intermediate between the two modes. A bimodal

FIGURE 1–1
Histogram of the Data Contained in Table 1–2

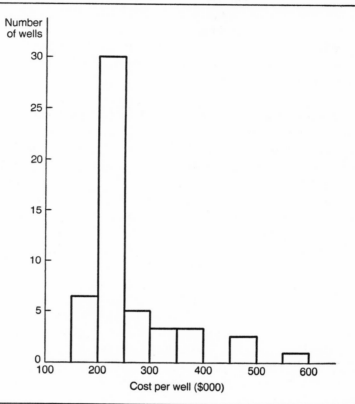

distribution frequently indicates that two or more sets of disparate data have been aggregated together. Gas wells are typically deeper and more expensive than oil wells. If the data pertained to both oil *and* gas wells the distribution of the data would be bimodal, and the measures of central tendency for the aggregated data would be fairly meaningless.

A major property of both the median and the mode is insensitivity to extreme values in the data. This fact is said to be a major argument in favor of these measures over the simple average as a measure of central tendency. However, is this lack of sensitivity necessarily a good thing? Implicit in the decision to ignore these values is the assumption that wells 1, 17, and 18 are somehow different from the other wells and should not enter into consideration. Suppose, however, that there was an equipment breakdown on well 1, a lost bit on well 17, and a flaming blowout on well 18. To the extent that these are reasonable contingencies for the proposed well they *should* enter into consideration. Unlike the median and the mode, the sample mean accounts for these contingencies relative to the frequency of their occurrence in the data, and for this reason it is not such an unreasonable measure of central tendency. Good practice, however, is to examine the facts surrounding each outlier.

Measures of Dispersion. The analyst interested in having one number represent an entire distribution of data ought to understand the extent to which the data can deviate from that measure of central tendency.

The *range*, the difference between the maximum and the minimum of the observed data ($372,292 in the Table 1–2 example), is one such measure of dispersion. It does indicate the range of variation in the data but is highly affected by outliers. A more satisfactory variant of this measure, the *interquartile range*, is defined by the difference between the *lower quartile*, the number such that just 25 percent of the data are smaller, and the *upper quartile*, the number such that just 25 percent of the data are larger. In the Table 1–2 example a quarter of the wells had a cost less than that of well 6 ($211,014), and a quarter had costs exceeding $263,423 (the cost of well 39). Thus half of the data lies within the interquartile range given by the difference between the two, $52,418. This number is best thought of as a measure of dispersion to be associated with the median. In fact the relationship between the range, interquartile range, and median provides a succinct graphical representation of the entire distribution of the observed data, known as a *boxplot* (see Figure 1–2).

In the boxplot of the Table 1–2 data the horizontal dashed line represents the median, the box represents the interquartile range, and the vertical lines extending from the boxes or "whiskers" represent the range. The whiskers extend to the range of the data or 1.5 times the interquartile range, whichever is smaller, to allow the outliers to be plotted separately.

Inspecting this boxplot we note that the upper tail of the distribution of the data—values in excess of the median—is much more extensive than the lower tail of the distribution. Where this is the case the distribution is said to be skewed to the right, or *positively skewed*. The relationship we observed between the sample mean, median, and mode is characteristic of such distributions. Where the lower tail is more extensive than the upper the distribution is said to be skewed to the left, or *negatively skewed*.

Boxplots convey in abbreviated form information similar to that provided

FIGURE 1–2
Boxplot of the Table 1–2 Data

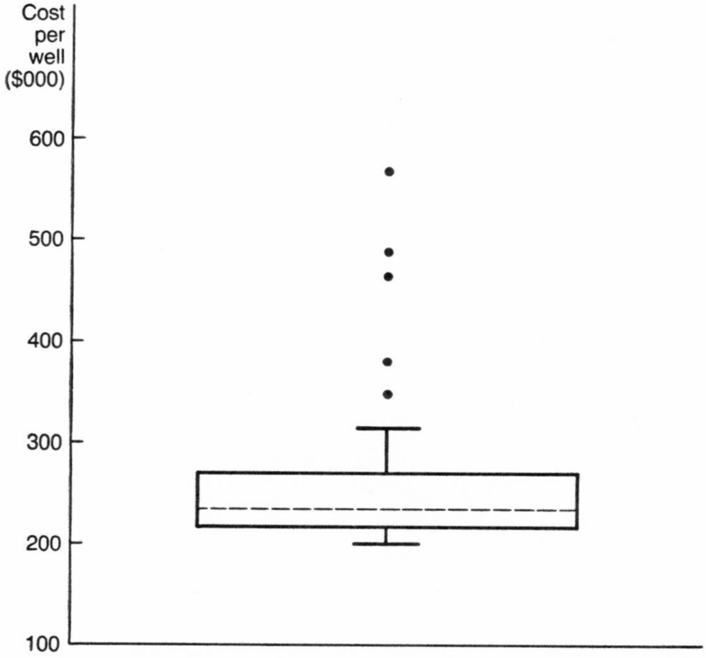

by the histogram. However, they are more useful than histograms in comparing distributions. By lining up boxplots against one another, one can gain an immediate visual impression of how distributions differ by their central tendencies, dispersion, and relative skewness. Figure 1–3 compares annual returns for three different classes of investment given in Table 1–1. We see immediately from this figure that small stock returns are more variable than common stocks in general, while corporate bond returns are less variable. While we saw in Table 1–1 that the average return (arithmetic return) is much higher for small stocks the median return is not that much greater than for common stocks in general. It seems that small stock returns are more highly skewed, with a higher degree of dispersion, than are stocks in general, again suggesting that the high arithmetic returns for these stocks should be interpreted with care.

Boxplots are used in several types of analysis. They are frequently used

FIGURE 1–3
Boxplot of Annual Returns by Investment Class, 1926–1984

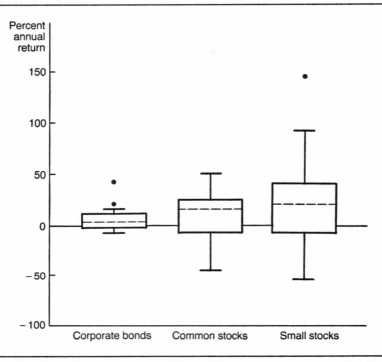

SOURCE OF DATA: Ibbotson Associates, *Stocks, Bonds, Bills and Inflation: 1985 Yearbook* (Chicago: Ibbotson Associates, Capital Management Research Center, 1986), pp. 94–99.

to compare the distribution of return by money managers. In another application they summarize succinctly the results of simulation experiments such as those designed to uncover the differences between alternative policies for asset and liability planning.

Just as the interquartile range is a measure of dispersion generally associated with the median, the variance and standard deviation are measures of dispersion associated with the sample mean.

Variance measures the average deviation from the mean *squared* (the deviations themselves unfortunately average to zero). For the Table 1–2 data,

$$\text{Variance} = \frac{(\$473,760 - \$256,770)^2 + (\$230,198 - \$256,770)^2 + \cdots}{50}$$

$$= \$6,151,215,000$$

or more generally,

$$\text{Variance} = \frac{(X_1 - \overline{X})^2 + (X_2 - \overline{X})^2 + \cdots + (X_N - \overline{X})^2}{N}$$

where

$\overline{X}$ = Average value of the variable of interest.
N = Number of observations.[5]

The *mean absolute deviation (MAD)*, on the other hand, averages the same deviations without respect to the sign of the deviation:

$$\text{MAD} = \frac{|\$473,760 - \$256,770| + |\$230,198 - \$256,770| + \cdots}{50}$$

$$= \$54,855$$

or

$$\text{MAD} = \frac{|X_1 - \overline{X}| + |X_2 - \overline{X}| + \cdots + |X_N - \overline{X}|}{N}$$

where

$\overline{X}$ = Average value of the variable of interest.
N = Number of observations.

and the vertical lines imply that the sign of the difference between the variable and its average value is ignored in the computation.

The variance is the most popular measure of dispersion. However, it is not expressed in dollar units. To remedy this problem take the square root of this value. This square root is referred to as the *standard deviation:*

Standard deviation = Square root of variance
Standard deviation = $\sqrt{6,151,215,000}$ = \$78,430

Referring back to Table 1–1 the standard deviation of annual returns is a useful summary statistic for the dispersion of returns. Small stocks experience returns that are more variable than those of stocks in general, while government bonds have returns that are less variable.

Sometimes analysts like to compare different standard deviations by expressing them in units of the mean value. This scaled standard deviation is referred to as a *coefficient of variation*. It is given by the formula

---

[5]Note that purists divide by $N - 1$ instead of by N to ensure that the estimate of the variance is an unbiased estimate of the true or underlying variance.

$$\text{Coefficient of variation} = \text{Standard deviation} \div \text{Sample mean}$$
$$= \$78,430 \div \$256,770 = .3054$$

Many analysts do not use this measure because the scaling by the sample mean appears somewhat arbitrary. Certainly we cannot measure the coefficient of variation if the sample mean is zero. However, it has one very important role in the context of performance measurement. The reciprocal of the coefficient of variation of fund *risk premiums* (returns in excess of the Treasury bill return) is known as the *Sharpe measure* where it is interpreted as the return per unit risk.[6]

As we shall see, the standard deviation and variance are particularly useful in the context of hypothesis tests and the definition of risk. For data analysis, however, they share the problem of sensitivity to outliers (these large values are squared before they enter the average and so will tend to dominate the measure). One approach to this problem is simply to exclude outliers. Standard deviations computed in this manner are called *trimmed standard deviations*. The MAD approach, which does not square deviations associated with large outliers, is less sensitive to this problem.

Measures of Association. Measures of central tendency and dispersion, boxplots, and histograms describe a complex set of data in a simple way. They do not describe the relationships between different sets of data upon which valuation frequently depends. The simplest descriptive tool for analyzing the relationship between sets of data is the *scatter plot*.

Figure 1–4 gives scatter plots of the relationships between annual returns of different investment classes given in Figure 1–3. These scatter plots (sometimes called *draftsman plots* when organized in this fashion) show that there is a strong positive relationship between the returns on common stocks in general and the returns on small stocks: when common stock returns are high, small stock returns are also high. There is, however, less relationship between common stock returns and the returns on corporate bonds and still less between the returns on small stocks and on corporate bonds.

A measure that captures the extent to which data are associated is the *covariance*. In the case of small stocks and common stocks, when common stock returns (R_c) were above average, so too were small stock returns (R_s). Similarly when returns were below average, so too were the returns on small stocks. Intuitively the covariance should be positive, and computing it as

---

[6]See William Sharpe, "Mutual Fund Performance," *Journal of Business*, January 1966, pp. 119–38. This and related measures are discussed in Chapter Seven.

FIGURE 1–4
Scatter Plots of Returns on Common Stocks, Small Stocks,
and Corporate Bonds

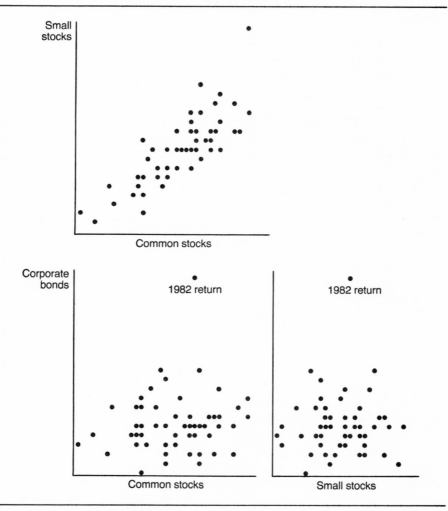

SOURCE OF DATA: Ibbotson Associates, *Stocks, Bonds, Bills and Inflation: 1985 Yearbook* (Chicago: Ibbotson Associates, Capital Management Research Center, 1986), pp. 94–99.

the average product of deviations from average should come out as a positive number.[7]

---

[7]Note that, as with the variance formula, in finding the average value of the product, purists divide by $N - 1$ instead of by N, the number of observations on the two variables.

Covariance between R_c and R_s = Average value of $(R_c - \overline{R}_c) \times (R_s - \overline{R}_s)$

$$= .0639$$

Covariance between X and Y = Average of $(X - \overline{X}) \times (Y - \overline{Y})$

where

X = Value of the first variable of interest.
$\overline{X}$ = Average of the first variable.
Y = Value of the second variable of interest.
$\overline{Y}$ = Average of the second variable.

In a similar way, if the returns were negatively associated in the sense that when the change in one was positive the other was negative, the covariance would be negative. However, the actual magnitude of the number is difficult to interpret.

The *correlation coefficient* is a measure of association that is a little easier to interpret. It is obtained by normalizing the covariance by the standard deviations of the variables under consideration. In other words, in the example above,

$$\text{Correlation} = \frac{\text{Covariance}}{\text{Standard deviation } R_c \times \text{Standard deviation } R_s}$$

$$= \frac{.0639}{.212 \times .363} = .83$$

$$\text{Correlation between } X \text{ and } Y = \frac{\text{Covariance between } X \text{ and } Y}{S_X \times S_Y}$$

where

X = First variable of interest.
S_X = Standard deviation of X.
Y = Second variable of interest.
S_Y = Standard deviation of Y.

If two sets of data were perfectly correlated in the sense that movements in one data series were exactly matched by corresponding movements in another, the correlation coefficient would be one. If there were no association the correlation would be zero. If the data were perfectly negatively associated in the sense that movements in one series were matched by corresponding but opposite movements in the other, the correlation coefficient would be minus one. Table 1–4 gives what is termed the *correlation matrix* of the data depicted in Figure 1–4.

TABLE 1–4
Correlation Matrix of Annual Returns, 1926–1984

	Common Stocks	Small Stocks	Corporate Bonds
Common stocks	1.00		
Small stocks	.83	1.00	
Corporate bonds	.15	.08	1.00

SOURCE OF DATA: Ibbotson Associates, *Stocks, Bonds, Bills and Inflation: 1985 Yearbook* (Chicago: Ibbotson Associates, Capital Management Research Center, 1986), pp. 94–99.

Table 1–4 can be compared directly to Figure 1–4. The returns on common stock seem to be closely associated with the returns on small stocks (correlation = .83) but less associated with the returns on corporate bonds (correlation = .15), while the degree of association between small stocks and corporate bonds (correlation = .08) is even more attenuated.

We conclude from Table 1–4 that common stocks and small stocks are closer together as investments than either is to corporate bonds. In this sense, common stocks and small stocks form a natural group, or *cluster*. Of course we did not need the correlation matrix to tell us this. However, the correlation matrix of returns or other quantifiable characteristics is important for determining natural groupings or sectors that would otherwise not be obvious to the analyst. Table 1–5 illustrates a somewhat broader set of investments.

There are many different ways of classifying securities on the basis of the observed correlation structure. Traditional *cluster analysis*, which we discuss here, is a very intuitive procedure that defines sectors on the basis of the pattern of correlations. If the analyst has some prior basis for determining the sectors, analysis of the correlation structure can yield a *discriminant function* to predict whether a particular security belongs to a given sector. This is a particularly useful method for predicting financial distress. First we examine the financial correlates of distress. Then we derive a discriminant function that lets us know whether a particular firm will fall into the financial distress category. Finally, the relatively sophisticated factor methods to be discussed later in this chapter are a way of classifying firms based on their exposure to economy-wide sources of uncertainty.

Cluster analysis attempts to form clusters of securities that correlate highly with one another in important attributes and have relatively low correlation with securities classified into different clusters. This analysis is at least implicit in the ways most analysts study sectors and form portfolios.

TABLE 1–5
Correlation Matrix of 13 Asset Classes

	NYSE Equities	AMEX Equities	OTC Equities	European Equities	Asian Equities	Treasury Bonds	Long-Term Corporate Bonds	Foreign Government Bonds	Business Real Estate	Residen-tial Real Estate	Farm Real Estate	Treasury Bills	Gold
NYSE equities	1.000												
AMEX equities	0.851	1.000											
OTC equities	0.900	0.897	1.000										
European equities	0.618	0.689	0.651	1.000									
Asian equities	0.237	0.123	0.244	0.391	1.000								
Treasury bonds	0.091	-0.153	-0.094	-0.130	-0.005	1.000							
Long-term corporate bonds	0.341	0.058	0.110	0.095	0.022	0.912	1.000						
Foreign government bonds	0.010	0.078	0.097	0.345	0.084	0.190	0.269	1.000					
Business real estate	0.159	0.227	0.138	0.268	0.218	0.036	0.107	0.249	1.000				
Residential real estate	0.123	0.213	0.090	0.207	-0.080	-0.039	-0.039	0.293	0.493	1.000			
Farm real estate	-0.164	-0.093	-0.223	-0.097	-0.003	-0.256	-0.255	0.103	0.016	0.214	1.000		
Treasury bills	-0.055	-0.063	-0.160	-0.169	-0.157	0.111	0.094	0.244	0.685	0.428	-0.053	1.000	
Gold	-0.094	-0.024	-0.067	0.032	0.046	-0.252	-0.316	0.107	0.219	0.586	0.517	0.179	1.000

SOURCE OF DATA: Roger G. Ibbotson, Laurence B. Siegel, and Kathryn S. Love, "World Wealth: Market Values and Returns," *Journal of Portfolio Management*, Fall, 1985.

FIGURE 1–5
Hierarchical Cluster Analysis of 13 Asset Classes

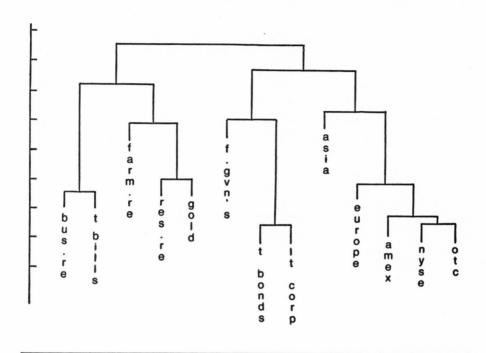

The particular method we will present here is known as the *hierarchical* approach.

The hierarchical approach to cluster analysis combines securities on the basis of correlation. The method can most easily be illustrated in terms of the correlation matrix given as Table 1–5 and shown in Figure 1–5. The most highly correlated asset classes are long-term corporates and U.S. Treasury bonds (correlation = .912) and New York Stock Exchange (NYSE) and Over-the-Counter (OTC) equities (correlation = .900). By allowing the within-group correlation to fall somewhat we can include American Stock Exchange (AMEX) equities in the equity group. The smallest correlation between any asset class in that group is now .851. Allowing this minimal correlation to fall, European and eventually Asian equities will be included in this sector. At that level of generalization foreign government bonds fall into the debt sector. Other groupings are less immediately obvious. Business real estate will correlate with Treasury bill returns, due to the inflation sensitivity of both asset classes, although it is difficult to motivate a strong relationship between gold and residential real estate. However, from the pattern of correlations we see clear evidence of real estate, debt, and equity sectors within the set of 13 asset classes of Table 1–5.

One major caveat is that this method, and indeed every other such classification technique, is meant only as a descriptive tool. There are many forms of cluster analysis, and it is an unfortunate fact that the results of the analysis do depend on the precise method used. Of course, the best test is that of common sense. Are the clusters or sectors that are identified using the procedure reasonable? An unreasonable group (residential real estate and gold, perhaps) may not be a particularly stable group. It may not survive slight differences in the way the cluster analysis is carried out or in the correlation assumptions made.

The correlation matrix and resulting classification tools are widely used in investment analysis. However, it should be treated with care. Referring back to Figure 1–4 we see that much of the apparent positive association between common stock returns and corporate bond returns can be attributed to just one abnormally high return on bonds (43.79 percent experienced in 1982) that happened to occur at a time when the common stock return of 21.41 percent was slightly above average. If this one outlier were excluded, the evidence of a positive relationship between the total returns on stocks and bonds would be reduced.

Another common measure of association is the *simple regression*. It is very tempting to describe the relationship between returns on small stocks and on common stocks in general in terms of a line that best fits through the scatter plot of returns on the two classes of investment. Such a line, termed a *regression line*, is depicted in Figure 1–6. It is obtained by means of *regression analysis*, which minimizes the squared differences between the actual observations and the regression line. This technique is available in many statistical computer software packages. Such software takes as input the data for the variables in question and provides as output estimates that are used to construct the line.

Output for a typical regression software package is given as Table 1–6. The coefficient column describes the line drawn in Figure 1–6. "Intercept" is the starting value of the line: If one knew that the return on common stocks was 0.0 percent one might predict that small stocks would earn a ¹.698 percent return. In other words, in Figure 1–6 the line would cross a vertical line drawn at zero common stock return, at a 1.698 percent return on small stocks. "Common stock returns" gives the slope of the line: We

FIGURE 1–6
Regression of Small Stock Returns on Common Stock Returns

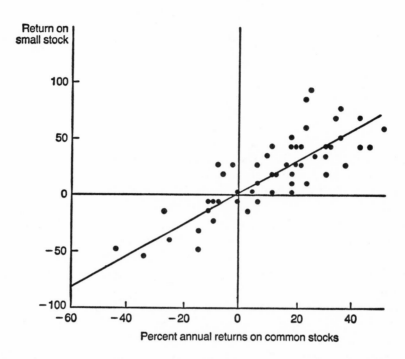

would expect that small stock returns would increase by 1.417 percent for every 1 percent rise in common stock returns. In the case of simple regressions involving asset or asset class returns, the 1.417 number is referred to as the *beta* of the asset. In short the relationship between small stock returns and common stock returns may be represented as

$$R_s = 1.698 + 1.417 \times R_c + e$$

where the line is given by the 1.698 and 1.417 numbers and e represents the error, or *residual,* which gives the difference between the actual small stock return and the return that would be predicted given the line.

The multiple R-square item (sometimes referred to as R-squared or simply r^2) is a simple summary measure of the relationship between small stocks and the returns on common stocks. It says that 68.53 percent of the variability in small stock returns can be explained by the variability of common stock

---

TABLE 1–6
Regression of Small Stock Returns on Common
Stock Returns: Sample Output

	Coefficient	Standard Error	t-Value
Intercept	1.698480	3.0786	0.5517
Common stock returns	1.416735	0.1272	11.1403

Residual standard error = 20.71715.
Multiple R-square = 0.6852.
N = 59.
F-value = 124.1068 on 1, 57 degrees of freedom.

---

returns. It is also the square of the correlation coefficient between small stock and common stock returns ($.6853 = .83 \times .83$).

The residual also indicates how well the regression line explains the observed data. The standard deviation of these residuals is also a measure of the extent to which the relationship describes the data. This standard deviation is referred to as the residual standard error (sometimes also referred to as the *standard error of the regression*), which in this instance is 20.72 percent. Even if we were to know the return on common stocks in general, there is a large degree of uncertainty about possible returns on small stocks. The remaining statistics, the standard error and *t*-value columns and the *F*-value item, give indications as to the reliability of these results and will be discussed separately below.

One might conclude from this analysis that small stock returns are "caused" by common stock returns. However, one could argue equally well that small stocks "cause" common stock returns. The truth lies somewhere in between. Both small stocks and common stocks in general are affected by the state of the economy, and there is a certain degree of variability the investor cannot avoid by simply switching from small stocks to a broadly diversified common stock portfolio. This exposure to common factors of variability, we shall see, is at the heart of an appropriate definition of the risk faced by investors.

Hypothesis Tests

Data analysis provides procedures to describe a set of data; *hypothesis tests* provide techniques for examining theories or hypotheses about how the data came into being. In the oil example at the beginning of the chapter the given $1.6 million was a reasonable estimate of how valuable the oil venture would be at year-end. Suppose that the promoter of the venture had been involved in 30 recent ventures, each of which struck oil. The estimated value of each venture at the initial offering and the ultimate value at the end of each project are given in Table 1–7.

These estimates do not appear to have been very reliable. The standard deviation of the difference between the estimate and the ultimate value of the oil venture (the last column in Table 1–7) is $277,460. When confronted with this data, the promoter might argue that the oil exploration business is very risky. It is difficult to estimate with any degree of precision the actual worth of an oil well before it is drilled. However, in 20 out of 30 cases the estimated value was too high; in addition the average difference was − $166,366. Are these data sufficient to conclude that the promoter systematically overestimates the ultimate value of the oil ventures in the offering prospectus?

In this context it is useful to draw a distinction between the *empirical distribution* (the distribution of the observed data) and what is termed the *theoretical probability distribution* (the distribution that could be said to give rise to the observed data).[8] The data in Table 1–7 pertain to the empirical distribution of the errors the promoter makes in estimating the ultimate value of the well. These data are essentially retrospective. They are relevant to current decisions only to the extent that they allow us to infer future conduct of the promoter. The promoter might argue that the reason the ultimate value fell short of expectations to the average amount of $166,366 was bad luck on ventures 14 and 28 rather than a predisposition on the part of the promoter to overestimate systematically. After all, the − $166,366 average difference was based on results for only 30 oil ventures. If we had data for other ventures, the promoter would claim, we would find that the difference would eventually average to zero. In other words, the data in Table 1–7 merely represent 30 cases drawn from a theoretical distribution for which the mean difference is zero. If this were the case the estimates would be said to be *unbiased*.

Unfortunately we do not get to observe the theoretical probability distribution directly. To assess the promoter's claim we need to *infer* its properties from the empirical distribution. The promoter claims that the estimates are unbiased, that the true mean difference in fact is zero. In the parlance cf statistics this is said to be the *null hypothesis:*

Null hypothesis: Mean difference = $0.00

---

[8]Probability distributions are introduced and motivated for the financial analysis context in the Appendix.

TABLE 1–7
Estimated and Actual Value of 30
Related Oil Ventures ($000)

Venture	Estimate	Actual	Difference
1	$1,600	$1,425	$ – 175
2	1,800	1,440	– 360
3	1,600	1,587	– 13
4	1,600	1,746	146
5	1,500	982	– 518
6	1,500	1,128	– 372
7	1,600	1,147	– 453
8	1,600	1,662	62
9	1,600	1,610	10
10	1,300	1,531	231
11	1,700	1,688	– 12
12	1,700	1,841	141
13	1,500	1,248	– 252
14	1,800	1,161	– 639
15	1,600	1,545	– 55
16	1,400	1,732	332
17	1,700	1,712	12
18	1,800	2,069	269
19	1,700	1,568	– 132
20	1,600	1,255	– 345
21	1,700	1,572	– 128
22	1,600	1,706	106
23	1,800	1,509	– 291
24	1,600	1,143	– 457
25	1,700	1,258	– 442
26	1,500	1,174	– 326
27	1,600	1,241	– 359
28	1,700	959	– 741
29	1,600	1,673	73
30	1,600	1,297	– 303

This null hypothesis is to be set against our initial reaction, that the promoter has a predisposition to overestimate the value of oil ventures. In other words, the *alternative hypothesis* is

Alternative hypothesis: Mean difference < $0.00

This formalization of null and alternative hypotheses is referred to by statisticians as a *hypothesis test*, or *significance test*. The object is to examine how far the sample mean is from the null hypothesis and to measure the significance of the difference.[9]

One of the attractive features of the sample mean as a measure of central tendency is that we know something of the way in which it is affected by the exigencies of a particular sample of data. The sample mean will of course vary around the true mean of the data from one particular sample to the next. It is highly unlikely that in another sample of 30 oil ventures the average error would turn out to be exactly −$166,366. The sample mean varies with each sample, and its variance turns out to be the variance of the underlying data divided by the number of items of data on which the sample mean is based. It is not surprising that the reliability of the sample mean as an estimate of the true or underlying mean should increase with the size of the sample used to estimate it: As the sample size increases, the sample mean will close in on the true mean of the underlying data:

$$\text{Mean of sample means} = \text{Mean of data}$$
$$\text{Variance of sample means} = \frac{\text{Variance of data}}{N}$$

The standard deviation of the sample mean is given by the square root of the variance and is referred to as the *standard error*. For the example given above, the standard error of the mean is

$$\text{Standard error} = \sqrt{\frac{\$277,460^2}{30}} = \$50,657$$

or in general,

$$\text{Standard error} = \text{Square root of} \frac{\text{Variance}}{N}$$

where N = Number of observations used to estimate the mean of the data.

The standard error is then a natural measure of the extent to which the sample mean differs from the mean under the null hypothesis. We see that −$166,366 differs from the null hypothesis of zero to the extent of 3.28 standard errors. This 3.28 number is referred to as the *t-value* or *t-statistic*:

---

[9]In this particular application we care only about large negative differences. Statisticians refer to such tests as *one-sided* or *one-tailed*. If the issue were the general reliability of the promoter, we would be as concerned with large positive differences as well. The test would then be referred to as *two-sided*, or *two-tailed*.

$$t\text{-value} = \frac{-\$166,366 - \$0.00}{\$50,657} = -3.28$$

or in general,

$$t\text{-value} = \frac{\text{Sample mean} - \text{Null hypothesis mean}}{\text{Standard error of sample mean}}$$

Since the t-value has a theoretical distribution approximated by a normal or bell-shaped distribution for which a difference greater than 1.65 standard errors occurs less than 5 percent of the time (this number can be found from tables published in most elementary statistics books),[10] a difference of 3.28 standard errors is "large."[11]

Thus the average error is too large to be accounted for by the exigencies of the particular sample of 30 oil ventures. In the parlance of statistics we say we reject the null hypothesis of a zero mean error at a 5 *percent level of significance.* In plain English we say the promoter significantly overestimates the ultimate value of the oil ventures he promotes.

The same analysis can be used to evaluate claims by a money manager that he or she can outperform some popular index of returns. In this instance the average error (the difference between the fund return and the index return) is referred to as the *alpha,* or value added, of the fund. The null hypothesis is that the true alpha is zero, and the alternative hypothesis is that the true alpha is positive, that the money manager can indeed outperform the index. Unfortunately the variability of returns is frequently so great that an extensive track record is necessary to show evidence that the manager can significantly outperform the index, at least using this simplest form of analysis. Risk adjustment procedures and procedures for reducing the apparent variability of returns lie at the heart of sophisticated procedures for performance measurement.

Multiple Regression Analysis

In the oil drilling example of Table 1–2 there was no adjustment for the fact that the different wells might not have been drilled to the same depth. It

---

[10]Actually the exact distribution is what is termed a *student-t distribution* with (30 −) 'degrees of freedom." For about 30 or more degrees of freedom, this is for all practical purposes identical to the well-known normal distribution.

[11]A t-value of 3.28 is large by any reckoning. The 1.65 number refers to a one-tailed test; in a two-tailed test, where we allow for the possibility that the main difference can be large in either a positive or negative direction, the critical number is 1.96. Treat with caution any finding of "significance" that depends on this distinction!

TABLE 1–8
Results from Regression of Cost per Well on
Average Depth of Well
(all onshore oil, gas, and dry wells, United States,
1959–1983)

	Coefficient	Standard Error	t-Value
Intercept	− 192,588.0000	110,368.0000	− 1.7450
Depth	72.5784	22.8501	3.1763

Residual standard error = 132,790.9.
Multiple *R*-square = 0.1214.
N = 75.
F-value = 10.08872 on 1, 73 degrees of freedom.
Durbin-Watson statistic = .2914.

SOURCE OF DATA: American Petroleum Institute, *Basic Petroleum Data Book*, vol. 5 (Washington, D.C.: American Petroleum Institute, May 1985), tab. 9.

---

seems reasonable to suppose that drilling costs increase with the depth of the well. If we have some idea of how deep the well might be, we might be able to get a more precise idea of the costs of this particular oil venture.

Using annual estimates of the cost per well and the average depth of all onshore oil, gas, and dry wells drilled in the United States from 1959 through 1984 we find that cost per well (in dollars) is indeed positively correlated with the depth of the well (in feet) with a correlation coefficient of .348. Further, regressing cost per well on the average depth per well, we find the results given in Table 1–8. In that table the standard error and *t*-values have the same interpretation as in the previous section, where the *t*-value pertains to the hypothesis that the coefficient in that particular row is in fact zero. The *F*-value, which in this particular case represents the *t*-value squared, provides another way of testing this hypothesis.

Thus we find that not only is there evidence of a positive association between depth and the cost per well but the association is significant. We might conclude from Table 1–8 that the best estimate of cost of the well is given by taking $72.5784 per foot of the projected depth of the well minus the amount $192,588.

This interpretation of the results is correct as far as it goes, but it does not go far enough. Regression analysis is no substitute for thought. To see how deceptive such analyses can be, consider the relationship between the predictions of the regression model (sometimes referred to as the *fitted values*) given by

Estimated costs $= -\$192,588 + (\$72.5784 \times$ Depth of well)

and the residuals or errors given by

Residual costs $=$ Actual costs $-$ Estimated costs.

This relationship is plotted in Figure 1–7. On careful examination we see that the model makes systematic, predictable errors for both oil and gas wells and that the model seriously underpredicts high costs for both well classifications (the errors are positively skewed). Furthermore, successive estimates of residual costs are highly correlated (the correlation coefficient is .8591). This correlation is disturbing because it suggests that the residual costs are related to some common factor currently excluded from the analysis. Regression analysis assumes these residuals bear no systematic relationship to one another. The *Durbin-Watson statistic* reported in the table provides a way of determining just how large this correlation is. It is approximately twice the quantity one minus .8591, the correlation between successive residual values.[12] In the sense referred to above in the context of cluster analysis, it measures the distance in terms of degree of association between successive residual values. It can be used to construct statistical tests of this association—numbers less than one or greater than three generally lead us to reject the hypothesis of "no association."[13] Based on the Durbin-Watson statistic of.2914 we find that the successive residuals are indeed associated, leading us to the conclusion that the model is misspecified. What is going on here?

The Table 1–8 results cover a period of rising costs for all types of productive activity. The producer and wholesale price indexes of the U.S. Bureau of Labor Statistics increased threefold from 1959 to 1983. Drilling technology became more sophisticated over that period, and costs per well rose as a result. The rise in energy prices in the late 1970s and early 80s prompted more than twice the number of wells to be drilled in 1982 than were drilled in 1975, straining the labor and material resources and again

---

[12]The exact formula is a measure of the appropriately normalized difference between successive residual values. It is given as the ratio of two quantities. The numerator is the sum of squared *differences* between successive residuals, and the denominator is simply the sum of squared residual values.

[13]The *critical value* of the Durbin-Watson statistic depends on the number of data points and the number of variables used in the analysis and is available in many statistics texts. However, a statistic less than one or greater than three will generally lead to a rejection of the hypothesis of "no association" at a 5 percent significance level. Numbers outside the range 1.5 to 2.5 are generally troubling, while a value of 2 for this statistic would correspond to no association.

FIGURE 1–7
Plotting Residuals against Fitted Values for Table 1–8 Results

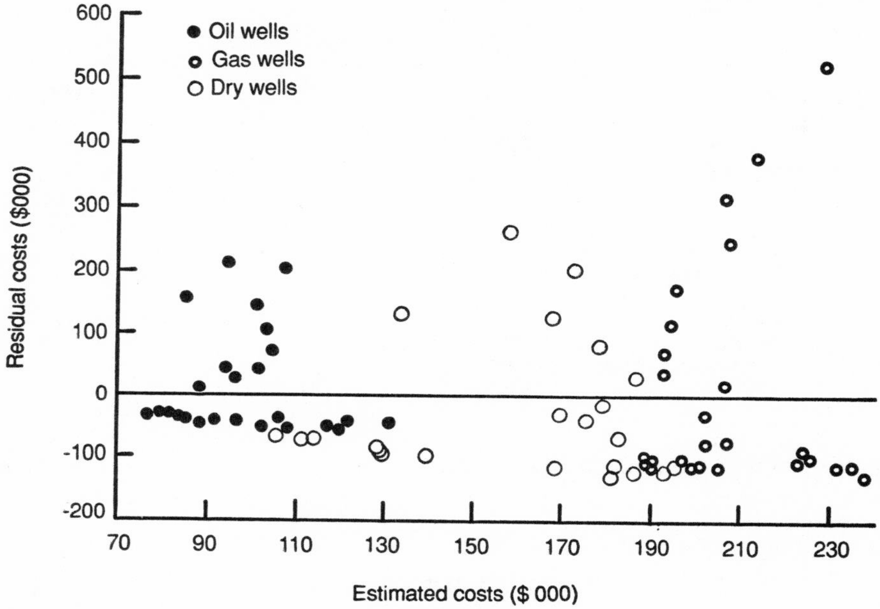

SOURCE OF DATA: American Petroleum Institute, *Basic Petroleum Data Book,* vol. 5 (Washington, D.C.: American Petroleum Institute, May 1985), tab. 9.

causing costs to rise. These effects would appear to swamp the modest changes in the depth per well over that interval.

How can these different effects be isolated? Just as simple regression examines the relationship between one variable and another, multiple regression examines the relationship between one variable and potentially many others. In addition to depth per well we may consider additional variables: time (the date of the observation, 1959, 1960, . . . 1983); the total number of wells drilled in the United States each year; whether the well was a gas well (zero if the datum in question belonged to an oil or a dry well, one if it pertained to a gas well); and whether the well turned out to be dry. Variables of this sort that classify the data are referred to as *dummy variables.* The variation in producer prices can best be accounted for by expressing all costs in *constant dollar* amounts. That is, each cost figure is expressed as a fraction of the producer price index for the year in question.

Results from regressing constant dollar costs against depth, time, the

TABLE 1–9
Regressing Constant (1983) Dollar Costs against Depth, Time,
Number of Wells, and Well Classification, 1959–1983

	Coefficient	Standard Error	t-Value
Intercept	−11,636,450.0000	1,482,837.0000	−7.8474
Depth	89.1725	18.7627	4.7527
Time	5,753.8280	777.8590	7.3970
Number of wells	3.2795	.3594	9.1251
Gas	52,063.1400	29,894.9600	1.7415
Dry	−5,789.7840	18,156.3300	−3.1889

Residual standard error = 35,611.66.
Multiple R-square = 0.9224.
N = 75.
F-value = 164.2498 on 5, 69 degrees of freedom.
Durbin-Watson statistic = 1.1178.

number of wells, and the well classification are contained in Table 1–9. This table reveals that:

1. Each additional foot of depth costs $89.17, other things equal.
2. Costs per well have increased an average of $5,753.83 per annum.
3. Every additional well drilled increases the cost per well $3.28.
4. At any given depth the average gas well costs $52,063 more than an oil well, and a dry well costs $5,789 less.
5. These numbers are significant at the 5 percent level (from the t-values), but the gas differential is only barely significant if we consider a one-tailed test.

In short, these results imply that expected costs will be given by the formula

$$\text{Expected costs} = -11,636,450 + (\$89.17 \times \text{Depth})$$
$$+ (\$5,753.83 \times \text{Year})$$
$$+ (\$3.28 \times \text{Total number of wells drilled})$$
$$+ \left(\$52,063 \times \begin{cases} 1 \text{ if well is gas} \\ 0 \text{ otherwise} \end{cases} \right)$$
$$+ \left(\$5,789 \times \begin{cases} 1 \text{ if well is dry} \\ 0 \text{ otherwise} \end{cases} \right)$$

This formula explains 92 percent of the observed variability in costs. In addition the F-value is very high. One can see from examining the t-values

FIGURE 1–8
Residuals Plotted against Fitted Values for Multiple
Regression in Table 1–9 ($000)

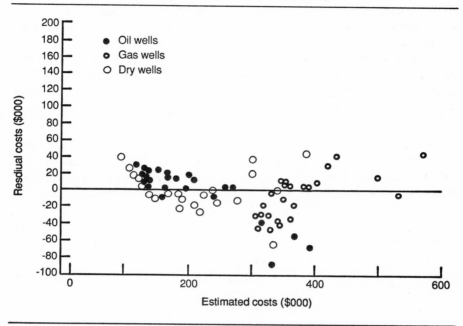

SOURCE OF DATA: American Petroleum Institute, *Basic Petroleum Data Book*, vol. 5 (Washington, D.C.: American Petroleum Institute, May 1985), tab. 9.

in the table that all the variables, with the possible exception of the gas dummy variable, are individually statistically significant. The F-value statistic is an analogous measure to a t-value in that it tests whether all coefficients are *jointly* significant in explaining the cost numbers. Where there is only one explanatory variable, as in Table 1–8, the F-value is equal to the t-value squared. Otherwise this statistic provides insights in addition to those given by studying the t-values alone.[14]

These results look impressive, but again one should look at the residuals from the regression, plotted in Figure 1–8. Things do not look good. Even

---

[14]The critical value of the F-value test statistic depends on the *degrees of freedom* given as 5 and 69, which are tabulated in most statistics texts. In this instance, the critical value for testing at the 5 percent level is 2.5. The observed value is 164.2, which is greater than 2.5, so we say that the regression is "significant." Of course, what we mean by significant is statistical significance. The coefficient values we estimate may have little economic significance.

though the model explains a higher percentage of the variability in costs, the errors for oil well costs appear even more predictable than before. Furthermore there is a distinct pattern to the residuals. They seem to fan out.[15] When estimated costs are low the residuals appear less variable than when estimated costs are high. In addition the residuals tend to be positive when estimated costs are very low or very high.

There is some evidence of a cyclical pattern to the residuals when they are plotted against time. The Durbin-Watson statistic of 1.1178, while higher than before, is still less than the 5 percent critical value of 1.49 appropriate for this number of data points and regression variables. Factors still appear to be omitted from the analysis.

Residuals fanning out as they appear to do in Figure 1–8 suggest a *logarithmic,* or ratio, *transformation* of the data. While the variability of the error measured in dollars may appear to increase with expected costs, perhaps the variance measured in terms of *percentage error* is more stable. The cyclical pattern to the residuals suggests that last year's cost figure may provide a better explanation of this year's cost than does the dummy variable identifying gas wells.[16]

Table 1–10 summarizes results from such a regression, which is a little more difficult to interpret. The time coefficient (note that time was *not* in logarithm form) is interpreted to mean that there is an average growth in constant dollar costs of 1.9 percent per year, other things equal. Costs depend on depth to the extent of the depth taken to the power 1.65, and they depend on the number of wells to the extent of that number raised to the power .33. Dry wells are significantly cheaper than other types of wells.[17] Finally, we find that last year's cost figure does explain a significant part of this year's cost number. The scatter plot of residuals to fitted values (in terms of the

---

[15]Statisticians refer to this phenomenon as *heteroscedasticity.*

[16]Statisticians worry that the use of such a so-called *lagged dependent variable* will lead to a downward biased estimate of the coefficient of the lagged cost variable. However, this bias is very small in terms of practical orders of magnitude so long as the coefficient is smaller than one (as is the case here). If the coefficient is close to one, the analyst would be better off studying *changes* in the cost numbers rather than costs themselves. Explaining a variable of interest in terms of past values of that variable and other related variables is one of the most popular simple methods for forecasting macroeconomic trends. This technique is called *vector autoregression.*

[17]This analysis shows that other things equal, dry wells cost 76 percent of the cost of other types of wells. This number is obtained by raising the exponential constant e to the power $-.2699$. For those unfamiliar with the use of logarithms and the relationship between logarithms and the exponential constant, see the Appendix, where these matters are discussed.

TABLE 1–10
Regressing the Logarithm of Constant Dollar Costs
against Time, Well Classification, and the Logarithms
of Depth and the Number of Wells, 1959–1983

	Coefficient	Standard Error	t-Value
Intercept	−45.0359	4.8510	−9.2839
Logarithm of depth	1.6502	0.1549	10.6517
Time	0.0190	0.0023	8.4203
Logarithm of number of wells	0.3305	0.0434	7.6209
Dry	−0.2699	0.0313	−8.6106
Lagged cost	0.2107	0.0738	2.8533

Residual standard error = 0.071217.
Multiple R-square = 0.9742.
N = 72.
F-value = 498.758 on 5, 66 degrees of freedom.
Durbin-Watson statistic = 1.8615.

logarithms) given in Figure 1–9 shows that this regression finally appears well specified.[18]

UNCERTAINTY AND VALUATION

Factor Methods and the Theory of Value

This chapter started with the proposition that investments can be characterized by the cash flows they generate and that valuation is a problem of comparing alternative cash flows. In the oil venture example it was assumed that the venture would be worth exactly $1.6 million one year from today. In reality, of course, there is considerable uncertainty about what such a venture would be worth at that time. The Table 1–7 numbers are perhaps a more realistic representation of what the venture may be worth. It is indeed possible that investors may lose part or all of their investment by year-end. What effect can or should this uncertainty, or risk, have on the valuation process?

Oil exploration is a very risky process. In a largely undeveloped field there is considerable uncertainty about whether a given well will actually strike oil and if so what the flow rate and proven reserves will turn out to

---

[18]The intercept, the logarithm of the constant term, would be close to zero if expressed in dollar terms.

FIGURE 1–9
Residuals Plotted against Fitted Values (in Terms of Logarithms) for Regression in Table 1–10

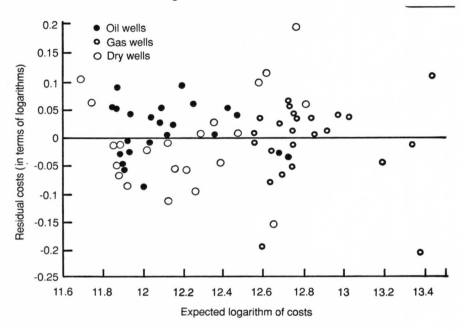

SOURCE OF DATA: American Petroleum Institute, *Basic Petroleum Data Book,* vol. 5 (Washington, D.C.: American Petroleum Institute, May 1985), tab. 9.

be after the well is drilled. For this reason the value of the well before it is drilled may appear somewhat imponderable. However, suppose the investor already owns shares in a well that is being drilled in an immediately adjacent area. The ultimate value of that well is also highly uncertain; but whatever it turns out to be, it should be very highly correlated with the ultimate value of the well in question. If the investor could sell those shares for $1,333 per share today and buy shares in the new venture for $1,000 per share, he would be better off by $333 per share today and as well off a year from today. At $1,000 per share, the shares of the new venture are significantly undervalued. Valuation remains a problem of comparing alternative cash flows.

This oil well example may appear a little too neat. Surely there are few examples where investments exist that are exact duplicates, in a sense, of the investment in question. Most investors hold portfolios of securities rather than individual securities. In the Table 1–7 example the uncertainty concerning the ultimate value of the venture, measured by the standard deviation of the error estimating this value, was on the order of $277,460. If the investor chose instead to hold a portfolio consisting of an equal investment in each of the 30 ventures, he or she would thereby *diversify* the risk. This *diversification* would be as if the investor held a share in the mean value of the different ventures; as we saw, the standard deviation would fall to $50,657. By holding a sufficiently large portfolio, such an investor can be shielded from the exigencies of a particular venture. The investor should not be in a position to care if a bit is lost or there are labor problems with a particular crew. These things should average out. Even if the well is dry, the dry well represents only one 30th of the original investment. What the investor cares about is the risk that cannot be diversified away. If oil prices fall, *all 30* oil ventures will be worth less. It is at this portfolio level that investments can be matched and hence valued in terms of their exposure to common factors of variation in the economy as a whole.

Factor methods provide techniques and procedures for evaluating the impact of factors of variation that affect all securities. The well-known *capital asset pricing model* can be thought of as corresponding to a model where there is only one factor of variation affecting the returns on all securities. In this model, securities are valued so that their return over and above the Treasury bill, or *riskless* return, is expected to be proportional to the degree to which they are exposed to all common stocks, the so-called *market factor*. This model is referred to as a *single-factor model*. The *arbitrage pricing theory* introduced by Stephen A. Ross derives similar results for the case where there is more than one factor affecting the returns on securities, called a *multiple-factor model*.[19]

Single-Factor Models

In single-factor models it is assumed that the uncertain returns on different securities are related only to the extent that they are all related to some common market factor. In other words, investors can reduce their risk by diversifying their portfolios; but there is an essential risk that cannot be diversified away, a risk that arises from the uncertainty of the economy as a whole. This market factor can thus be measured by the returns on a broadly diversified portfolio, usually identified with a capitalization-weighted port-

---

[19]See Stephen A. Ross, "The Arbitrage Theory of Capital Asset Pricing," *Journal of Economic Theory*, December 1976, pp. 343–62.

folio such as the Standard & Poor's 500. This insight gives rise to the *market model* introduced by William Sharpe.[20]

In Table 1–6, a simple regression appeared to capture the relationship between the returns on a portfolio of small stocks R_s and the returns on a broadly diversified common stock portfolio R_c:

$$R_s = 1.698 + (1.417 \times R_c) + e$$

This is an example of a market model where, in this context, the error *(e)* is termed the *nonsystematic,* or *idiosyncratic, component of returns.* The 1.417 number is referred to as the beta of the small stock portfolio. The nonsystematic component of returns can be diversified away within a large portfolio. The beta, which measures the extent to which the returns on the security depend on the market factor, thus represents a measure of the risk that cannot be diversified away. The beta of a broadly diversified market fund is one. An asset or portfolio more risky than the market has a beta greater than one. As we would expect, small stocks are riskier than the market as a whole, with a beta of 1.417. A beta less than one indicates a security less risky than the market as a whole. (Public utility stocks typically fall into this latter category.)

To estimate beta, one could simply use a regression analysis like the one presented in Table 1–6. Most investigators usually regress *monthly* or *daily* returns, where available, to obtain the most precise estimate of this quantity. There are several caveats to this approach. In periods when interest rates are highly volatile (such as the late 70s and early 80s in the United States) a large part of the variability in stock returns could be accounted for by this phenomenon. If this is the case, then the returns on the security and on the market should be measured in excess of the yield on Treasury bills with the same time to maturity as the holding period over which the returns are defined. Beta is not stable over extended periods of time, since the operations of firms change. Sixty months of data is the maximum that should be used to estimate this parameter, and there are a variety of ways one can adjust beta to account for changes in the firms that issue the securities in question.

A variety of services provide periodic estimates of beta for a wide range of equities. These data can be used to construct the beta of a portfolio as a weighted average of the betas of the component equity securities in the portfolio, using as weights the percentage of the current value of the portfolio

---

[20]See William Sharpe, "A Simplified Model for Portfolio Analysis," *Management Science,* January 1963, pp. 277–93.

invested in each equity issue. Few services provide estimates of beta for other than equity issues.

The major advantage of this class of single-factor models is that it is very easy to use in a variety of applications. It is well understood, and the data used in its estimation are readily available, at least for the equity markets. The major disadvantage is that it may not be descriptively accurate. If there exist more than one factor of variation affecting broad classes of securities, then the beta measure will systematically over- or underestimate the risk of particular securities. Furthermore the implicit assumption that the S&P 500 is the "market" is at least to be questioned. It is not clear that such a portfolio is sufficiently diversified, as it contains only equity issues and excludes small equity issues at that.

Multifactor Models

Multifactor models attempt to address the principal drawbacks of the single-factor models: the assumption of only one factor and the reliance on the return on a particular market composite as the single factor. However, they do so at the cost of some increase in the difficulty of estimation and application.

Formally the multifactor model can be expressed as

$$\text{Return on asset} = \text{Constant} + (b_1 \times \text{Factor 1}) + (b_2 \times \text{Factor 2})$$
$$+ \cdots + \text{Idiosyncratic component of return}$$

where

Factor 1, factor 2, and so forth represent factors of variation in the economy as a whole that are common across all assets.

$b_1, b_2, \ldots$ represent the extent to which the particular asset in question is exposed to each of the factors. (The factors and factor exposures are analogous to the market factor and beta of the single-index model.)

Idiosyncratic component of returns represents the part of returns that is not related to the common factors and that can be diversified away in large portfolios.

The relationship between single- and multifactor models is similar to the relationship between simple and multiple regression. In fact, multiple regression may be used to estimate the coefficients of the multifactor model. To do this, one would first specify the factors of variation such as unexpected changes in unemployment, interest rates, and inflation. Then, for each asset, one would regress the time series of returns on that asset against the factors specified by the investigator. The coefficients obtained from such a time-series regression analysis would represent the factor exposures b_1, b_2, and so forth, for each asset under study.[21] However, it is difficult to specify all the potential common factors of variation on some a priori basis.

Another approach to estimating the multifactor model is to use *factor analysis,* which does not require the investigator to specify in advance what the factors of variation represent. Such analysis can be performed using many standard computer software packages. If a multifactor model generates observed returns, we should be able to infer factor exposures from the extent to which the time series of returns for different securities are correlated with each other. This is precisely what factor analysis does. It takes as input the correlation matrix of security returns and as output yields the factor exposures for each asset. In the parlance of factor analysis, the factor exposures are called *factor loadings,* and the factors themselves are referred to as *factor scores.* Given the ready availability of computer software, this procedure is very easy to apply. However, the results of such analysis are sometimes difficult to interpret. In addition, the factors identified by such an approach may not be particularly stable over time.

These procedures assume there is a large quantity of historical data on security returns. For this reason the formalization of multifactor models has been largely restricted to the study of equity markets. However, the insights of the approach are clearly not limited to such markets. The study of term structure issues (in the case of bond markets) and real estate issues is amenable to this kind of analysis.

Where there is insufficient data for explicit estimates of factor exposures using multiple regression or factor analysis, other methods are available. *Scenario analysis* that asks "what if" questions that relate the possible returns of the security to the state of the economy within a top-down securities analysis approach can be best thought of in terms of such a multifactor model.

The factor exposures estimated for single- or multifactor models represent measures of risk specific to each security. These measures of risk reflect the extent to which the returns on that security relate to factors of variation in the economy as a whole. With sufficient data they can be estimated by regressing the *time series* of returns on the security against a *time series* of factor values. In the case of the single-index model the factor values represent returns on some market index. In the case of the multifactor model the factor

---

[21]This approach has been outlined in Nai-fu Chen, Richard Roll, and Stephen A. Ross, "Economic Forces and the Stock Market," *Journal of Business,* July 1986, pp. 383–403.

values represent unexpected changes in macroeconomic factors, which in the case of factor analysis are in turn measured by the factor scores.[22]

The importance of each of these measures of risk can be weighted by the extent to which investors in the capital markets require a premium over and above the riskless return in order to bear such risks. Both the capital asset pricing model and the arbitrage pricing theory predict that the return investors expect to receive is given by the riskless return plus a measure of the quantity of risk (given by the risk exposures of the particular security) times a measure of the "price" of risk (given by the risk premiums that may differ according to the measure of risk but are constant across securities). In principle, with sufficient data the risk premiums can be estimated by regressing the *cross section* of average security returns against the *cross section* of factor exposures.[23] *Cross-sectional regressions* of this type can be used to estimate the investor's required return on risky investments. In addition such regressions are used in the context of performance measurement to measure the performance that may be attributed to the risk borne by a particular money manager (see Chapter Seven).

CONCLUSION

This chapter is meant to serve as an overview of the quantitative methods used in the context of financial analysis. The mathematics of valuation and statistics and data analysis are tools to which every analyst should have ready access. This is not to say that every analyst needs to make frequent use of these tools, and it is not to suggest that use of the tools will unambiguously lead to large and positive returns. In the remainder of this book we show how the tools can be applied in a variety of specialized areas of analysis.

---

[22]The measure of risk specific to a *portfolio* of assets is given at a point in time by a weighted average of the measures of security risk, where the weights are simply the percentage of the portfolio invested in each of the assets. In other words, the beta of a portfolio is simply the "portfolio" of the betas.

[23]Strictly speaking, this regression should be in the form of a *weighted least-squares* regression where the weights are given by the reciprocal of the estimated standard deviation of the idiosyncratic component of each security's return. In other words, the constant term, measures of risk, and average return for each security should be divided by the standard deviation of the idiosyncratic term prior to running the regression. If this is not done the residuals from the cross-sectional regression will be said to be *heteroscedastic* (see footnote 15).

PROBLEMS
1. Suppose you are currently negotiating a financial settlement and as part of this settlement you need to determine the present value of a pension that pays $200 per month for 10 years beginning 10 years from now. What is the value of this pension today, assuming a constant annual interest rate of 10 percent?

Answer: The present value of a 20-year annuity based on the above information equals:

$$PV = \$200 \times \left[\frac{1}{.1/12} - \left(\frac{1}{.1/12} \times \frac{1}{(1 + .1/12)^{(12 \times 20)}} \right) \right]$$

$$PV = \$20,725$$

The present value of a 10-year annuity based on the above information equals:

$$PV = \$200 \times \left[\frac{1}{.1/12} - \left(\frac{1}{.1/12} \times \frac{1}{(1 + .1/12)^{(12 \times 10)}} \right) \right]$$

$$PV = \$15,134$$

Therefore the present value of a 10-year annuity 10 years from now equals $5,391 ($20,725 − $15.334).

2. Suppose a portfolio manager generates a 16-percent annualized return over a five-year period and a 12-percent annualized return during the first two years of this period. What was the manager's annualized return for the last three years of this period?

Answer: 18.75 percent.

$$\left(\frac{1.16^5}{1.12^2} \right)^{1/3} - 1 = .1875$$

CHAPTER TWO

Quantitative Methods in Equity Analysis

H. Russell Fogler and Mark P. Kritzman

This chapter, which demonstrates the application of quantitative methods to equity analysis, begins with an exploration of equity valuation within the context of the present value formula. Following that, a discussion of anomalies demonstrates the use of data analysis to uncover peculiarities in equity returns. The final section of the chapter shows how factor analysis can be used to select stocks and to attribute return.

The focus of this chapter is on the merits and limitations of quantitative analysis. One should not assume that quantitative techniques are a substitute for sound fundamental analysis. Rather these two disciplines complement each other. Fundamental analysis can be thought of as a process for refining the information on which estimates of key financial variables are based, while quantitative analysis can be thought of as a method for translating this information into estimates of value and return.

EQUITY VALUATION

As mentioned in Chapter One, valuation is a problem of comparing alternative streams of cash flows, and a common basis for comparing these cash flows is *present value*. In general, the present value of a stream of cash flows is equal to

$$PV = \frac{C_1}{1 + r} + \frac{C_2}{(1 + r)^2} + \frac{C_3}{(1 + r)^3} + \cdots + \frac{C_N}{(1 + r)^N}$$

where

PV = Present value.
C = Cash flows.
r = Rate of return used to discount cash flows.

In the case of a common stock, the cash flows equal the dividend payments in each period, and, if we assume a finite investment horizon, the price for which the stock is sold at the end of our investment horizon. For example, in order to estimate the present value for a stock, given a five-year investment horizon, we can rewrite the generalized present value formula as

$$PV = \frac{D_1}{1 + r} + \frac{D_2}{(1 + r)^2} + \frac{D_3}{(1 + r)^3} + \frac{D_4}{(1 + r)^4} + \frac{D_5 + P_5}{(1 + r)^5}$$

where

PV = Present value of stock.
D = Dividend payments.
p = Stock price at end of horizon.
r = Rate of return used to discount cash flows (which also equals the stock's expected return).

Suppose that a company earned $10 per share in the previous 12 months and that we expect earnings to grow 8 percent per year for the next five years. Also let us assume that this company has consistently paid out 40 percent of its earnings as dividends. From this information we can estimate the dividend payments in years one through five.

We still need to estimate the stock's price at the end of the fifth year. One approach for estimating the future stock price is to estimate an equilibrium price-earnings multiple for the stock and apply this multiple to the estimate for earnings at the end of the fifth year. For example, if earnings grow at 8 percent for five years they will increase to $14.69 by the end of the fifth year. Suppose we estimate the equilibrium price-earnings multiple to equal 12. Then the stock's price at the end of the fifth year will equal $176.28.

The final input that we need to estimate is the rate that we use to discount the dividends and fifth-year stock price. A reasonable point of departure for estimating the *discount rate* is the yield to maturity on long-term bonds. We may wish to start with this value and adjust it in accordance with the historical *risk premium* of stocks over bonds to arrive at a discount rate for the overall stock market. Then once we have estimated the stock market's discount rate, we can adjust it to reflect the systematic risk of the particular stock we are analyzing. The intuition behind this adjustment is that investors require compensation for bearing systematic risk, since this risk cannot be diversified away. As a consequence the expected cash flows from a risky company are discounted at a higher rate than are the expected cash flows from a less risky company.

We can estimate a company's systematic risk by regressing the company's historical returns on the overall stock market's historical returns. The slope of the regression line is called *beta*, and it measures the sensitivity of a stock's return to the market's return. The table below shows the results of regressing the returns of our hypothetical company, which we creatively call XYZ Company, on the returns of the Standard & Poor's 500 Index, which we use as a proxy for the stock market. This table shows that XYZ's beta equals 1.15.

	Coefficient	Standard Error	t-Value
Intercept	−.252	1.014	.25
Slope	1.150	.204	5.62

Residual standard error = 0.0444.
Multiple R-square = 0.2015.
N = 60.
F-value = 31.5844 on 1, 58 degrees of freedoms.
Durbin-Watson statistic = 2.0801.

Now suppose that the yield to maturity for bonds equals 9 percent and we determine that stocks historically have returned 2 percent more than bonds; hence we choose 11 percent as the discount rate for the overall stock market. We can determine the discount rate to apply to XYZ's cash flows simply by multiplying the market's discount rate by the XYZ's beta, which in this case results in a discount rate of 12.65 percent (11 percent × 1.15).[1]

We now have all of the required inputs to estimate XYZ's present value. First we compute the expected dividend payments by growing the earnings at 8 percent each year and multiplying this value by the payout ratio. Thus the expected dividend payments in years one through five are:

---

[1]This calculation assumes we estimate beta precisely. Beta could be as much as 1.15 plus or minus .408 (twice the standard error).

Year 1: $10 × (1.08) × .4 = $4.32
Year 2: $10 × (1.08)² × .4 = $4.67
Year 3: $10 × (1.08)³ × .4 = $5.04
Year 4: $10 × (1.08)⁴ × .4 = $5.44
Year 5: $10 × (1.08)⁵ × .4 = $5.88

and XYZ's price at the end of the fifth year equals $176.32 ($10 × (1.08)⁵ × 12).

To determine the present value of each of these payments we divide them by the quantity one plus the discount rate, raised to the power of the period in which the cash flow occurs, and then sum these values:

Year 1: $ 4.32 ÷ 1.1265   = $ 3.83
Year 2:   4.67 ÷ (1.1265)² =   3.68
Year 3:   5.04 ÷ (1.1265)³ =   3.53
Year 4:   5.44 ÷ (1.1265)⁴ =   3.38
Year 5:   5.88 ÷ (1.1265)⁵ =   3.24
          176.32 ÷ (1.1265)⁵ =   97.20
                                 $114.86

Based on our assumptions the sum of these discounted cash flows, and hence the present value of XYZ Company, equals $114.86. This value is often thought of as a stock's fair value. Thus if XYZ's current price in the market is above its fair value it is considered overvalued, whereas if its current price is below this value it is considered undervalued.

This same general framework can also be used to compare stocks according to their *expected returns*. Instead of solving for the stock's fair value we substitute its current price for the present value to determine the discount rate that equates its expected cash flows with its current price. For example suppose that XYZ sold for $105. A discount rate of 14.83 percent equates the cash flows with this value. It should make sense that, since the price is lower than the present value we derived by using a 12.65 percent rate, XYZ's expected return is higher. If XYZ instead sold for $120 its expected return would equal 11.60 percent. From this perspective we should consider a stock undervalued if its expected return is higher than its beta times the market's expected return, while we should consider it overvalued if its expected return is lower than its beta times the market's expected return.

Thus far we have concentrated on the analytical framework of equity valuation rather than the estimation of the required inputs. We have taken this focus because fundamental analysis, which is used to estimate the required inputs, is outside the scope of this discussion. Nonetheless a few observations are in order.

Within the valuation framework we have just presented, the most reliable input that we need to forecast is the dividend payout ratio, since this value is fairly stable for most companies. Thus we are usually safe to extrapolate historical data. We may wish to superimpose our subjective views, however, if we feel it appropriate to do so. For example, if we expect a company's earnings to grow sharply, we may wish to lower our forecasted historical payout ratio, whereas if we expect earnings to fall sharply, we may choose to raise our forecasted payout ratio. The rationale for these adjustments is that companies manage dividends so that they tend to be less volatile than earnings.

The growth rate of earnings is typically less predictable than the payout ratio. Research-oriented organizations focus most of their efforts on forecasting earnings growth. In the absence of this research, we can base our estimate of earnings growth on the consensus forecast of the research community. Various organizations collect and tabulate these estimates and then make them available to subscribers.

The most difficult value to forecast is the equilibrium value for a stock's price-earnings multiple. Again we may wish to start with historical values and adjust them based upon fundamental considerations. For example we might use the historical average for the company's particular industry as a point of departure and adjust it according to our expectation about the company's return on equity and debt-equity ratio. In general we may wish to raise the equilibrium price-earnings multiple above the industry average if a company has a higher than average return on equity, and we may wish to lower it if a company has a higher than average debt-equity ratio.

Dividend Discount Model

If we assume that dividends will grow at a constant rate indefinitely and that the rate used to discount these dividends remains constant, the valuation model just presented can be simplified to

$$PV = \frac{D}{r - g}$$

where

PV = Stock's present value.
D = Dividend payment at the end of the first period.
r = Discount rate.
g = Growth rate of dividends.

This simple model is commonly referred to as a *dividend discount model*. For example, if we expect a dividend payment of \$4.20 at the end of the first period and believe that the dividend payment will grow at an annual rate of 8 percent, and that these payments should be discounted at a rate of 12.65 percent, the present value of this stock equals \$90.32:

$$90.32 = \frac{4.2}{.1265 - .08}$$

The dividend discount model is recommended by its simplicity and the ease with which we can implement it. However, the assumption that dividends will grow at a constant rate for infinity is less than plausible, not to mention difficult to verify. Moreover this assumption leads to some strange results if we are not careful about our inputs. For example, as the growth rate approaches the discount rate, the stock's present value approaches infinity, and the model explodes when the two rates are equal.

As an alternative to the assumption that dividends grow at a constant rate for infinity many analysts use a three-stage model. For example it is typically assumed that young companies' dividends do not grow at all in the first stage, since earnings are reinvested to promote growth. In the second stage, dividends are assumed to grow at an above-average rate as the company reaps the benefits of its prior reinvestment. In the third stage it is assumed that the growth rate stabilizes at a steady state usually somewhere between the growth rates in the first and second stages. This analysis is very sensitive to assumptions about these growth horizons, which can be extremely difficult to determine.[2]

Single-Period Valuation Model[3]

As an alternative to the constant growth model and the three-stage model, we may wish to focus on a single, finite investment horizon. In fact the typical institutionally managed equity fund is turned over completely within a single year, implying an average holding period of one year. With some simple algebra and a few accounting identities, we can rearrange the present value formula to develop a model of expected return assuming that our investment horizon is a single year.

Let us start with the definition of return for a one-year holding period.

[2]For example, see "Valuation Models: The Key Considerations," Harvard Business School Case Study no. 9–281–067.

[3]This particular model was introduced by Jarrod W. Wilcox, "The P/B–ROE Valuation Model," *Financial Analysts Journal*, January–February 1984, pp. 58–66.

Return equals the dividend income we receive plus the change in price that occurs while we hold the stock, all divided by the stock's price at the beginning of our holding period.

$$\text{Return} = \frac{\text{Dividend} + (\text{Ending price} - \text{Beginning price})}{\text{Beginning price}}$$

We can restate this identity as dividend yield plus percentage change in price. Further, we can restate a stock's percentage change in price as approximately equal to growth in book value plus the percentage change in the stock's price to book value ratio.[4] Therefore we can write

$$R = \frac{D}{P} + g + \frac{PB' - PB}{PB}$$

where

R = Stock's expected return.
D = Dividend payment.
P = Current stock price (the beginning price).
g = Growth in book value (not earnings).
PB = Current price-to-book value ratio.
PB' = Price-to-book value ratio in one year.

We can rearrange this expression further by rewriting dividend yield as earnings times the payout ratio, divided by current price, and by rewriting growth in book value as earnings times the retention rate (one minus the payout ratio), divided by current book value.

With this final rearrangement, our expression for a stock's single-period return is

$$R = \frac{E \times p}{P} + \frac{E \times (1 - p)}{B} + \frac{PB' - PB}{PB}$$

where

E = Earnings.
p = Dividend payout ratio.
B = Current book value.

For this expression we must forecast three values: earnings, dividend payout ratio, and the price-to-book value ratio at the end of the year. The

---

[4]The exact formula for the percentage change in price is growth in book value plus the percentage change in the stock's price to book ratio *times* one plus the growth in book value. This one plus growth factor is typically small and usually ignored. In the numerical example reported on the next page, the exact formula yields 15.35 percent, as opposed to 15.03 percent for the approximate formula.

stock's current price and book value, and thus the current price-to-book value ratio, are known values.

To illustrate this model suppose that we observe the following known values:

Current price = $50.
Book value = $42.

and suppose we forecast the following values:

Earnings = $4.50.
Payout ratio = 40 percent.
Price-to-book value ratio = 1.25 (one year hence)

These values imply an expected return for the next 12 months equal to 15 percent:

$$.15 = \frac{4.5 \times .4}{50} + \frac{4.5 \times .6}{42} + \frac{1.25 - 1.19}{1.19}$$

Moreover we can partition return into three components: yield, growth, and revaluation. In the above example the stock's total expected return of 15 percent comprises an expected contribution of 3.6 percent from yield, 6.4 percent from growth, and 5.0 percent from revaluation or the percentage change in the stock's price-to-book value ratio.

Since this forecast of return depends on forecasts of three unknown values, it is valuable to determine how sensitive our estimate of return is to each of these inputs. We can measure these sensitivities by taking the derivative of return with respect to earnings, the payout ratio, and the price-to-book value ratio to which the stock reverts. In so doing we may find, for example, that a small error in our earnings forecast will lead to a large error in our estimated return, whereas a fairly large error in the payout ratio will only have a minimal impact on our estimate of return. This information is extremely useful because it helps us to channel our research effort efficiently. In the above case, we would concentrate our efforts on ensuring the quality of our earnings forecast.

In general we should seek a high degree of reliability for those forecasts to which our return estimate is most sensitive. In the case of earnings, we may wish to examine the dispersion of the analysts' forecasts if our estimate is based upon consensus of the analysts. If there is wide disagreement among the analysts, we should be less confident in our forecast. If on the other hand the analysts' forecasts fall within a narrow range, we should be more confident (assuming our forecast falls within this range). Similarly we could examine the historical pattern of earnings. Again a high degree of variability in past earnings as measured by their standard deviation should tend to reduce our confidence, whereas low historical variability should tend to increase our confidence. Of course, if we believe something we know about the company is not reflected in the analysts' forecasts and is not a function of past earnings, we must evaluate our information on its own merits.

ANOMALIES

In recent years researchers have discovered a variety of attributes that seem to coincide with abnormal returns—returns that more than compensate for a stock's systematic risk. The presence of excess returns associated with certain attributes is referred to as an *anomaly*.

One of the first documented anomalies is the P/E effect:[5] the notion that stocks with low price-earnings multiples tend to produce higher than average returns, even after accounting for their betas. A related anomaly is the yield effect, which holds that stocks with high dividend yields produce above-average returns.[6] Of course the fact that low P/E stocks typically have high dividend yields makes disentangling one effect from the other difficult. Both attributes may in fact be proxies for a low-price effect. Many studies have also supported the notion that small capitalization stocks perform better than large capitalization stocks.[7] More recently, however, investigators have discovered that S&P 500 stocks produce higher returns than stocks not a part of that index.[8]

In addition to the many anomalies associated with company attributes, numerous studies have detected the presence of calendar anomalies. For example, stocks have been widely documented to have higher returns at the turn of the year—the so-called January effect.[9] In fact some researchers have argued that the size anomaly only occurs at the turn of the year.

---

[5]S. Basu, "Investment Performance of Common Stocks in Relation to Their Price-Earnings Ratios," *Journal of Finance*, June 1977.

[6]R. Litzenberger and K. Ramaswamy, "The Effects of Dividends on Common Stock Prices: Tax Effects or Information Effects," *Journal of Finance*, May 1982, pp. 429–43.

[7]M. Reinganum, "Misspecification of Capital Pricing: Empirical Anomalies Based on Earnings' Yields and Market Value," *Journal of Financial Economics*, 1981, pp. 19–46.

[8]W. Jacques, "The S&P 500 Membership Anomaly, or Would You Join This Club?" *Financial Analysts Journal*, November–December 1988, pp. 73–75.

[9]D. Keim, "Size-Related Anomalies and Stock Market Seasonality: Further Empirical Evidence," *Journal of Financial Economics*, June 1983, pp. 12–32.

What constitutes an anomaly? Clearly if we test enough phenomena we are bound to uncover something unusual. Moreover, suppose that through statistical inference we validate as best we can that a result is indeed anomalous. Is there possibly an explanation for this result that makes it normal?

Typically the criterion for an anomaly is that the returns for stocks that share some common characteristic are significantly greater than the stocks' betas times the market's return; that is, their returns more than compensate for their systematic risk. For example supppose we observe that stocks with low price-earnings multiples have higher returns than stocks with high price-earnings multiples, based on a decile ranking of the New York Stock Exchange stocks according to P/E. This result may be perfectly reasonable if low-P/E stocks tend to be riskier than high-P/E stocks. Thus the first adjustment we must make is to control for their riskiness. We can control for risk simply by subtracting the product of the stock's beta times the market's return from the stock's total return. If, on average, stocks with low P/Es have a higher risk-adjusted return (alpha) than stocks with high P/Es, then we have evidence of a P/E effect.

The next question is whether or not the alpha associated with low-P/E stocks is statistically significant. We can test for statistical significance by dividing the stock's alpha by the standard error. If this value, referred to as a *t-statistic*, is greater than 1.96, then we are 95 percent confident that the alpha associated with low-P/E stocks is significantly different from zero. If on the other hand the high return to low-P/E stocks disappears or becomes insignificant when we adjust for risk, then it is reasonable to assume that the apparent P/E effect is simply a risk premium.

Suppose we also notice that small capitalization stocks seem to produce above-average returns even after we take risk into account. Moreover suppose we notice that the average P/E of small stocks is lower than the average P/E of large stocks. How can we distinguish a P/E effect from a small-stock effect? One approach is to rank stocks into deciles or some other percentile grouping according to P/E and according to capitalization. We can construct a matrix in which each row represents a decile of capitalization and each column represents a decile of P/E. Then we can examine whether the risk-adjusted returns for each row differ with statistical significance as a function of P/E and whether the risk-adjusted returns for each column differ with statistical significance as a function of capitalization. We may find that one effect disappears or that both effects survive.

We can also use multiple regression analysis to determine whether or not there are anomalous returns to various attributes. For example we may hypothesize that stock returns in a given period vary according to the stock's exposure to various attributes at the beginning of the period, such as market risk, yield, growth, price-earnings multiple, capitalization, financial risk, and industry affiliation. We can compute these attributes for each company and use a dummy variable to indicate industry affiliation. Then we can perform the following cross-sectional regression:

$$R_i = \alpha + \beta_M M_i + \beta_Y Y_i + \beta_G G_i + \beta_{PE} PE_i + \beta_C C_i + \beta_F F_i + \beta_I I_i + e_i$$

where

$\quad R_i =$ Monthly total return of the ith company.
$\quad \alpha =$ Constant term.
$\quad M_i =$ Market exposure.
$\quad Y_i =$ Yield.
$\quad G_i =$ Historical growth in earnings.
$PE_i =$ Price-earnings multiple.
$\quad C_i =$ Capitalization.
$\quad F_i =$ Debt-equity ratio.
$\quad I_i =$ Industry affiliation, which is denoted by one if the company is a member of a particular industry and zero if it is not.
$\quad e_i =$ That part of the company's total return that cannot be explained by exposure to these attributes and is therefore specific to the company.

and where the i subscript refers to numbers specific to a particular company.

Suppose we determine these values for all of the companies in our sample as of the beginning of each month for the prior 10 years and perform 120 cross-sectional regressions. In each regression, the stocks' returns for the month are regressed on these attributes and industry affiliations. If after we perform these regressions we observe that the t-statistics for each of the attributes are significant in more than 5 percent of the regressions, we can conclude that differences in exposure to these attributes help to explain cross-sectional differences in company returns.

Next we can look at the time series of the coefficients for each attribute. These coefficients represent the marginal returns to the attribute. That is, they represent the return of a hypothetical portfolio exposed only to that particular attribute or industry, with zero exposure to all other attributes and industries. (For example, if we observe a marginal return equal to .03 percent we would expect a .03-percent return to be generated in that month by a portfolio with an exposure to this attribute that is one standard deviation above the average exposure of the sample and with a zero standard deviation exposure to all other attributes.) If we believe that returns are proportional to market risk, then we should expect that the average marginal return through time to each attribute except market risk will be close to 0 percent. However, the marginal returns to each attribute might be very high or very low in a particular month (or else their *t*-statistics would not have been significant in more than 5 percent of the regressions).

If instead of an average return close to 0 percent we observe a value that is significantly nonzero, this result is anomalous within the paradigm of the *capital asset pricing model*. For example, if there were indeed a small capitalization anomaly, we should observe a statistically significant negative coefficient for the capitalization attribute; that is, a low average marginal return for large companies and a high average marginal return for small companies after controlling for the presence of other attributes such as yield and price-earnings multiple. To determine if an attribute has a significantly anomalous return we simply divide the geometric marginal return to the attribute by the standard deviation of the marginal returns. If the absolute value of the *t*-statistic is greater than 1.96, we should be 95 percent confident that the marginal return to the attribute is significantly different from zero. Since this approach measures the return to each attribute in the presence of all the other attributes, we are able to disentangle the various anomalies.

FACTOR ANALYSIS

In our discussion of anomalies we sought evidence of persistent return biases associated with attributes or factors that explain return differences. Even if we fail to uncover anomalous results, we can use *factor analysis* to select stocks by identifying factors that affect stock returns and then by anticipating changes in these factor values. To illustrate, let us consider a hypothetical stock, the broadcast media giant XYZ.

Suppose that in estimating the beta of XYZ its returns and residuals seemed related to at least two factors: the market return and an index of broadcast industry return. Thus we might have hypothesized a two-factor model to explain differences in return through time:

$$R_{\text{XYZ},t} = R_{f,t} + b_{\text{XYZ},1}f_{1,t} + b_{\text{XYZ},2}f_{2,t} + e_{\text{XYZ},t}$$

where

$R_{\text{XYZ},t}$ = XYZ's return in time period t.
$R_{f,t}$ = Return on a riskless asset during t.
$b_{\text{XYZ},i}$ specifies the percentage change in XYZ's return for a given level of f_i.

TABLE 2–1
First Four Factor Loadings

	Factor 1	Factor 2	Factor 3	Factor 4
Standard & Poor's 500 Index	0.97	−0.04	0.09	−0.01
Cash equivalents	−0.30	0.09	0.29	0.61
Salomon Brothers Bond Index	0.30	0.43	0.57	0.05
American Stock Exchange Index	0.86	−0.22	0.00	−0.09
New York Stock Exchange Index	0.98	−0.04	0.08	0.02
Wilshire 5000 Index	0.98	−0.06	0.05	0.03
XYZ	0.37	0.61	−0.32	0.33
CBS	0.58	0.48	−0.24	0.19
Cox Communications	0.59	0.21	−0.15	0.23
Exxon	0.64	−0.52	0.31	0.02
Schlumberger	0.65	−0.47	0.26	0.20
American Brands	0.44	0.40	0.50	0.02
Avon Products	0.43	0.33	0.06	0.36
Chase Manhattan Bank	0.75	−0.19	0.18	0.02
Diamond Shamrock	0.75	−0.19	0.18	0.02
Charming Shoppes	0.60	0.13	−0.34	0.24
Manor Care	0.64	0.30	−0.23	0.26
Gerber Scientific	0.69	−0.06	−0.27	0.33
Atlantic Richfield	0.49	−0.54	−0.02	0.44
Variance explained	0.43	0.11	−0.08	0.06
Cumulative variance	0.43	0.54	0.62	0.68

Note: The above loadings and indexes would be calculated by *principal components* analysis, which can be considered a special case of factor analysis. In principal components, no specification of the number of factors is made; rather, successive sources of variation are calculated until all variation is explained. By contrast, factor calculations parcel variation into systematic factor-explained variation and residual idiosyncratic variation. Generally, the factor interpretations will not depend on the technique chosen if samples are large, although the loading estimates will vary.

$e_{XYZ,t}$ is a random error term.

$f_{1,t}$ might represent the excess market return over the riskless rate, as proxied by Standard & Poor's index.

$f_{2,t}$ might be an index of excess returns on major broadcasting stocks.

Factor analysis is a mathematical procedure for calculating indexes that best explain the variation within a sample set of data. Table 2–1 contains a set of such indexes for several stock and bond indexes as well as individual stocks, including our hypothetical XYZ. Each of the coefficients might be considered as a beta that varies between plus and minus one. For example the first factor index has a correlation of 97 percent with the S&P 500 Index. Hence this might be thought of as the market effect. XYZ's returns have a correlation of 37 percent with the index. The second factor is harder to interpret; its heaviest loadings are Salomon Brothers Bond Index, XYZ, CBS, EXXON (negative), Schlumberger (negative), American Brands, and Atlantic Richfield (negative). This second index may reflect oil and commodity price inflation, as a drop in such prices might raise bond prices, lower interest rates, and reduce oil company profits relatively. The third index may be long-term interest rates (the Bond Index and American Brands load positively), while the fourth may be short-term rates.

The above analysis has some very important implications—or good news! Because the indexes were calculated by *principal components analysis,* they successively explain the greatest amount of remaining variation, independent of the other indexes. The amounts of variation explained by each of the four indexes were 43 percent, 11 percent, 8 percent, and 6 percent—a cumulative total of 68 percent of the variation in the indexes and stocks. Thus we start to see that there are a few really important factors in the return-generating process. Numerous other studies also document the presence of three or four general factors related to market effects, interest rates, inflation, and so on.[10]

Unfortunately such factor indexes have important limitations—the bad news! First, although they explain past movements exactly it is hard to know what economic forces are influencing them. Second, because they explain the past movements exactly, indexes (other than the first) are often nonstationary over time.[11] Third, to be very accurate one needs to prespecify the exact number of factor indexes, and there is no way to do this precisely.[12]

The Theory behind the Factors[13]

Factor models have just two purposes: (1) to attribute portfolio returns and (2) to adjust returns for systematic risk.

Factor models for attributing return are merely linear equations that express the statement

---

[10]See Nai-fu Chen, Richard Roll, and Stephen A. Ross, "Economic Forces and the Stock Market," *Journal of Business,* July 1986, pp. 383–403.

[11]See Stephen R. Cosslett and H. Russell Fogler, "Factor Nonstationarity in Large Samples: A Note" (Unpublished manuscript, 1986).

[12]Various statistical tests are available to test the hypothesis that k factors are sufficient to explain returns. Yet, if the true process has five factors but the fifth's explanatory power is small the tests may not reject a hypothesis that the true underlying process is a four-factor process.

[13]For a simple discussion of the relationship of the arbitrage pricing theory to factor models, see H. Russell Fogler, "Common Sense on CAPM, APT, and Correlated Residuals," *Journal of Portfolio Management,* Summer 1982, pp. 20–28.

$$R_i = E_o + b_{i1}f_1 + b_{i2}f_2 + \ldots + b_{ik}f_K + e_i$$

where R_i is the return on the ith stock, E_o is the expected return, plus the price change represented by the ith stock's return sensitivities (b_{ik}) to k factors multiplied by the factors' changes (f_k), plus e_i, which is some idiosyncratic return not explained by the other terms.

Factor models for risk adjusting are also linear equations but with systematic factors only; thus

$$R_i = E_o + b_{i1}f_1 + b_{i2}f_2 + \ldots + b_{is}f_S + e_i$$

where S is the number of systematic factors. *Systematic factors* are sources of variation that cannot be diversified away. For example, an economic depression affects virtually all stocks, as does unanticipated inflation; thus overall economic activity and inflation would be systematic factors. *Unsystematic factors* are sources of variation that can be diversified away. For example, building stocks may be highly correlated, but one's portfolio can hold just one or two such stocks in combination with other stocks that do well when building stocks do poorly (possibly stocks that do well when interest rates rise). Finally, according to theory, higher *systematic* risk causes higher long-run returns, so that the return expected in the future (ex ante return) will be related to these systematic factors:

$$E_i = g_o + g_1 b_{i1} + g_a b_{ia} + \ldots g_s b_{is}$$

where E_i represents the stock's ex ante *expected return*, g_o represents the implied riskless rate, g_1 through g_n represent the market prices of risk, the quantities of which are represented by the stock return sensitivities b_{i1} through b_{is}. In a present value model the ex ante expected return determines the appropriate discount rate r to be used in the analysis.

What are the systematic factors? Frankly we do not know, and ultimately this is an empirical issue.[14] The most obvious sources of greatest nondi-

---

[14]Two concepts are crucial to understanding the empirical issue. First, theory is based on return-risk trade-off for expected (ex ante, or future) return although hypothesis testing can only be conducted with actual (ex post, or after the facts are in) data. Second, *any* two or more sets of data can be used to explain ex post results, *if* the data sets have the same number of dependent factors. This is a subtle point that is best illustrated by the two equation systems:

$$2X + 3Y = 12 \qquad 1A + 1B = 12$$
$$2X + 1Y = 8 \qquad 2A + 1B = 8$$

Although the solution values for (X,Y) are different than for (A,B), both systems are equal to (12,8); then both systems can be said to "explain" (12,8).

In our world of uncertainty the empirical issue becomes a choice of variables—which variables $(X,Y$ versus $A,B)$ provide the most stable relationship with the greatest explanatory power.

versifiable variation can be hypothesized from the dividend discount model. Obvious candidates are changes in real economic activity, interest rates, inflation, and dividends. Evidence suggests that at least three or four systematic factors exist. Two popular four-factor name tags are (1) growth–cyclical–stable–energy and (2) real production–inflation–credit premium–term structure slope.[15] Yet, while research on verifying systematic factors may continue for long into the future, use of simple and straightforward factor models for return attribution and portfolio management is currently very effective.

How to Use Factor Models for Attributing Return

Suppose you wanted to attribute the S&P return to its factor composition. To do so, you would need the average effect of each factor (that is, the *factor sensitivity* coefficient) and the characteristics of the S&P index's factors. These values are presented in Table 2–2.

With only four common factors (beta, yield, size, and price) the small unexplained return of 0.64 percent is rather good. Of course you may ask "Why is there any error for a portfolio as large as the S&P average?" There are several important causes:

- *Only a few factors were included.* Many common factors and sector/industry factors generate returns. Only four sector effects were included, as a first-step regression showed that the other sector effects were not statistically significant.
- *The estimates were from a different set of stocks than the S&P.* The sample was 1,249 companies with equity capitalization over $25 million.
- *Ordinary least-squares regression was used.* Each stock was weighted equally although the S&P total return depends on the capitalization weight of each stock. Also all estimates have some sampling error as well as implicitly assuming independence and normality in the residuals (an unlikely result, given the effects from missing factors).
- *Rounding and averaging may cause some slight amount of error.* Although this effect is almost negligible, one should remember the logarithm of an average size will be less than the average of the logarithms of size.

---

[15]See, for example, James L. Farrell, Jr., *Guide to Portfolio Management* (New York: McGraw-Hill, 1983), pp. 205–13; Chen et al., "Economic Forces."

TABLE 2–2
Factor Sensitivity Coefficients of the S&P Index

	Factor Sensitivity	S&P Average, Third Quarter 1986	Return Attribution
Starting point (intercept)	15.22%		15.22%
Beta	− 5.67	1.00	− 5.67
Yield	− .58	4.18	− 2.42
Size (in natural logarithm)	− 1.06	14.85	−15.74
Price	.12	.39	4.68
Sectors:			
Capital goods	2.76	.05	.14
Materials and service	1.96	.10	.20
Energy	2.55	.14	.36
Financial	− 3.76	.07	− .26
Consumer nondurables	0	.29	.00
Utilities	0	.13	.00
Transportation	0	.03	.00
Consumer durables	0	.04	.00
Technology	0	.15	.00
Unexplained return			.64
S&P return			− 4.13%

Given the above limitations, should such factor attribution be discarded? The answer is no, not if it adds useful information. But one must be careful in using it. First, the amount of return explained (R^2) in *individual stocks* was only about 8 percent, which is similar to the results found by others in cross-sectional regressions although about 40 percent is explained over a number of years. And for *portfolios* the explanatory power will be much higher. Also, if a "normal portfolio" is specified as a manager's benchmark, then a manager's ability can be understood by examining how much more or less return is attributed to each factor in his portfolio relative to the factor exposure of the benchmark. Such analysis may help to distinguish whether a portfolio's return is attributable to luck or to skill.[16]

CONCLUSION

In this chapter we demonstrated the application of quantitative methods to equity analysis. We showed how the generalized present value framework

---

[16]For a discussion of the theory of such performance measurement see Mark Kritzman, "How to Detect Skill in Management Performance," *Journal of Portfolio Management*, Winter 1986, pp. 16–20.

TABLE 2–3
Factor Sensitivities of an Equally Weighted Portfolio

	Portfolio	S&P
Expected return (DDM forecast)	12.57%	13.10%
Yield	3.09%	4.28%
P/E ratio	12.86	11.14
Growth	9.60%	8.30
Factor price sensitivities		
Real GNP	26.53	21.48
Short-term interest rates	− 2.77	− 2.76
Inflation	− 10.09	− 8.37
Oil prices	.64	1.20
Defense spending	− 1.26	− 1.20

could easily be customized to estimate a stock's fair value or expected return. We also showed how data analysis and regression analysis provide the tools to uncover and disentangle anomalies. Finally, we discussed the application of factor analysis to stock selection and to performance attribution.

PROBLEMS

1. Suppose that a stock generated $7 in earnings per share in the prior 12 months, that these earnings are expected to grow 8 percent annually for the next three years, and that 50 percent of these earnings will be paid out as dividends. Also suppose this stock has a beta of 1.05 and the expected return for the overall stock market is 10 percent per year for the next three years. Finally suppose the stock's price-earnings multiple on trailing 12-month earnings will equal 13 at the end of three years. What is the present value of this stock?

   $$Answer: \quad PV = \frac{\$7 \times (1.08) \times .5}{[1 + (.10 \times 1.05)]} + \frac{\$7 \times (1.08)^2 \times .5}{[1 + (.10 \times 1.05)]^2}$$
   $$+ \frac{[\$7 \times (1.08)^3 \times .5] + [\$7 \times (1.08)^3 \times 13]}{[1 + (.10 \times 1.05)]^3}$$

   $$PV = 83.59$$

2. Suppose you hypothesize that differences in stock returns in a given month across a wide sample of stocks are explained by differences in several attributes, including capitalization and price-earnings multiples. You test this hypothesis by regressing monthly returns against these attributes for five years of monthly observations. All of the

coefficients are more statistically significant than would occur by random process. The average capitalization coefficient from the 60 regressions equals − .6 percent, which is statistically different from zero. The averages of the other coefficients are not distinguishable from zero. Interpret these results, assuming no important variables were omitted from this model.

Answer: The selected attributes explain cross-sectional differences in stock returns, as evidenced by the fact that their coefficients are statistically significant more often than expected by random process. However, only the capitalization attribute produces persistent results in the sense that, controlling for the other attributes, small companies tend to outperform large companies on average. Specifically these regressions suggest that a hypothetical stock with a capitalization that is one standard deviation greater than the average capitalization of the sample used to estimate the model, and whose other attributes are zero standard deviations away from the sample averages, is expected to return − 60 basis points per month.

CHAPTER THREE

Quantitative Methods in Fixed-Income Analysis

Roger G. Ibbotson and Margaret A. Corwin

Fixed-income securities are contracts that usually entitle the holder to a series of cash flows or interest payments as well as a return of principal. This chapter addresses the quantitative methods that may be used to analyze such contracts. The first part of the chapter addresses bond valuation issues and the measurement of returns. The second part addresses bond yields. The final two sections address portfolio considerations and how interest rate sensitivity can be managed.

VALUATION OF FIXED–INCOME SECURITIES

Elements of Bonds

The *par value* of a bond is the value printed on the face of a bond certificate. This principal (face) amount is the amount that must eventually be repaid

NOTE: This chapter is adapted with permission from a chapter in Roger G. Ibbotson and Gary P. Brinson, *Investment Markets: Gaining the Performance Advantage* (New York: McGraw-Hill Book Company. Copyright © 1987, McGraw-Hill, Inc.).

and approximates the amount borrowed by the issuer. The most common par value of U.S. government and corporate bonds is $1,000. In this country, bond prices are usually quoted in a price per $100 of face value. Suppose United Utilities issues 10 percent bonds, maturing in 20 years. These bonds might sell for $90 or about 90 percent of face value, which means they have an actual price of $900 per $1,000 bond.

As the United Utilities example illustrates, a bond's market *price* is usually not equal to its face value. This price is determined in the market by the bond's coupon rate, maturity date, call provisions, tax status, and default risk, as well as prevailing interest rates. Each of these factors is considered in turn.

In addition to a return of principal, most bonds promise a series of cash payments. The amount of those payments is determined by the *coupon rate*, usually expressed as a percentage of the principal (par) amount. For example the United Utilities bond with a 10 percent coupon produces 10 percent interest on the $1,000 face value, or an annual interest of $100. If the bond sells above or below $1,000 the coupon remains at $100. The bond would have an annual yield greater than 10 percent if the bond were to sell for less than $1,000. If the bond sold above $1,000 the annual yield would be less than 10 percent. Coupons are usually paid semiannually, and such yields are slightly higher because the interest compounds.

When bonds are sold between interest dates, they are usually priced to include part of the interest payment that the new owner will receive. Consequently the seller must allocate part of the purchase price to *accrued interest*. The *flat price* of a bond is the quoted price plus accrued interest.

A bond's *maturity date* is the date on which the issuer must repay the bond's principal value. Long-term debt is usually considered to be any obligation repayable more than 10 years from the date of issue, while medium-term debt is longer than 1 year and less than 10 years. Short-term debt is debt due in less than one year.

Types of Bonds

A bond's principal and interest payments can take one of three forms: a coupon bond, a zero coupon bond, or an annuity. The focus of this chapter will be on the first two, which are generally thought of as bonds.

Coupon bonds, the most common type, have already been described. Typically these are issued near face value. Coupon bonds also pay a fixed dollar amount of interest determined by the coupon rate. Such payments are made to bondholders, usually semiannually, until maturity.

A *zero coupon*, or *discount*, *bond* is a bond issued below its par value, or at a discount. For example a $1,000 zero coupon bond that matures in three years might sell for $780 for an annual yield to maturity of 8.6 percent. Its return comes from an increase in principal value alone, for this type of bond pays no interest on face value. The price of such a bond without default risk is the present value of the face amount, assumed to be received with complete certainty. Some corporate bonds and all U.S. Treasury bills (but not Treasury notes or bonds) are issued at a discount. Some investors find "zeros" advantageous because most are not callable before maturity and because, over the investment horizon, they have no reinvestment risk. Zeros were developed for investors with well-defined time horizons. Strictly speaking, zeros are called *original-issue discount* bonds that distinguish them from coupon bonds selling below face value, since bond traders sometimes refer to the latter as *discount* bonds.

An *annuity* is the third type of bond payment scheme. A house mortgage and an insurance annuity contract are examples of annuities. Each payment contains principal and interest. Payments are level over a finite term, and there is no "balloon" payment of principal at maturity. The amount of principal and interest changes because the interest is computed on a decreasing outstanding balance; the interest portion is less and the principal portion greater with each payment.

The Present Value Formula

As with other investments, the value of a bond can be expressed as the present value of the payments to which the bondholder is entitled. Suppose an investor purchased on the coupon payment date a bond paying an annual coupon. Expressed in terms of a par value of 100 the present value is given by

$$PV = \frac{c}{(1 + r_1)} + \frac{c}{(1 + r_2)^2} + \frac{c}{(1 + r_3)^3} + \ldots + \frac{100 + c}{(1 + r_T)^T}$$

where

$$c = \text{Coupon.}$$
$$r_1, r_2, \ldots r_T = \text{Appropriate discount rates for one year, two years, through } T \text{ years.}$$
$$T = \text{Time to maturity of the bond.}$$

The value of 100 in the last term of the formula reflects the repayment of principal at maturity. In many applications it is assumed that all the discount rates are equal. In that case the (single) discount rate that sets the present value equal to the current price of the bond is said to be the *yield to maturity* (or simply the *yield*) of the bond.

Few bonds actually pay annual coupons, and rarely are bonds purchased on coupon payment dates. For this reason it is sometimes convenient to express the present value formula as

$$PV = [c \times d(t_1)] + [c \times d(t_2)] + [c \times d(t_3)]$$
$$+ \ldots + [(100 + c) \times d(T)]$$

where $d(t_1)$, $d(t_2)$, . . . $d(T)$ represent the appropriate *discount factors* associated with payments received t_1, t_2, through T years from today. These discount factors are given by the formula

$$d(t) = \frac{1}{(1 + r_t)^t}$$

where t now refers to the year or fractional part of the year at which the payments occur.[1]

It is evident from the present value formula that the value of a bond varies inversely with the interest rates that are represented as the discount rates in the formula. As interest rates decline, the value of the bond rises because the fixed coupon and principal payments associated with the bond become more valuable. Likewise, when interest rates rise these payments become less valuable, and bond prices fall.

Bond Yields and Returns

Yield to Maturity. A bond's yield to maturity (or simply its yield) is its internal rate of return, or the single discount rate that equates the present value of future income to the bond's current market value. This calculated return of a bond relates to three factors:

---

[1]Since many bonds pay coupons on a semiannual basis the industry convention is to assume that rates are expressed on a semiannual compounded basis. In other words,

$$d(t) = \frac{1}{\left(1 + \dfrac{r_t}{2}\right)^{2t}}$$

This is a complication we shall ignore for the remainder of the chapter.

1. The money received in the form of a periodic coupon payment.
2. The difference between purchase price and redemption value.
3. The number of years to maturity.

In bond trading, yields to maturity are typically quoted on a semiannual compounding basis.

Consider again the United Utilities bond with a 10 percent coupon, a face value of $1,000, a term of 20 years, and a market value of $900. (For ease of explanation assume annual coupons instead of the more prevalent semiannual coupons observed in the marketplace.) The present value of the bond's income is the value of an income stream of $100 annually plus the value of the $1,000 principal payment 20 years later. (The interest has a present value of $781.85 while the principal has a present value of $118.15, summing to $900.) If the security's market value is $900 its yield to maturity is determined by iteration, or trial and error—that is, by trying various discount rates to see which rate equals that market value. Using present value tables or a calculator in such a process, the discount rate is found to be about 11.3 percent. Thus the bond's yield to maturity is about 11.3 percent. A bond's yield to maturity changes if interest rates change, if its default risk increases, or if expectations about inflation change.

Expected Return. A bond's yield to maturity would be the bond's *expected return* if there is no expected default and if interest rates are constant through time. If default is expected the bond's expected return will be less than its yield to maturity, because of the expected loss from default.

Yet there is a problem with thinking about yields as constant returns. The calculation assumes that the same rate is used to discount all payments, but bondholders may demand different rates over different future periods. The yield is really an average and hides the variability of rates at which interest payments might be reinvested. The return expected by investors may vary from period to period in the future.

Actual Return. A bondholder's *actual return* is the amount of money received from holding the bond over a period, divided by the investment at the beginning of the period. Only if the bond is held to maturity is the bond's actual return equal to its expected return or yield. If sold before maturity the bond's actual return includes the capital gain or loss on its sale. If interest rates change at any time during the period, interest payments may be reinvested at rates higher or lower than expected.

Consider yet again the United Utilities bond, this time one year later. The coupon is still 10 percent, and the face value is still $1,000. But now the remaining term is 19 years, and the market price is $950. Assuming the bond is then sold, its actual return can be calculated as the difference between purchase price ($900) and the sale price ($950), or $50, plus the income from the period ($100), both divided by the purchase price. Therefore the actual return is 16.7 percent in that year, while its yield to maturity at the end of the year has fallen to 10.6 percent.

Aftertax Return. So far the before-tax returns on bonds have been described. To obtain the *aftertax returns* the taxes on interest income and on capital gains or losses from principal must be taken into account. The interest income from coupon bonds, determined by the coupon rate, is all subject to tax. Likewise the increase in a discount bond's principal value over its purchase price must be treated as interest income. In addition the difference between a bond's purchase price (less accrued interest if any) and its sales price is taxed at capital gains rates, which are usually lower than ordinary rates.

Discount Yield. The yields on short-term bonds are often quoted as discount yields. This is the annual interest over par, divided by the time to maturity. For example a bond with a 7 percent coupon selling at $93 with one year to maturity is quoted as having a yield of 7 percent, which is approximately $70/$1,000, divided by 1, which equals 7 percent. A more correct computation would be $70/$930, divided by 1, or 7.5 percent. Because long-term bond yields include compound interest, short- and long-term bond yields are not directly comparable. Of course short-term bond yields can be converted to the yield to maturity and then referred to as *bond equivalent yields*, which are comparable.

Current Yield. Sometimes people measure a bond's *current yield*, which is the ratio of its promised or current income to its current market price. Again, this is not to be confused with a bond's yield to maturity. If the 10 percent United Utilities bond sells for $950 its current yield would be the coupon ($100) divided by the market value ($950), or a current yield of 10.5 percent in contrast to its yield to maturity of 10.6 percent. In this example the yield to maturity is higher than the current yield because the investor expects a $50 capital gain at maturity, which is included in the yield to maturity.

Note that a bond's coupon rate is different from its current yield. The coupon rate is the bond's return as a percent of its par (principal) amount, while its current yield is the income return on the investment at the market

TABLE 3–1
Different Durations of a Four-Year Discount and a Four-Year Coupon Bond
(with annual compounding)

(1) *Type of Bond*	*(2)* *Time* *(years)*	*(3)* *PV of* *Payment*	*(4)* *PV of Payment* *as Fraction of PV* *of Bond*	*(5)* *(2) × (4)*
Discount bond				
Coupon = 0 percent	4	$635.50	1.00	4 years
Annual yield to maturity = 12 percent				
Coupon bond				
Annual coupon = 9 percent				
Annual yield to maturity = 12 percent				
interest	1	$ 80.36	.088	.088 years
	2	71.75	.079	.158
	3	64.06	.071	.213
	4	57.20	.063	.252
Principal	4	635.50	.699	2.796
Total		$908.87	1.000	3.5 years

price. Yield to maturity, however, measures the total expected return—including both income and capital gain or loss—on the overall investment. To reiterate: when the term *yield* is used in this chapter, yield to maturity is implied.

A Bond's Duration

The *duration* of the bond is a weighted average of the times when payments are due. Each payment's weight is determined by its present value as a percentage of the present value of the bond as a whole. Consider two bonds, both with four-year terms and 12 percent yields to maturity. The first is a four-year zero coupon bond with a price of $635.50. This bond had a duration of four years because there is a single payment at maturity that makes up 100 percent of its present value. By contrast the second is a four-year bond with a 9 percent coupon and a price of $908.87. This bond has a shorter duration—3.5 years—because each coupon payment (compounded annually to simplify the illustration) figures into the weighting. The calculation of these bond durations is shown in Table 3–1.

The formula for duration is

$$\text{Duration} = \left(t_1 \times \frac{c \times d(t_1)}{PV} \right) + \left(t_2 \times \frac{c \times d(t_2)}{PV} \right)$$
$$+ \ldots + \left(T \times \frac{(100 + c) \times d(T)}{PV} \right)$$

TABLE 3–2
Maturities and Durations of Selected Bonds
(with semiannual compounding)

Coupon	Yield to Maturity	Maturity	Price	Duration
12%	12%	5 years	$1,000.00	3.901 years
12	12	10	1,000.00	6.079
12	12	20	1,000.00	7.975
12	12	30	1,000.00	8.566
6	12	30	515.14	9.196
0	12	30	33.40	30.000

where

$$d(t_1), d(t_2), \ldots d(T) = \text{Discount factor for payments to be received}$$
$$t_1, t_2, \text{ through } T \text{ years from today.}$$
$$c = \text{Coupon.}$$
$$PV = \text{Present value of the bond.}$$

Since the present value of the bond is nothing more than the sum of the discounted payments to be received from the bond, the formula says simply that duration is a weighted average of the time until payment dates, where the weights are given by the fraction of the present value arising from that period's payment.

Duration thus measures the average time investors have money owed to them in present value terms. In Table 3–2 the effects of increasing maturity and decreasing coupon rates on a bond's duration are illustrated. When a bond's yield and coupon are held constant but its maturity is increased, its duration increases but much more slowly than the bond's maturity in years. While a 5-year, 12 percent bond has a duration of 3.9 years, a similar 10-year bond has a duration of 6.1 years, and a comparable 20-year bond has a duration of only 8.0 years.

The higher the bond's coupon rate, the shorter its duration. This is because the higher the coupon rate, the larger the coupons' weights relative to the present value of the bond. A 30-year bond with a coupon of 12 percent has a duration of 8.6 years, while a 30-year bond with a coupon of 6 percent has a duration of 9.2 and a 30-year discount bond with a zero coupon has a duration of 30 years.

While the expression for duration given above is completely general, in practical applications measures of duration differ according to assumptions that are made about the appropriate discount rates. They also differ according to uses to which measures of duration are put.

If the discount factors are computed assuming the discount rates are all equal to the yield to maturity *(ytm)* on the bond:

$$d(t) = \frac{1}{(1 + ytm)^t}$$

then the resulting measure of duration is referred to as *Macaulay's Duration* after Frederick Macaulay who originally developed this measure.[2] So-called *second generation duration* measures compute the discount factors *d(t)* on the basis of the zero coupon yield curve, using methods to be discussed later in this chapter.

The extent to which bond prices are affected by changes in interest rates depends on the length of time investors have their funds committed to such investments. Thus duration is a natural measure of interest rate sensitivity. For this purpose, analysts use a measure of *adjusted duration* given as duration divided by the quantity one plus the yield to maturity of the bond, since it can be shown that the percentage change in bond price is approximately equal to the adjusted duration times the change in yield to maturity. Take a bond with a duration of five years, a coupon of 12 percent, and a yield to maturity of 12 percent, selling at par, or 100. If the yield to maturity rises 10 basis points, or .10 percent, to 12.10 percent, the price will fall approximately 5/1.12 times .10 percent, or .446 percent, to 99.554.

Analysts should treat this measure of adjusted duration with some care. Since duration falls as interest rates rise, the measure *overestimates* the fall in prices as interest rates rise and *underestimates* the rise in prices when interest rates fall. This property, known as *convexity,* needs to be adjusted for when interest rates change by more than an insignificant amount. Another limitation of adjusted duration as a measure of interest rate sensitivity is an implicit assumption that short term rates of interest move in lockstep with long-term rates. More advanced measures of duration are being developed to account for these difficulties.[3]

---

[2]Frederick Macaulay, *Some Theoretical Problems Suggested by the Movement of Interest Rates, Bond Yields, and Stock Prices since 1865* (New York: National Bureau of Economic Research, 1938).

[3]Other complications arise where the bonds in question may be called by the issuer prior to maturity. Adjustments for these optionlike characteristics (see Chapter Five) are described in Alden Toevs, "Hedging Interest Rate Risk of Fixed Income Securities with Uncertain Lives," in *Controlling Interest Rate Risk,* ed. Robert Platt (New York: John Wiley & Sons, 1986), pp. 176–96.

DETERMINANTS OF BOND YIELDS

Bonds with the same yield to maturity are not necessarily equivalent. Bonds differ according to coupon rate and time to maturity. They also differ with respect to credit risk, taxable status, call terms, conversion options, and other special features. The interpretation of the yield to maturity depends on an understanding of the effect these variables have on the value of bonds.

Yield Curves—The Term Structure of Interest Rates

The yield to maturity measure is easiest to interpret where the appropriate discount rates that enter into the present value formula are in fact the same for all maturities. The appropriate discount rates typically rise with time to maturity. Investors seem to demand a difference in yield between long-term and short-term bonds even where there is no risk of default and the bonds are otherwise equivalent. If two bonds have the same yield to maturity and are the same except for time to maturity, such an investor would prefer the shorter time to maturity. The reason is that the later payments would be valued less than they would be if the discount rates were the same for all maturities. The yield curve describes the way that rates vary with time to maturity.

The yields to maturity on default-free bonds of various maturities are shown together in Figure 3–1 to portray what is called the yield curve on Treasury securities. In June 1986, 30-day Treasury bills are shown to yield about 6.1 percent while five-year notes yield about 8.1 percent, the 2.0 percent difference being the yield spread between these two securities. The yield curve on such riskless securities is also called the *term structure of interest rates*.

The yield curve, or term structure, takes three basic forms, as also shown in Figure 3–1. In an upward sloping curve such as the June 1986 curve, short-term rates are lower than long-term rates. When the curve is downward sloping, as in the January 1981 curve, short-term rates are higher than long-term rates. The curve can also be humpbacked, as it was in October 1981; here short-term rates are low, medium-term rates are high, and long-term rates are in between. The shape of the yield curve can indeed change over time. However, the upward sloping curve depicted for June 1986 is found most frequently.

Economists are interested in this curve chiefly because it contains within it some indication of the future course of interest rates. To give a concrete example, suppose that at a recent Treasury bill auction one-year Treasury

FIGURE 3–1
Term Structure of U.S. Treasury Yields

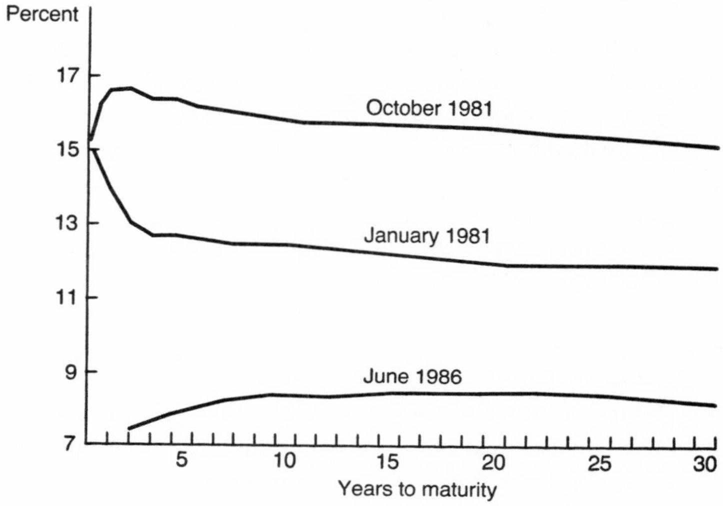

SOURCE: Ibbotson Associates, *Stocks, Bonds, Bills and Inflation: 1986 Yearbook* (Chicago: Ibbotson Associates, Inc. 1986).

bills were sold to yield 6 percent to their maturity in one year. At the same time, a zero coupon Treasury stripped certificate is trading at a price to yield 8 percent to its maturity in two years. This yield spread reflects the fact that the yield curve is upward sloping.

Under what conditions would the average investor consider the two investments equivalent? If the investor were to invest in the two-year paper, $100 of initial investment would grow to $116.64 in two years:

$$\$116.64 = \$100 \times (1 + .08)(1 + .08)$$

On the other hand the investor who invested in the Treasury bill would have to reinvest the proceeds at the end of the year to match the two-year investment. In fact the investor would require a return of 10.04 percent on the reinvested funds to match the two-year investment:

$$\$116.64 = \$100 \times (1 + .06)(1 + .1004)$$

In other words, for a 6 percent, one-year investment to exactly match an 8 percent, two-year investment, the investor would require an annual return of 10.04 percent one year from today. The 10.04 percent number implied by the yield spread between 6 percent on one-year investments and 8 percent on two-year investments is referred to as a *forward rate*. The current rate of 6 percent is referred to as the *spot rate*.

One theory that would explain the upward-sloping yield curve is that investors expect interest rates to rise. In other words, they expect the spot rates in the future to match the forward rates implicit in the yield curve. This view, known as the *expectations hypothesis*, is necessarily incomplete, as few investors can assess precisely what will happen with interest rates in the future. Investing in the two-year instrument ties up money for that period of time. Investors are unable to take advantage of favorable changes in interest rates and are, moreover, subject to the possibility of capital loss if interest rates rise and they have to sell their investment prior to maturity. Hence investors require some kind of premium on longer-term paper to account for this risk. This view, known as the *liquidity preference hypothesis*, would predict that the forward rate exceeds the market's expectation of the future expected spot rate by the measure of this premium. It would predict that the yield curve would be upward sloping even if expected spot rates were equal to the current spot rates and would explain why yield curves generally slope in an upward direction. The fact that yield curves are sometimes sloped downward, as in January 1981, is a strong indication that the market expected interest rates to decline. Finally there is the *preferred habitat theory*, which suggests that the market may be dominated by individuals and institutions with very particular maturity preferences. This view might explain why the yield curve sometimes exhibits "bumps" in its shape.

Credit Risk and Default Premiums

Other than the time to maturity, the credit or default risk is usually the most important characteristic of a bond. U.S. government bonds are usually assumed to be default free. If a bond is subject to default, the promised yield to maturity must be high enough not only to cover this probability but also to provide compensation for taking default risk. The total of these compensations is the *default premium*. If the expected loss from default is 1 percent and if the compensation for taking default risk is 1 percent, then the total default premium would be 2 percent. When a riskless bond yields 10 percent, the corresponding yield on a bond subject to the default probability described above would be 12 percent. The expected return would be approximately 12 percent conditional on no default but only 11 percent after allowing for the probability of default.

The *yield spread* between a bond and a comparable government bond is in large part a measure of the market's assessment of default risk. In addition, various rating agencies rate the creditworthiness of most bonds. For example, Moody's rates bonds Aaa, Aa, Baa, and so forth, with the lower-rated bonds having the higher likelihood of default.

Taxable Status

Major categories of bonds are treated differently for tax purposes. The income from municipal bonds is exempt from U.S. federal income tax and also, in many cases, from state and municipal taxes. The income from U.S. Treasury issues is typically subject to federal taxes, and the income from corporate bonds is also subject to state taxes. This difference alone explains a yield spread between municipal bonds and other bonds of a similar risk.

To the extent that capital gains are taxed at rates that differ from those applied to income, high-coupon bonds have different aftertax returns than low-coupon bonds. Historically, corporates with low coupons have low yields that may in part be explained by the fact that investors expected part of their return in the form of capital gains that were taxed at a lower rate. In the past, bond premiums and discounts were treated asymmetrically for tax purposes;[4] for the same yield to maturity, other things equal, the investor would prefer the bond trading at a discount to one trading at a premium.

Even among U.S. Treasury issues, there are important differences in tax status. Aside from the wide range of coupon rates, premiums, and discounts, some Treasury issues have special estate tax characteristics. Known as flower bonds these bonds are redeemable at par to pay estate taxes in the event that the holder dies. One type of flower bond requires the bond to be held at least six months prior to the death of the holder, while another requires only that the bond be held at the time of death. While these bonds typically have a long term to maturity, few investors would purchase them with the intent of holding them to maturity. For this reason the high price and low yield to maturity of such bonds are deceptive.

Callable Bonds

Most long-term bonds are callable by the issuer after some grace period. Corporates are usually callable at par plus the coupon, and government bonds with call provisions are callable at par.[5]

---

[4]With the notable exceptions of Treasury bills and original-issue discount bonds.

[5]Most Treasury bonds are not callable.

The call term is in fact an option that the issuer holds. The option has value; the bond sells at a lower price and has a higher yield to maturity than a comparable bond issued without the call terms. The issuer will tend to call the bonds if interest rates fall and he or she can refinance at a lower rate. Call terms make bond valuation complex, since a delayed option has to be valued. The theory of options discussed in Chapter Five can be applied in this context.

Convertible Bonds

Convertible fixed-income securities are corporate bonds or debentures that may be exchanged at a specified price for a certain number of shares of the corporation's common stock. Convertible bonds have two characteristics: a claim on a preset stream of cash flows and an option to purchase the common stock of the firm. The value of a convertible bond is thus related to these two components: the bond's value as a straight debt instrument and the value of the option on the firm's stock. Such instruments have unlimited potential for price appreciation. As the value of the corporation's stock increases, so will the value of the convertible debt security. This security also provides investors with limited downside risk, or limited loss of principal. The risk of loss is minimized because the value of a convertible bond is bounded below by the value of a straight bond; if the firm's stock falls in price so as to make the option worthless the convertible bond is still worth the same amount as other nonconvertible debt securities of the corporation.

Convertible bonds are sometimes sold as a way to "have your cake and eat it too." To be sure, the conversion terms are valuable; but they are also built into the price, giving convertibles lower yields than they would otherwise have. The conversion feature is in fact an option; and again, the theory of options discussed in Chapter Five can be used to value the privilege of conversion.

DATA ANALYSIS

Historical Returns

In the previous section we discussed the extent to which the yield to maturity could be used to compare and analyze different bond issues. Another approach is to compare these issues on the basis of their historical returns. Historical returns are not the same as the yield to maturity, since total returns include both the yield to maturity and the return in excess of yield. Stated another way, total returns include both income and capital gains or losses over specified holding periods.

TABLE 3–3
U.S. Bond Market: Total Annual Returns, 1960–1984

	Compound Return	Arithmetic Mean	Standard Deviation
Corporate			
Intermediate-term	6.37%	6.80%	7.15%
Long-term	5.03	5.58	11.26
Corporate total (including preferreds)	5.35	5.75	9.63
Government			
Treasury notes	6.32	6.44	5.27
Treasury bonds	4.70	5.11	9.70
U.S. agencies	6.88	7.04	6.15
Government total	5.91	6.10	6.43
Cash equivalents			
U.S. Treasury bills	6.25	6.29	3.10
Commercial paper	7.03	7.08	3.20
Cash total	6.49	6.54	3.22

SOURCE: Roger G. Ibbotson, Laurence B. Siegel, and Kathryn S. Love, "World Wealth: Market Values and Returns," *Journal of Portfolio Management,* Fall 1985.

The total returns on U.S. Treasury and corporate bonds, and cash equivalents, are measured annually from 1960 to 1984 and presented in Table 3–3. The geometric mean or compound annual return, the arithmetic mean return, and the annual standard deviation are given for each bond category.

The period 1960–1984 was generally a period of rising interest rates. Therefore capital losses were incurred on net, especially for those who held longer-term bonds. The capital losses on longer-term bonds more than offset the higher yields earned over the period. Thus, over the 25-year period, cash equivalents tended to outperform notes and intermediates, which in turn tended to outperform longer-term bonds. The other important variable explaining the historical returns is credit risk. The higher credit risk of corporates caused them to have higher returns. This risk was rewarded over the period, since there were very few defaults. Thus commercial paper outperformed Treasury bills, corporate intermediates outperformed Treasury notes, and long-term corporates outperformed Treasury bonds.

Correlations

Table 3–4 presents the correlation matrix of total annual returns for the 10 bond categories. Note that the highest correlations of bond returns are for those bonds with similar maturities. Treasury bills and commercial paper

TABLE 3–4

U.S. Bond Market: Correlation Matrix of Total Annual Returns

	Treasury Notes	Treasury Bonds	Total U.S. Agencies	Intermediate Government Bonds	Long-Term Corporate Bonds	Total Corporate Bonds	Corporate Bonds	Treasury Bills	Commercial Paper	Total Cash
Treasury notes	1.000									
Treasury bonds	0.904	1.000								
U.S. agencies	0.962	0.904	1.000							
U.S. total government bonds	0.972	0.950	0.964	1.000						
Intermediate-term corporate bonds	0.900	0.865	0.848	0.887	1.000					
Long-term corporate bonds	0.858	0.912	0.808	0.859	0.941	1.000				
U.S. total corporate bonds	0.865	0.902	0.809	0.863	0.960	0.996	1.000			
Treasury bills	0.395	0.111	0.328	0.325	0.336	0.094	0.135	1.000		
Commercial paper	0.394	0.115	0.348	0.330	0.313	0.070	0.108	0.990	1.000	
U.S. total cash	0.400	0.119	0.340	0.332	0.339	0.096	0.136	0.999	0.995	1.000

SOURCE: Roger G. Ibbotson, Laurence B. Siegel, and Kathryn S. Love, "World Wealth: Market Values and Returns," *Journal of Portfolio Management,* Fall 1985.

have a correlation of .99, Treasury notes and corporate intermediates have a correlation of .90, and Treasury bonds and long-term corporates are also correlated .90. To a somewhat lesser extent corporates correlate with each other across maturities. Naturally the total categories are highly correlated with their subcomponents.

These results demonstrate quite clearly that interest rate sensitivity at different maturities is the primary factor responsible for bond returns over any given period. Despite the differences between government and corporate issues, bonds that promise similar cash flows have returns that are similar to the extent that they are subject to the same interest rate factors.

Regression Analysis

In order to analyze further how bond returns relate to each other and to economic phenomena, *regression analysis* is used. First the excess returns over Treasury bills (held to be riskless) are computed for total corporate bonds and total government bond portfolios. These excess returns are re-gressed on the excess returns on a portfolio consisting of all bonds; the results are reported in Table 3–5. Note that the alphas, the intercepts from these regressions, are near zero, and the betas that represent the slope coefficient are quite significant. The beta of corporate bonds is 1.33, and the beta of governments is only .84. At least one explanation for the higher beta of the corporate bond portfolio is the fact that this portfolio has a longer average term to maturity.

Each of the bond categories is regressed on the inflation rate. Note that the betas of the cash equivalents are positive while the other betas are negative—and more negative the longer the maturity. Recall that the total returns consist of a yield component plus the return in excess of yield. Yields tend to go up with inflation, leading to higher income but to capital losses. Cash equivalents are good inflation hedges, while long-term bonds are negative hedges against inflation for short-term investors.

Estimating the Term Structure

Most accounts of the mathematics of bond valuation assume the analyst can simply observe the term structure of interest rates and use this information to compute the discount factors that appear in the present value formula. Figure 3–2 gives the yield curve as measured by the yields to maturity on Treasury bills, bonds, and notes implied by the mean of bid and ask price

TABLE 3–5
Bond Regressions: Total Annual Returns

Dependent Variable	Independent Variable	Alpha (Percent)	Alpha t Statistic	Beta	Beta t Statistic	Adjusted R²	Standard Deviation of Residuals	First-Order Autocorrelation of Residuals
Corporate bonds	U.S. total bonds	− 0.05	− 0.10	1.33	18.35	0.933	2.56	− 0.28
Government bonds	U.S. total bonds	0.12	0.36	0.84	18.61	0.935	1.60	− 0.28
U.S. corporate bonds								
Intermediate-term	Inflation	7.45	2.82	− 0.16	− 0.39	− 0.037	7.43	0.37
Long-term	Inflation	10.42	2.61	− 0.91	− 1.46	0.046	11.23	0.18
Total corporate bonds	Inflation	9.49	2.75	− 0.70	− 1.31	0.029	9.69	0.26
U.S. government bonds								
Treasury notes	Inflation	6.72	3.44	− 0.05	− 0.18	− 0.042	5.49	0.15
Treasury bonds	Inflation	8.59	2.46	− 0.66	− 1.21	0.019	9.81	− 0.01
U.S. agencies	Inflation	7.33	3.22	− 0.05	− 0.15	− 0.042	6.40	0.05
Total government bonds	Inflation	6.58	2.76	− 0.09	− 0.24	− 0.041	6.70	0.14
U.S. total bonds	Inflation	7.56	2.88	− 0.31	− 0.75	− 0.018	7.38	0.22
U.S. cash								
Treasury bills	Inflation	3.11	3.77	0.60	4.66	0.464	2.32	0.74
Commercial paper	Inflation	3.63	4.48	0.65	5.14	0.514	2.28	0.74

SOURCE: Roger G. Ibbotson, Laurence B. Siegel, and Kathryn S. Love, "World Wealth: Market Values and Returns," *Journal of Portfolio Management,* Fall 1985.

quotations as of December 31, 1985.[6] While it is clear from this figure that the yield curve is upwardly sloping, a number of bonds with the same maturity seem to trade at different yields. As one example two Treasury bonds, both set to mature on November 16, 1986, trade to yield 6.3 percent and 7.6 percent, respectively. Should the analyst use the 6.3 percent number or the 7.6 percent number? Some of these differences can be explained. The bond yielding 6.3 percent trades at a discount, whereas most of the other bonds trade at a premium; the 6.3 percent number reflects some of the tax advantages associated with bonds that are purchased at a discount. Some differences may be due to pricing errors and would represent arbitrage opportunities, although many other differences simply reflect the fact that many bonds are not frequently traded. The mean of the bid and ask prices does not always represent an accurate assessment of what the bond could actually trade for in the market. Finally, some of the differences may simply reflect quotation errors.

One obvious approach to the problem is to fit some kind of smooth curve to the data represented in Figure 3–2. Few yield curves rise as steadily as does the one depicted in that figure; as indicated earlier in this chapter, yield curves can take quite a variety of shapes. For this reason simple linear regression procedures are often not appropriate. Many analysts simply fit a smooth curve by eye through the points depicted in such figures; others employ more sophisticated procedures that use computer technology to do essentially the same thing. Such procedures are called *spline smoothing* (we shall refer to them later in this section).

This approach is not altogether satisfactory for several reasons. On a purely practical level it is sometimes difficult to fit a smooth curve to this data. Figure 3–3 illustrates the difficulties associated with fitting such a curve to the Treasury bill data. It is much easier to fit the discount factors directly to this data. Since Treasury bills are zero coupon bonds, the price today expressed as a fraction of par is the discount factor associated with the time to maturity of that bill:

$$\text{Price today} = \text{present value} = \$1 \times \frac{1}{(1 + r_t)^t} = d(t)$$

where

$r_t = $ Yield of the Treasury bill to a maturity of t.

$d(t) = $ Discount factor associated with this maturity.

---

[6]The yield to maturity of flower bonds and other bonds with special tax treatments are excluded from this figure as are the yields to maturity of callable bonds. These bonds have yields to maturity that systematically differ from those of other bonds, for reasons outlined earlier in this chapter.

FIGURE 3–2
Yield Curve of Treasury Bills, Bonds, and Notes, December 31, 1985

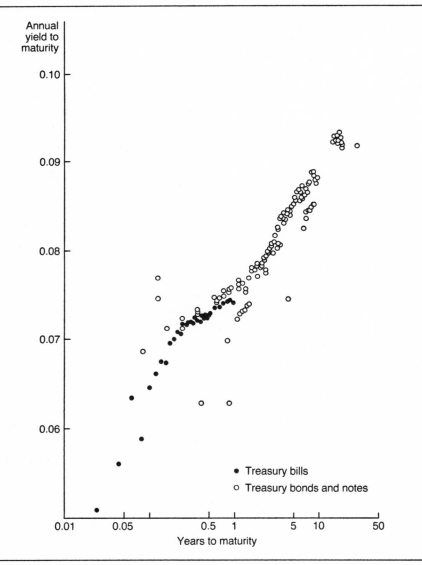

Figure 3–4 illustrates the Treasury bill discount factor as a function of the time to maturity for the same data reported in Figure 3–2. Unlike the yield to maturity the discount function is a smooth function of time and can be easily estimated. Since many applications only use the yield to maturity as a way of obtaining the discount function, it seems sensible to estimate the discount function directly.

Unfortunately the Treasury bill data extend only as far as one year to maturity. The yield to maturity on coupon bonds represents a complicated average of yields to maturity on each of the coupons associated with the bond. As such it cannot be used to construct discount factors.[7] This is another argument against fitting a smooth curve to coupon bond yields: such yields are often difficult to interpret. Recently rights to the coupon and principal repayment of par have been issued separately in the secondary markets as zero coupon CATS, TIGRs and STRIPS. With such data one can estimate the discount factors directly for more than one year to maturity.

To this point we have not discussed in detail the methods to be used for fitting smooth curves to this kind of data. There are almost as many procedures as there are statistics software packages that implement them. The most common family of procedures falls under the general rubric of spline smoothing. The idea behind spline smoothing is a very simple one. If one were to consider the discount factor $d(t)$ as a cubic function of the time to maturity,

$$d(t) = a + bt + ct^2 + dt^3$$

it would be possible to estimate coefficients a, b, c, and d directly, using multiple regression methods. Within certain ranges of the time to maturity the fitted function might approximate relatively closely the actual discount function, to work adequately for all possible times to maturity. The spline procedure estimates the cubic function for ranges of the time to maturity, constraining the coefficients so that the function encounters a smooth transition between ranges.

This procedure has been criticized by H. Gifford Fong and Oldrich

---

[7]However, it is possible to write the value of the coupon bond as the sum of discount factors times the payments to be received at each of the coupon payment dates. If each of the discount factors can be expressed as a function of the time to each coupon payment date, it is possible to use econometric methods to estimate the discount factors on the basis of coupon bond prices as well as on the basis of discount bond prices. This procedure is discussed in Stephen J. Brown and Philip H. Dybvig, "The Empirical Implications of the Cox, Ingersoll, Ross Theory of the Term Structure of Interest Rates," *Journal of Finance*, July 1986, pp. 617–30.

FIGURE 3–3
Treasury Bill Yield Curve, December 31, 1985

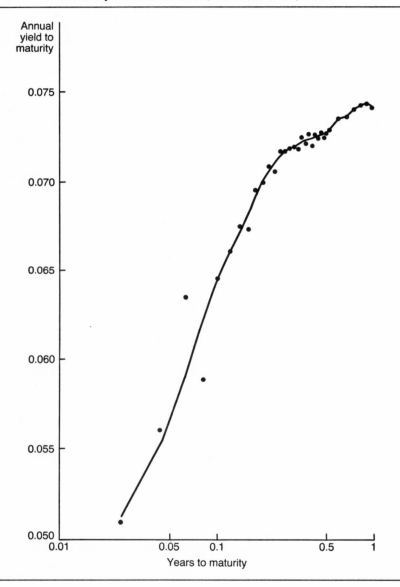

FIGURE 3–4
Treasury Bill Discount Factors, December 31, 1985

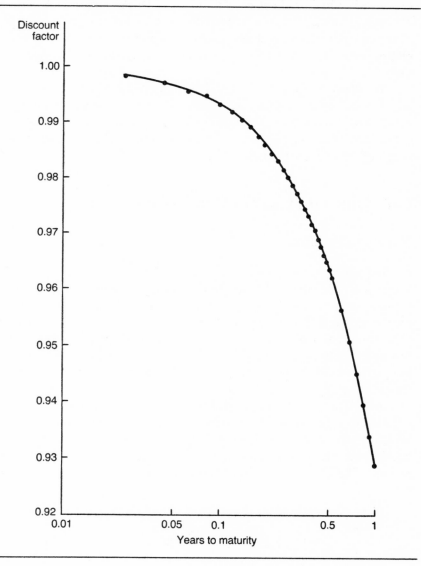

Vasicek on the grounds that the approximation has no basis in theory and does not seem to be adequate at long times to maturity.[8] They suggest fitting exponential functions in place of the cubic functions within each of the ranges of time to maturity. Their approach does not necessarily address the problem of imposing ad hoc smoothness constraints on the functions to be estimated. One approach is to base these constraints on an equilibrium theory of interest rates.[9]

An alternative approach that does not involve the necessity to impose any constraints on the data has been suggested. Instead of fitting a yield curve or a discount function to the data as a smooth curve, the analyst should estimate the sequence of forward rates as a series of constants, one for each series of periods out into the future.[10]

FACTORS THAT AFFECT BOND MARKETS

Horizon Premiums

A bond's maturity—or more precisely its duration—significantly affects its sensitivity to prevailing interest rates. Long-term bond prices are more sensitive to interest rate changes than those of short-term bonds. As previously indicated, the difference between the yields in long- and short-term bonds or between any two bond yields is called a yield spread. Investors seem to demand such a spread, or premium, for assuming the interest rate risk of long-term bonds. This spread is called the bond *maturity premium, horizon premium,* or *liquidity premium.*

In economic terms the yield on a default-free bond is equal to the expected inflation plus the expected real interest rate plus the bond's horizon premium. With inflation of 6 percent, a real interest rate of 3 percent, and the bond's horizon premium of 1 percent, such a default-free bond should yield 10 percent. The horizon premium constitutes the compensation for interest rate risk.

---

[8]H. G. Fong and O. Vasicek, "Term Structure Modeling," *Journal of Finance,* July 1982, pp. 339–48.

[9]See Brown and Dybvig, "Empirical Implications."

[10]Thomas Coleman, Lawrence Fisher, and Roger Ibbotson, "Estimating Forward Interest Rates and Yield Curves from Government Bond Prices: Methodology and Selected Results" (Working paper, Yale University, 1986, unpublished).

Inflation and Real Returns on Bonds

Changes in expected inflation cause changes in nominal interest rates and consequently in bond yields. The economist Irving Fisher was the first to observe that the nominal rate of interest must equal the real rate of interest plus the prospective rate of inflation. Thus if investors generally revise their estimates of expected inflation downward by 1 percent, the nominal interest rate may also fall by 1 percent.

In practice, changes in expectations about inflation often do cause a shift in bond yields. In fact the change may affect bonds of different durations in different ways. If investors expect that near-term inflation will increase, the yields on bonds of short duration rise. If investors do not increase their expectations about long-term inflation as much, yields on bonds of longer duration will increase but less sharply.

Bond Dedication and Immunization Strategies

Liabilities in essence are the obligation to make payments in the future. An individual might be planning to put a child through college, or a pension fund manager might anticipate paying pension benefits to retirees. Both invest their assets in the interim to meet these future demands. Shrewd investors have observed that matching the duration of such assets to that of anticipated liabilities reduces the risk of insufficient wealth to meet these obligations.

Dedication. When the liability is known and its amount fixed, certain assets can be set aside, or *dedicated,* to meet that liability. To continue the above examples, the parent may buy a zero coupon bond to assure that funds will be available when a child reaches college age, and the pension fund manager may buy bonds with interest payments that exactly match the monthly amount of expected retirement obligations to retired employees. For example, a portfolio of zero coupon bonds with durations of six, seven, and eight years can be used to meet a series of liabilities with maturities of six, seven, and eight years.

Immunization. If liabilities of differing amounts mature at different times, the matching of cash flows can be complicated or impossible. In this situation it is possible to immunize the liabilities with a portfolio. The objective of the procedure known as *immunization* is to insulate the investor from adverse changes in interest rates. Obviously this objective can be accomplished by dedication strategies but is a little more difficult to achieve using coupon bonds, as one is concerned with minimizing the risk associated with reinvestment of the coupon payments.

Fortunately it is possible to immunize a coupon bond portfolio by so arranging the portfolio that the duration of the portfolio matches the desired holding period of the investor. In this procedure, if interest rates rise investors benefit by the fact that they can reinvest coupons at a higher rate, but they incur a capital loss. On the other hand, if rates fall investors reinvest at a lower rate but experience a capital gain. If the investor were to hold bonds to maturity, capital risk is minimized but reinvestment risk is high. If on the other hand the investor were to roll over investments on a short-term basis, reinvestment risk is minimized but capital risk is high. There is thus a trade-off. Under certain conditions to be discussed later, reinvestment risk and capital risk are equal and exactly offsetting at the duration of the bond (as discussed earlier, duration can be thought of as the midpoint of the bond payments measured in present value terms). Thus if the investor chooses a portfolio such that the duration exactly matches the desired holding period, perhaps dictated by the liabilities the investor faces, such an investor will be *immunized* against unforeseen changes in interest rates.

This analysis assumes that the long-term rates, which chiefly affect the capital risk component, move in lockstep with the short rates that affect reinvestment risk. Investors who look to duration-based immunization as a way of locking in abnormally high short rates are liable to be disappointed. If short rates fall, leaving long rates largely unaffected, reinvestment value will fall without a corresponding rise in capital value.

Immunization and Interest Rate Elasticity. When long and short interest rates change by the same amount, the yield curve shift is parallel. In this case, as discussed before, only a bond's *adjusted duration* need be known in order to determine the effect on a bond's price. Typically, however, long-term rates are more stable than short-term rates. Thus the short end of the yield curve is more volatile and sensitive to interest rate changes. In economic terms, short-term rates are more interest rate elastic than long-term rates.

Empirically, short rates usually adjust by a greater amount than long rates. For every 1 percent change in the yield to maturity on a one-year bond, two-year bond yields change about 0.8 percent on average. For longer-term bonds the changes are smaller: 5-year bond yields change about 0.4 percent relative to 1-year bonds, and 15-year bond yields change only 0.2 percent.

When elasticity factors are computed, long-term bonds are less elastic than short-term bonds. If the factor was one for short-term bonds, the factor will be less than one for long-term bonds. When such factors are multiplied by a bond's duration, the expected change in price can be determined. Specifically the expected change in price is equal to the elasticity factor (expressed as a negative number) times the bond's adjusted duration times the expected short-term change in yield.

CONCLUSION

The analysis of fixed-income securities is especially amenable to quantitative methods because unlike equities, for example, their cash flows are highly predictable. Therefore the linkage between present value concepts and bond valuation is fairly direct. This convenient linkage, together with some data analysis, leads to several observations and suggests certain fixed-income strategies.

The yield to maturity of a bond best measures its approximate expected return. This is true especially for a default-free bond over the life of the bond, ignoring reinvestment risk. For bonds with default risk, the bond's expected return will be below its promised yield to maturity because there is some probability that the bond will default.

The actual return on a bond equals its yield to maturity plus the return in excess of this yield, whether positive or negative. Gains and losses on bonds occur primarily because of changes in prevailing interest rates.

The adjusted duration of a bond measures its price sensitivity to changes in its yield to maturity. Long-term bond prices are more sensitive to changes in yield to maturity than short-term bonds. On the other hand this is partially offset by the empirical fact that short-term interest rates fluctuate more than long-term interest rates.

Dedication and immunization are techniques to protect a bond portfolio's nominal value from changes in interest rates over a given horizon. When the liabilities are fixed, zero coupon bonds can be dedicated so that their maturities match the horizon. In this way nominal risk is eliminated at the end of the horizon.

Immunization is desirable when there are many liabilities with complicated payment schedules and when coupon bonds are used to match these liabilities. As interest rates change, there is a trade-off between the bond's price and the rate at which coupon payments are reinvested. Immunization is a mathematical procedure for balancing such trade-offs.

PROBLEMS

1. One year ago you paid $8,000 for a two-year coupon bond with a face value of $10,000 and an annual coupon rate of 10 percent. Now (just after payment of the first annual coupon) the bond has a yield to maturity of 8 percent. What is the price of the bond today, and what was the return on holding the bond over the past year?

   Answer: The yield to maturity is the internal rate of return on the bond. In other words it is that discount rate which sets the present value (PV) equal to the current price. The cash flow on the bond after one year is simply $10,000 (return of principal) plus $1,000 (coupon payment). Thus the current price is given by the formula

   $$\text{Price} = \frac{\$10,000 + \$1,000}{1 + .08} = \$10,185.18$$

   The return on the bond over the first year is given by the formula

   $$\text{Return} = \frac{\$10,185.18 - \$8,000}{\$8,000} = 27.31\%$$

2. What is the duration as of today for the bond mentioned in problem 1 above?

   Answer: The duration is one year; there is only one cash flow remaining on the bond.

3. In addition to the bond mentioned above, you just paid $6,001.37 for zero coupon bonds maturing two years from today with a total face value of $7,000. These bonds also yield 8 percent to maturity. What is the duration of these bonds? What is the duration of the overall bond portfolio?

   Answer: The duration of the first bond is one year, and the duration of the second is two years. To determine the duration of the portfolio, note that the current value of the bond portfolio is $16,186.55. The Macaulay measure of duration is obtained by first determining the yield to maturity on the bond portfolio. This is 8 percent since

   $$\$16,186.55 = \frac{\$11,000}{1 + .08} + \frac{\$7,000}{(1 + .08)^2}$$

   Then we use the formula for duration:

$$\text{Duration} = \left[1 \times \left(\frac{\$11{,}000 \times [1 \div (1 + .08)]}{\$16{,}186.55}\right)\right]$$
$$+ \left[2 \times \left(\frac{\$7{,}000 \times [1 \div (1 + .08)^2]}{\$16{,}186.55}\right)\right]$$
$$= 1.37 \text{ years}$$

The so-called second generation measure of duration is obtained by the formula

$$\text{Duration} = \left[1 \times \left(\frac{\$10{,}185.18}{\$16{,}186.55}\right)\right] + \left[2 \times \left(\frac{\$6{,}001.37}{\$16{,}186.55}\right)\right]$$
$$= 1.37 \text{ years}$$

The two answers are the same, because the zero coupon yield curve is flat. The first bond is actually an 8 percent zero coupon as of the end of the first year (only one payment remaining). The second bond is also a zero yielding 8 percent.

CHAPTER FOUR

Quantitative Methods in Real Estate Analysis

Susan Hudson-Wilson

Valuation in the context of real estate can be very complex and difficult. However, the general principles of valuation are similar to those that apply in other investment contexts. Moreover the general perception that real estate markets are inefficient creates opportunities for those with special knowledge of such markets or special access to pertinent information. Use of quantitative methods will aid though not, of course, guarantee performance.

This chapter begins by introducing some of the issues of property valuation, using a simplified property analysis that focuses on the application of concepts of present value and measures of return. (This treatment is not meant to be exhaustive; the interested reader is referred to other texts for further reading on these issues.[1]) The chapter then addresses some of the ways in which methods of statistics and data analysis are used in the valuation context and concludes with a brief review of portfolio design considerations.

PROPERTY VALUATION ISSUES

Valuation

There are several traditional approaches to valuation in real estate analysis. These are known as the cost approach, the market data or comparable ap-

---

[1]See for example Paul F. Wendt and Alan R. Cerf, *Real Estate Investment Analysis and Taxation* (New York: McGraw-Hill, 1979).

proach, and the income approach. They are used to obtain an appraisal meant to approximate market value closely if the property were to be sold today for what is referred to as its highest and best use. The highest and best use reflects the most valuable use to which the property may be put. In other words an apartment building may be worth more to a prospective purchaser who intends to convert it into a condominium than to a purchaser who intends to operate it as a rental building. It is as a condominium (net of the costs of conversion) that the property should be valued.

The cost approach represents an approach to valuation that stresses the physical value of the structure and the land over the economic value of the property's leasing and management and the value of the alternate uses to which the property can be put. Essentially the appraiser calculates the replacement cost of the property and subtracts an amount that reflects the fact that the property is not newly constructed. The adjustment tends to be somewhat subjective and typically does not allow for the income that can be generated by the property. This approach cannot be used for the valuation of the land component, for which a separate calculation has to be made.

The market data approach is closer to a concept of market value of the highest and best use of the property. In this approach, comparable properties are defined for which market prices are available. An adjustment (or a series of adjustments) is made for the fact that the property in question is not exactly the same as the properties to which it is compared. The adjustment process is again somewhat subjective.

The income approach values the highest and best use in terms of the present value of the cash flows resulting from such a use. Simple applications assume that the cash flows are to be received in perpetuity either by the owner of the property or by the person to whom the property is eventually sold. This is a simple application of the perpetuity formula discussed in Chapter One:

$$\text{Present value} = \frac{C}{r}$$

In this context the cash flow quantity C is often referred to as *net operating income (NOI)*, and the discount rate r is referred to as the *capitalization rate*. If we were to assume that the cash flow C were to grow at a constant rate g over time, then the appropriate formula would be

$$\text{Present value} = \frac{C}{r - g}$$

and the quantity *(r − g)* would be interpreted as the capitalization rate.

The capitalization rate is generally held to include some kind of risk premium. To estimate this quantity many analysts invert the present value formula above to find the capitalization rates that may be inferred from the prices at which properties currently trade:

$$\text{Capitalization rate} = \frac{\text{Cash flow}}{\text{Present value}} = \frac{\text{Net operating income}}{\text{Current price of property}}$$

and properties can be compared on the basis of their implied capitalization rates. The analysis of capitalization rates is analogous to the analysis of the equity price-earnings model discussed briefly in Chapter One (the capitalization rate can be thought of as the reciprocal of the price-earnings ratio).

Net operating income is generally defined as rental and nonrental income (gross potential income) less an allowance for vacancy and other losses and for operating expenses that include maintenance and repair expenses, payroll, real estate taxes, utility costs, insurance, and so forth. While it is typically measured net of extraordinary items (is "stabilized"), it in many instances is only a benchmark of value, as estimating many of the expense items with any degree of precision is difficult. In most cases several costs of ownership and sale at the end of the holding period are ignored. Many analysts are beginning to lean toward the inclusion of costs such as transfer taxes, brokerage commissions, and hazardous substance removal. These costs are uniformly covered by sales prices.

A variant of this approach is known as the *gross income multiplier*, where the expense items are neglected altogether and the measure of cash flow is simply the gross rental and nonrental income from the property in question.

The simplifications used to construct cash flow measures are often made necessary by the paucity of data in many real estate applications. Of what value is analysis based on such numbers? So long as the measures of income are proportional to some well-defined measure of aftertax cash flows, it is perfectly appropriate to use the implied capitalization rates for comparison purposes. However, where simplifications are used, valuations derived from such numbers should be treated with a due degree of caution.

Such valuations are appraisals of value for the "typical" investor and are presumably reflected in the price at which the property could be sold. They may not represent measures of value for a particular investor. To value a property from that perspective it is necessary to construct pro forma income statements for each year of the holding period. This enables the analyst to estimate accurately revenues and expenses and to assess the tax consequences for a particular investor. The aftertax cash flows for each year of the holding period, plus some estimate of the value of the property less transaction costs

TABLE 4–1
Annual Pro Forma Income Statement

	Years 1 through 5
Lease 1 (20,000 square feet)	$ 340,000
Lease 2 (30,000 square feet)	510,000
Lease 3 (50,000 square feet)	850,000
Gross potential income	1,700,000
Less:	
Vacancy factor	0
Reserve (.10 per square foot)	10,000
Net operating income	$1,690,000

if sold at the end of that period, are discounted at the required rate of return for that investor. A simple example should make this clear.

Simplified Valuation Example. This example represents a significantly "stripped-down" case. An actual valuation would be concerned with taxes and other considerations such as expenses and expense inflation, market rents when leases expire, inflation rates, condition of the local market, construction costs, and the nature of the sale (timing, leverage, partnerships, etc.). Later we will add some complexity to the problem, but it should be clear that there is a significant subjective element to real estate valuation that can only be captured imperfectly by use of quantitative methods.

The hypothetical property under analysis is a 100,000-square-foot office building. Three "credit" tenants lease 100 percent of the space under 10-year, triple-net leases at fixed rental rates of $17 per square foot. In other words the tenants are regarded as financially secure and pay all of the expenses associated with the space rented in addition to the rent itself. Inflation and market vacancy are assumed to be zero, and a $.10 per square foot structural reserve[2] constitutes the only expense to the building's owner. The asking price for the building is $18,777,777, or $187 per square foot. (See Table 4–1.)

Assume that the investor contemplating a purchase has determined that the building will be worth $16,900,000 in five years, the assumed holding period.[3] The investor has arrived at this conclusion by capitalizing the fifth-

---

[2] This is an allowance to fund current capital expenses of the building. Here it is treated as an expense, so it is deducted from gross income.

[3] Actually, a 10-year holding period is more traditional in real estate analysis. We use a shorter time period for illustrative purposes.

year net operating income at a rate of 10 percent. That is, the fifth-year net cash flow of $1,690,000 ($17.00 per square foot rent times 100,000 square feet, minus the structural reserve) has been set equal to 10 percent of the market value of the building. This calculation assumes that the current use reflects the highest and best use at that point in time.

This investor, having determined the future value of the office building, determines the present value of the property by discounting the cash flows and the future value (called *reversion*), using his required rate of return. The required rate is generally determined as the risk-adjusted opportunity cost of the funds available for the purchase of the property. The case under analysis is a relatively low-risk transaction, so the required, or *hurdle,* rate of return would reflect this fact. The investor would set the fifth-year capitalization rate equal to the required rate in order to be consistent. Setting the hurdle rate at 10 percent and calculating the present value yields a present value of $16,900,000. Given the need to earn at least a 10 percent rate of return and given the assumed future value, the investor would be willing to pay up to $16,900,000 for the property. If the investor were able to conclude the transaction for less, the internal rate of return would rise above the required rate.

Recall that the asking price is $18,777,777. The investor and the seller are nearly $2 million apart because of different perceptions of risk or different assessments of the highest and best use. The investor's assessment is that the project is riskier than is perceived by the seller, not an unusual situation.

Another way to view this example is to assume that the property is being offered at a lower price, say $17,000,000. The investor would then capitalize fifth-year NOI as before and could calculate the *internal rate of return (IRR)* on the investment and compare this rate with the hurdle rate. In this case an asking price of $17,000,000 would yield an IRR of 9.84 percent, which is below the investor's required return. Unless the investor could complete the transaction at the present value price of $16,900,000, the investor's return requirement would not be met, even at this lower price.

Finally, let us assume that the asking price of the property is known, as is the investor's required rate of return. Assume the asking price is $17,000,000, and the required rate of return is 10 percent. Given these two pieces of information, the future value (after five years) of the property may be calculated. This future value represents the *required future value,* given the asking price and the cash flows, in order for the investor to attain his required rate of return. The required future value of $17,061,051 may then be compared with the likely future price as determined by capping fifth-year NOI, (that is, the "market" price of $16,900,000). In this case if the investor were to purchase the property at the asking price and then seek to attain his required rate of return he would need to set a selling price in the fifth year that would be above the expected market price. Thus the prospective investor would be attempting to set a lower cap rate (and so a higher price) than that which the market would be likely to bear. The investor's cap rate would be 9.9 percent (divide NOI by the required selling price) while the previously determined market cap was 10 percent. Again, unless the investor can attain a lower initial purchase price or can adjust the required rate of return downward, the property will not meet the investor's needs.

The analysis conducted above assumed zero vacancy and inflation rates, fixed lease rates, a static required rate of return and market cap rate, and a 100 percent equity purchase. A simple relaxation of the hurdle rate of return or any other assumption would be sufficient to generate a series of scenarios for purchase price and rate of return.

As mentioned before, accurate assessment of expenses is difficult at best in many property valuations. A large subjective element enters into the determination of the likely resale value of the property at the end of the assumed holding period. An approach suggested by James W. Hoag and more recently attempted by researchers at the University of North Carolina attempts to resolve this problem at least in part by using a regression approach that is in a sense a synthesis of the market value and income approaches to valuation.[4] They suggest regressing the prices at which properties trade against fundamental characteristics of value such as income and expenses in the year of purchase, net leases, capital improvements and so forth, national economic measures such as business inventories and volume of sales of industrial properties, and regional measures of locational and temporal value. Such a regression model could be used to estimate the market value of a portfolio of real estate holdings even though the individual properties do not come to market.

Return and Risk.   Real estate investments typically have been associated with large positive returns. In the period from 1947 to 1984 a dollar invested in real estate investments increased 20-fold, and (as can be seen from Table 4–2) returns were only exceeded by the returns on stock equity investments. Yet these investments appear to have very small risk. Note the low standard deviation of real estate returns and also the low correlation of

---

[4]See J. W. Hoag, "Towards Indices of Real Estate Value and Return," *Journal of Finance,* May 1980, pp. 569–80; David Guilkey, Rebel Cole, and Mike Miles, "The Motivation for Institutional Real Estate Sales" (Working Paper, University of North Carolina at Chapel Hill, 1988).

TABLE 4-2
Annual Returns for U.S. Real Estate and Other Investments, and Inflation, 1947–1984

	Real Estate	Stocks	Small Stocks	Corporate Bonds	Long-Term Government Bonds	Treasury Bills	Inflation
Mean and standard deviation of annual returns (percent)							
Arithmetic mean	8.30	12.58	17.81	4.23	3.56	4.69	4.33
Geometric mean	8.24	11.27	14.78	3.88	3.24	4.64	4.27
Standard deviation	3.67	17.13	27.03	9.24	8.69	3.43	3.67
Correlations of annual returns							
Real estate	1.000						
Stocks	−0.062	1.000					
Small stocks	0.029	0.786	1.000				
Corporate bonds	−0.060	0.124	0.013	1.000			
Long-term governments	−0.077	−0.013	−0.101	0.949	1.000		
Treasury bills	0.403	−0.231	−0.011	0.200	0.237	1.000	
Inflation	0.849	−0.274	−0.080	−0.187	−0.152	0.650	1.000

such returns with those of other assets. It would appear that real estate can add significant diversification within a large portfolio of assets.

The apparent high return and low risk of real estate investments seem inconsistent with the perception of risk associated with such investments. It is also difficult to reconcile the differences in risk measured for real estate investment trusts (REITs) versus their "hard asset" counterparts. Real estate looks too good to be true. Three theories may begin to explain the seeming inconsistency between risk and return: Risk may be understated by the valuation process. Leverage may not be reflected in the return measures. Returns may also be overstated as a result of the costs associated with information scarcity, illiquidity, and property management.[5]

The valuation process described earlier in the chapter tends to smooth returns. The process relies enough on comparables (in determining cap rates and rents) that it is somewhat adaptive or backward looking in nature. As true values fall in a market, appraised values adjust but with a lag. As true values rise the appraised values are similarly lagged. The lagging process is compounded by the political realities of falling values (one tends to hope the corner will be turned prior to having to recognize the decline in value) and rising values (one tends to take the gains conservatively for tax and hedging reasons).

In addition, changes in valuation may simply reflect inflation adjustments to income, expense, and highest and best use numbers. This factor alone may explain the high correlation between measured returns on real estate and the inflation rate observed in Table 4–2.

Most real estate return indexes report on unleveraged property held in institutional portfolios. This is certainly true of the most widely used measure, the Frank Russell Index produced by the National Council of Real Estate Investment Fiduciaries, and the data presented in Table 4–2. These indexes and others seek to measure the performance of the *property,* not the performance of the financial structure. NCREIF has attempted, without success to date, to devise a hybrid index to measure the impact of financial structure on returns.

Leverage increases expected return on the equity component of the investment, not only by concentrating return in the hands of equity holders but also by virtue of the favorable tax treatment of payments to debt holders. However, leverage increases risk. The risk of real estate equity is therefore higher than the numbers in Table 4–2 would indicate. Assuming the debt

---

[5]Mike Miles, "Real Estate as an Asset Class: A 25-Year Perspective," from *Bond Market Research: Real Estate,* Salomon Brothers, January 1989.

had no risk, the standard deviation of equity returns on a property financed by an 80 percent mortgage would increase by a factor of five (five being the reciprocal of the percentage of equity finance, which in this instance is 20 percent). Thus the 3.67 percent standard deviation (reported in the table) for unleveraged real estate investment returns would imply a 21.35 percent standard deviation of equity returns, given an 80 percent mortgage.

Ultimately it is the prices at which properties actually trade, rather than the current valuations, that are relevant for performance measurement and risk assessment. Returns based on valuation numbers should therefore be treated with care in a multiasset portfolio modeling context.

Market Analysis

The example of the previous section presented a highly simplified version of project valuation. Most actual cases are far more complex, dealing with more tenants, differing lease terms and conditions, variable inflation rates, and variable market conditions. Market conditions as represented by a market vacancy rate affect the length of individual leases and the rental rates at lease renewal. Market conditions may be simulated and applied to the analysis of a project in which the tenants are not yet signed up or existing tenants have lease expiration dates prior to the anticipated date of sale of a property. As will be demonstrated in the third section of this chapter, market conditions are also relevant to portfolio analysis.

The *vacancy rate* is a summary, or reduced form, statistic conveying information about the supply of and demand for various types of real estate in particular markets at particular times. The vacancy rate is calculated as total rentable space (in square feet) minus leased space, expressed as a percent of total rentable space. In theory all comparable space in a market should be individually measured and examined for occupancy in order to calculate the rate. In fact the rate is calculated by various groups and individuals for select markets and submarkets, structure types, and periods of time, using varying degrees of rigor. The two best-known sources for vacancy data are Coldwell Banker and Office Network. The former collects data on 31 cities for office and industrial space; the latter follows only office space in approximately 30 cities.

The vacancy rate, even in its reduced form, is able to provide useful information on current market conditions and the current market relative to its own norms, to the U.S. market as a whole, and to alternative investment locations.

Table 4–3 contains vacancy data for the nation and the cities of Atlanta

TABLE 4–3
Office Market Vacancy Rates, June 1978
to March 1985
(quarterly percents)

	Nation	Atlanta	San Francisco
1978			
June	6.9	17.8	0.9
September	6.2	14.2	0.7
December	5.6	13.3	0.4
1979			
March	5.2	12.5	0.5
June	4.8	10.0	1.6
September	4.2	12.0	0.2
December	3.6	11.6	0.4
1980			
March	3.4	11.9	0.2
June	3.4	12.5	0.2
September	3.9	13.1	0.1
December	4.1	13.9	0.1
1981			
March	3.8	12.1	0.1
June	4.1	11.6?	0.1
September	4.4	12.3	0.3
December	4.8	17.7	0.4
1982			
March	5.5	15.4	0.8
June	7.1	15.2	3.4
September	8.9	20.1	3.6
December	10.3	19.4	5.7
1983			
March	10.8	19.9	5.9
June	11.7	18.4	6.1
September	11.7	16.3	6.4
December	12.4	16.0	5.9
1984			
March	13.1	14.7	6.9
June	13.5	14.5	8.6
September	14.2	14.1	9.0
December	14.7	15.5	10.1
1985			
March	15.3	15.8	10.9
Mean	7.8	14.7	3.2
Median	5.9	14.4	.85
Standard deviation	4.0	2.7	3.5

SOURCE: Coldwell Banker.

FIGURE 4–1
Office Market Vacancy Rates: Nation, Atlanta, San Francisco

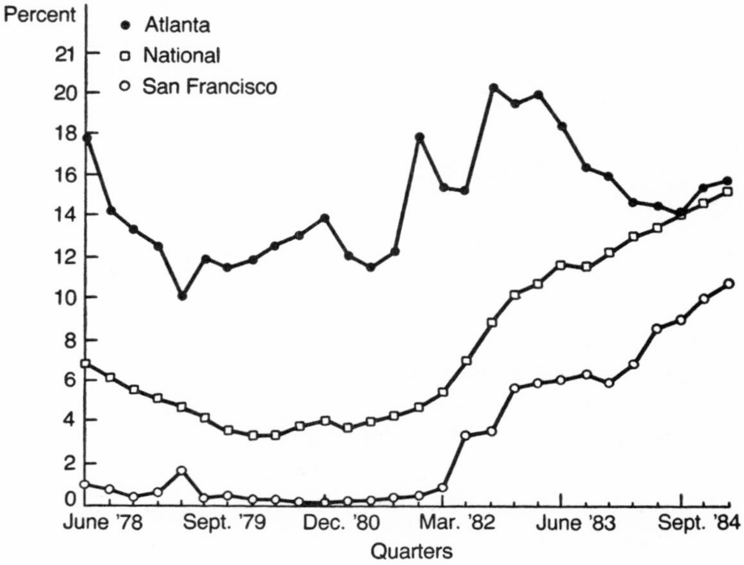

and San Francisco. A rapid scan of the data reveals that Atlanta generally experiences high vacancy rates, San Francisco experiences low rates, and the U.S. moves between the two. The mean values support this observation as do the medians. The median for San Francisco is significantly below its mean, indicating a nonnormal distribution. The mode for San Francisco consists of the 0 to .9 percent range, within which over half of the values fall. Three values each fall into the ranges of 5.0 percent to 5.9 percent and 6.0 percent to 6.9 percent, making this distribution somewhat bimodal. The San Francisco distribution is also characterized by a high standard deviation relative to its mean. An examination of the plot of San Francisco office market vacancies over time (see Figure 4–1) establishes that while there are no outliers, there has been an apparent shift in the behavior of the market. Vacancy rates have tended to increase over time in both the national and regional markets.

The Atlanta data present a more consistent portrait. The mean, mode, and median are quite similar. There are no outliers, and the standard deviation reflects variation around the mean over time rather than a major market shift.

TABLE 4–4
Correlation of National and Regional Vacancy Rates and Time
(second quarter 1978 through first quarter 1985)

	Vacancy Rate			
	Nation	Atlanta	San Francisco	Time
Vacancy rate				
Nation	1.000			
Atlanta	0.539	1.000		
San Francisco	0.979	0.461	1.000	
Time	0.843	0.465	0.874	1.000

The mean and standard deviation calculations indicate that normally (95 percent of the time) the national vacancy rate varies between a theoretical − .2 percent and a high of 15.8 percent. The March 1985 rate of 15.3 percent is therefore unusually high. This relationship between the "norm" and the current level may be a one-time market condition that may or may not continue into the future. The structure of the market would need to be analyzed to establish a behavioral cause and to assess the likely persistence of such behavior. Alternatively, current behavior does not represent a true aberration but rather a normal cyclical event that has not been captured by a time series that begins in the second quarter of 1978. A different statistic used for market analysis and discussed below would suggest the alternative explanation.

In sharp contrast the Atlanta vacancy rate varies within a theoretical range of 9.3 percent to 20.1 percent, with a March 1985 value of 15.8 percent. The current value is not out of line with normal behavior. A review of the data plot in Figure 4–1 would even suggest that a full market cycle is captured within the time period for which the data are available.

The correlation matrix in Table 4–4 provides some information useful for comparative purposes. Vacancy rates have tended to rise from 1978 to 1985, as reflected in the positive correlation between vacancy rates and time. This is less true of the Atlanta market, for which the correlation is smaller. Again, before a firm inference about the future could be based on this statistic, one would want to be sure that the data are representative of the behavior of each market. In fact there is reason to doubt that the steady rise in vacancies will persist at the national level; and as we shall see, these data are more indicative of longer-term cyclical movements in these rates. The correlation matrix also shows a very high correlation between national vacancy rates and those for San Francisco. Rather than indicating any causality, this cor-

TABLE 4–5
Regression of San Francisco Vacancy Rates
on National Rates
(second quarter 1978 through first quarter 1985)

	Coefficient	Standard Error	t-Value
Intercept	−3.47907	0.3058	−11.38
National vacancy rate	0.85898	0.0350	24.57

Residual standard error = 0.7429.
Multiple R-square = 0.9587.
N = 28.
F-value = 603.739 on 1, 26 degrees of freedom.
Durbin-Watson statistic = 0.8851.

relation probably indicates similar responses to various market factors. Although the San Francisco vacancy rate is included as a part of the national rate, each city is a small enough portion of the national vacancy rate that independent behavior is possible. The correlation between the nation and Atlanta is low, indicating that similar market factors are probably not governing the two markets.

The high correlation between San Francisco and the nation allows the employment of a useful modeling or forecasting procedure. It is possible to model (for analytical or forecasting applications) the national vacancy rate in as careful and detailed a fashion as possible and then to estimate a very simple equation for San Francisco, using national data. The estimated coefficients of such a relationship will capture differences in the responsiveness of San Francisco and the nation to an identical set of market factors.

Table 4–5 illustrates the result of a simple regression of the national vacancy rate on the San Francisco vacancy rate. The regression statistics confirm the strength of the relationship between the nation and San Francisco. The R^2 (.9587) is high, the t-statistic (24.57) on national is very strong, and the residual standard error is very low (.7429). However, the fact that the Durbin-Watson statistic is so low is disturbing:[7] the autocorrelation of the residuals is .49. Such a low Durbin-Watson statistic is a good indication that the regression model is misspecified: an explanatory variable has been left out of the analysis.

---

[7]The Durbin-Watson statistic of .8851 is less than the critical value of 1.10 (1 percent significance level). This indicates that the positive serial correlation of .49 is statistically significant.

TABLE 4–6
Regression of San Francisco Vacancy Rates on National
Rates and Rates for Previous Quarter
(third quarter 1978 through first quarter 1985)

	Coefficient	Standard Error	t-Value
Intercept	−2.11747	0.5797	−3.65
National vacancy rate	0.54001	0.1312	4.12
Previous-quarter rate	0.40703	0.1647	2.47

Residual standard error = 0.6277.
Multiple R-square = 0.9724.
N = 27.
F-value = 422.189 on 2, 24 degrees of freedom.
Durbin-Watson statistic = 1.8838.

It would seem reasonable that a good predictor of next month's vacancy rate is this month's rate. Including the lagged vacancy rate as an explanatory variable yields the results reported in Table 4–6. The Durbin-Watson statistic is no longer significant, and the autocorrelation of the residuals is − .004.

With time-oriented data it is sometimes useful to include an additional variable (here called time) in a regression equation. The correlation analysis presented in Table 4–4 would seem to indicate that such a variable would have significant explanatory power.

Table 4–7 presents the results of the regression including time. The additional variable is in fact not significant. Using the vacancy rate of the previous month as an explanatory variable appears to capture the fact that vacancy rates tend to move with time. Rather than indicating that San Francisco rates are merely trending upwards over time, these data seem more indicative of a cyclical pattern of movements in vacancy rates. A good predictor of next month's vacancy rate is this month's rate. However, 28 quarters of data cannot be conclusive here. With a more comprehensive data base, a more explicit time-series model of the data would be called for.

The stage is now set for the modeling and forecasting of the national office vacancy rate. These results would then be used in the San Francisco model to generate a forecast of the city's office market. At this point, unfortunately, the problems with vacancy rate data emerge. The fact that the rate is a summary statistic means that modeling will be difficult.

The vacancy rate summarizes the relationship between the supply of and demand for space. Since these two components are separately motivated it is preferable to analyze each separately and then form a vacancy rate or a proxy. A methodology that builds the vacancy rate (or a proxy) in this fashion

TABLE 4–7
Regression of San Francisco Vacancy Rates on National
Rates, Rates for Previous Quarter, and Time
(third quarter 1978 through first quarter 1985)

	Coefficient	Standard Error	t-Value
Intercept	−2.25254	0.5718	−3.94
National vacancy rate	0.47081	0.1358	3.46
Previous-quarter rate	0.39368	0.1606	2.45
Time	0.04759	0.0315	1.51

Residual standard error = 0.6115.
Multiple R-square = 0.9749.
N = 27.
F-value = 297.29 on 3, 23 degrees of freedom.
Durbin-Watson statistic = 2.0254.

has been developed and is in use. (This author constructs a statistic entitled the *Real Estate Market Index*, or *REMI*; others call it a vacancy rate. The basic techniques are similar.)

Essentially the REMI and its counterparts are constructed by first calculating construction contract awards in square footage on the demand side. The difference between square feet constructed and square feet demanded is then expressed as a percentage of square feet constructed. The data used by the various groups calculating this statistic vary, but generally F. W. Dodge–McGraw-Hill contract awards and Commerce Department construction permits dominate the supply side, while the demand side is dominated by standard employment data generated via government administrative programs at the Bureau of Labor Statistics. The primary advantage of the data is that they are available on a reasonably consistent basis over time, at great geographic detail, and for many structure types.

The historical supply-side data are generated by taking construction contract awards or permits issued and projecting them forward to a "put in place" concept. Thus the flow of new square footage available for lease is known. Clearly, a contract awarded today will become a building in the future, so the raw data provide an implicit short-run forecast. This flow series may be converted to a total-stock-of-space series only with difficulty or a set of assumptions. It is the author's practice to generate a five-year moving sum to create a stock series for space up to five years old.

The nature of the raw data provides a year or two of virtually known additions to stock. Projecting stock (or additions) beyond this is more difficult. What turns out to be useful is simply to rely on the historic mean as a "most likely" future scenario and then to develop high and low straight line projections around that mean. The standard deviation of the put-in-place series provides some guidance in setting the high and low construction scenarios. Again, to develop the most realistic bands it is critical to analyze the put-in-place series as the vacancy series were analyzed earlier. In addition contemporary knowledge of the market being analyzed is critical in order to anticipate shifts in market behavior.

The demand side requires a series on the population using the space in question. For example office demand may arise from employment in non-manufacturing sectors or from white-collar workers or from workers earning particular salary levels. The key here is not so much which cut is made of the universe of the work force but rather how the selected subset is translated into square-footage terms. Once the subset of the work force has been selected it must be modeled and forecast. National employment forecasts are available through nearly every major Wall Street economist's office, and subnational forecasts are available from a variety of economic consulting firms. Alternatively one can construct an employment demand model on a personal computer and can manage the forecast to meet one's own beliefs and theories. The employment data must be translated into square-footage terms with a square-foot-per-worker scalar or series. This author calculates the change in the selected employment level and multiplies it by a square-foot-per-worker number developed by analyzing the historic relationship between space and use. Thus a periodic new demand-for-space series is generated. This series is generated. This series is made equivalent to the supply series by calculating a five-year moving sum.

The supply and demand series have thus been created independently, and each has significant simulation capability. What-if scenarios may be created by manipulating the demand and/or the supply sides and *then* seeing the magnitude of effect on the vacancy, or a proxy statistic.

Since the national vacancy rate is not easy to model and forecast from a conceptual perspective, the REMI may be employed here as a forecasting tool for the vacancy rate. Table 4–8 contains a regression analysis relating the national vacancy rate to the constructed Real Estate Market Index series. The statistics confirm that the fit of the model appears to be acceptable, but the Durbin-Watson statistic of .1355 indicates that the positive serial correlation in the residuals is even more significant than before. The data at the national level appear to be far more cyclical than the data at the regional level. In addition there appears to be a significant seasonal component. Table 4–9 presents the results of regression analysis that indicate the significance of the national vacancy rate last quarter and last year as predictors of this

Quantitative Methods in Real Estate Analysis / **117**

TABLE 4–8
Regression of National Vacancy Rates on the Real
Estate Market Index
(second quarter 1978 through first quarter 1985)

	Coefficient	Standard Error	t-Value
Intercept	12.17044	0.3519	34.58
Real Estate Market Index	4.18101	0.2520	16.59

Residual standard error = 1.2244.
Multiple R-square = 0.9136.
$N = 28$.
F-value = 275.26 on 1, 26 degrees of freedom.
Durbin-Watson statistic = 0.1355.

quarter's vacancy rate. However, the market index remains a significant explanatory variable, and its coefficient (4.18829) is virtually unchanged from the results reported in Table 4–8. Clearly the importance of the market index has not diminished with the inclusion of other explanatory variables in the regression.

The careful analysis of subnational market conditions over time is possible using these tools. The addition of the REMI or its equivalent permits both the forecasting of vacancy rates (where available) and the independent analysis and forecasting of the REMI.

TABLE 4–9
Regression of National Rates on the Real Estate Market
Index, Current and Lagged One Quarter, and the National Rates
Lagged One Quarter and One Year
(third quarter 1979 through first quarter 1985)

	Coefficient	Standard Error	t-Value
Intercept	5.18411	1.9264	2.69
Real Estate Market Index	4.18829	0.8631	4.85
Lagged market index	−3.25101	1.0255	−3.17
Lagged national rate	0.65215	0.1448	4.50
National rate lagged one year	1.12589	0.4467	2.52

Residual standard error = 0.3199.
Multiple R-square = 0.9956.
$N = 23$.
F-value = 1030.825 on 4, 18 degrees of freedom.
Durbin-Watson statistic = 1.9041.

TABLE 4–10
Regression of Annual Phoenix Vacancy Rates on the Phoenix Real
Estate Market Index and Rates for Previous Year
(1979 through 1985)

	Coefficient	Standard Error	t-Value
Intercept	7.88833	5.8487	1.35
Phoenix Real Estate Market Index	3.01289	1.7915	1.68
Lagged Phoenix vacancy rate	0.77404	0.3765	2.06

Residual standard error = 3.1827.
Multiple R-square = 0.8522.
$N = 7$.
F-value = 11.53524 on 2, 4 degrees of freedom.
Durbin-Watson statistic = 1.9113.

The Phoenix, Arizona, REMI is used below to model and forecast the Coldwell Banker office vacancy rate for Phoenix. These two series are constructed for the Maricopa County area so they are comparably based, with a correlation of .824.

Table 4–10 presents results regressing the vacancy rate on the REMI and the vacancy rate measured for the previous year. The brief historical time series available obviously renders the equation less statistically reliable, but this data dilemma tends to occur with some frequency. In all of the analysis presented in this chapter the role of the analyst looms large. Clearly there is more than enough room for the application of experienced judgment.

Table 4–11 provides historical and forecast data generated by the preceding regression. The Real Estate Market Index for Phoenix was constructed using an employment (or demand) forecast in conjunction with the short-term projection of current construction contract awards and a longer-term, "most likely" projection of contract awards. The assumption underlying the demand forecast is that demand is likely to continue to be strong in the short run, trending slightly downward to 1990. The supply side is expected to cool down slightly from current high levels under the pressure of the unusually high level of vacancy rates that are causing declining effective rental rates and increased construction lender caution.

Integration of Property and Market Analysis

In this example the Phoenix vacancy rate analyzed above will be applied to the earlier property analysis. The market rental rate will be $17 per square foot, zero rent and expense inflation will be assumed, and expenses will be

TABLE 4–11
Actual and Predicted Vacancy Rates
for the Phoenix Area

	Vacancy Rate	Market Index
Historical data		
1978	10.500%	−1.097
1979	5.300	−2.036
1980	6.700	−2.654
1981	8.200	−2.104
1982	10.100	−0.913
1983	13.200	−0.342
1984	19.700	−0.198
1985	23.100	−0.371
Predictions		
1986	24.440	−0.441
1987	24.510	−0.762
1988	24.260	−0.863
1989	24.720	−0.646
1990	25.643	−0.458

limited to the $.10 per square foot structural reserve. The building will now be cast as a speculative development with no signed tenants. The prospective investor must analyze the market and this project's relationship to the market to generate realistic leasing scenarios in order to determine value and offering price. Although our focus is on the impact on the internal rate of return, it is clear from the first part of this chapter that offering price, rate of return, and future value are directly related.

Table 4–12 presents two leased-up scenarios. Scenario I assumes that the building will be fully leased upon completion and will remain leased except for a 5 percent vacancy factor. This vacancy factor does not imply that 95 percent of the building is occupied at all times. Rather it captures the effect of tenant mobility and the time required to refit space as each tenant leaves and is replaced by another. Scenario II hypothesizes that the building will perform similarly to the market. That is, in the first year of operation, occupancy of 79.5 percent could be anticipated; and by year 5, occupancy would decline to 74.2 percent as the entire market softens. It is unlikely that any one building would perform exactly like the carefully defined aggregate market, but scenario II provides a way to analyze the market's effect on the property and to contrast this with an optimistic (traditional in the real estate industry) view. While the point of this analysis is to be as

TABLE 4–12

Property and Market Analysis Scenarios

	Year				
	1	*2*	*3*	*4*	*5*
Scenario I					
Gross potential income	$ 1,700,000	$1,700,000	$1,700,000	$1,700,000	$ 1,700,000
Less: Vacancy factor (5 percent)	85,000	85,000	85,000	85,000	85,000
$.10 reserve	10,000	10,000	10,000	10,000	10,000
Net operating income	1,605,000	1,605,000	1,605,000	1,605,000	1,605,000
Present value at 10 percent capitalization rate	$16,050,000				$16,050,000
Scenario II					
Gross income	$ 1,700,000	$1,700,000	$1,700,000	$1,700,000	$ 1,700,000
Less: Vacancy factor	24.4%	24.5%	24.3%	24.7%	25.6%
$.10 reserve	10,000	10,000	10,000	10,000	10,000
Net operating income	1,275,200	1,273,500	1,276,900	1,270,100	1,254,800
Present value at 10 percent capitalization rate	$12,609,054				$12,548,000

120

accurate as possible it is equally important to assess sensitivities so that risk may be fully understood.

Suppose the asking price of the building were set at $16,050,000, assuming a 5 percent vacancy factor. The IRR on Scenario I would be 10 percent and the IRR on scenario II is 3.88 percent. Returns are quite sensitive to market conditions expressed as property vacancy rates.

This example could be used to demonstrate the importance of rental and expense inflation assumptions and capitalization rate assumptions. Each component of this seemingly straightforward spreadsheet is subject to considerable underlying analytic effort. The value of the analytics is generated both in the increased accuracy of the pro forma statement and in the heightened appreciation of the sensitivity of the key statistics to the assumptions driving the analysis.

PORTFOLIO ANALYSIS

Market analysis has a role in interproject or portfolio analysis as well as in project analysis. Essentially, the objective of portfolio analysis is to design a portfolio of real estate holdings that achieve an overall return commensurate with the level of risk selected by the portfolio manager. The optimal way to discharge this assignment would be to collect a long time series on each of the universe of properties' rates of return. These returns would then be used in a mathematical model designed to identify through the analysis of covariance a series of unique, efficient portfolios (each paired with a risk level) from which the manager could select a preferred portfolio.

The implementation of this ideal process is a fairly simple matter for common stocks. In real estate, as usual, the data are difficult to come by. Time series on returns that would permit the analysis of risk are not available for specific properties. The closest that one can come to time series on returns for various market segments is the index known as the FRC Property Index, which records the performance of properties managed by members of the National Council of Real Estate Investment Fiduciaries. The time series is quarterly, beginning in December 1977. One catch is that because the commingled funds involved cover only around 850 properties, the data can only be meaningfully disaggregated into five structure categories *or* four geographic categories. In addition the data are not representative of the universe of commercial properties. This lack of representation and degree of aggregation renders the data useless for any meaningful portfolio optimization exercise. Of greater concern though is the fact that the time series is based on appraised values rather than transaction prices. As noted earlier in this chapter, appraisals can smooth the true volatility by about a factor of five.

The other real estate return data sources (notably Evaluation Associates Inc.) report on the performance of particular funds. The composition of these funds changes over time; so while this data might be of use in the performance evaluation of portfolio managers it is of limited use in optimization efforts. It also suffers from the problems associated with dependence on appraisals.

A more recent approach to portfolio design begins with an intuitively plausible but impossible to verify assumption: vacancy rates and real estate returns are behaviorally related. Improvements in market vacancy rates are very likely to translate into rising market and property rental rates. As rents rise, net operating income should rise, and capitalized or discounted cash flows should follow. As vacancy rates rise, the reverse chain of events ought to occur. This approach is able to take advantage of the readily available vacancy rate data and constructed data such as the REMI. The virtue of data like the REMI and its counterparts is that the universe of real estate may be included in the optimizer and the analysis may be conducted by very disaggregated geographic and structure-type markets. While an individual property within a market might not behave precisely as indicated by the relevant REMI or vacancy rate it is highly likely that the two will be closely related.

CONCLUSION

Quantitative methods are rapidly emerging as a valuable tool in real estate analysis. Progress has been impeded, however, because high-quality data are scarce. Properties are infrequently turned over, and deals are usually negotiated privately. This forces analysts to rely on estimated values such as appraisals in their application of quantitative methods. The securitization of real estate in the form of REITS and mortgage-backed securities may yield some useful data for quantitative analysis. Moreover quantitative methods may be used to improve the quality of the raw data as suggested by the development of a real estate market index.

PROBLEMS

1. The present owners of Eagle Towers, an apartment building in Manhattan, think they will get $16.5 million for the structure if they put it on the market now and sell it by the end of this year. At that asking price you estimate the capitalization rate to be 25 percent. Comparable buildings located in the same Upper West Side neighborhood and changing hands in June through September of this year had a capitalization rate of 18 percent.

a. Treating the capitalization numbers at their face value, do they justify a buy decision? Why?

Answer: Yes. The capitalization rate for Eagle Towers is higher than the comparable properties, suggesting that the asking price on which the numbers are based is too low.

b. What would you estimate the annual net operating income of Eagle Towers to be?

Answer:

$$\text{Capitalization rate} = .25 = \frac{\text{NOI}}{\$16.5}$$
$$\text{NOI} = .25 \times \$16.5 = \$4.125$$

c. What special factors pertaining to Eagle Towers might lead you to question your decision in problem 1.*a* above, based solely on the stated capitalization numbers?

Answer: Are the properties indeed comparable in terms of structure of market condition? (Note the difference in time between September and end of year. What if the year in question were 1987?) The caveats to simple price-earnings comparisons apply here too.

2. Data show that real estate investment has lower risk (as measured by the standard deviation of returns) than any other investment with comparable returns. Therefore prudent investors should allocate almost all of their fund portfolios to the real estate area. Discuss.

Answer: This conclusion does not necessarily follow. Real estate return measures are largely based on appraisal numbers, which represent a lagged partial adjustment to changes in market values. Changes in appraisal numbers often represent a simple inflation adjustment to the valuation inputs. Returns on other comparable investments are typically based on market valuations. Hence quantitative return and risk measures are not perfectly comparable.

CHAPTER FIVE

Quantitative Methods in Derivative Security Analysis

Christopher B. Barry and Andrew H. Chen

Derivative securities have values and cash flows determined by the behavior of other securities, called the *underlying securities*. For example a common stock call option gives the owner of the option the right to buy a given number of shares of stock at a specified price within a specified time period. The value of the option depends on the value of its underlying asset, the common stock. Similarly a Treasury bill (T-bill) futures contract obliges the owner to purchase T-bills at a fixed price on a particular date. The value of the futures contract is derived from the value of the underlying asset, the T-bills. Derivative securities, then, are securities that allow the buyer or seller of the securities to arrange payoffs contingent on the values of other securities. As a result, derivative securities enlarge the opportunity set of payoffs that can be obtained by investors.

This chapter will introduce the basic concepts and results of applying quantitative methods to the analysis of derivative securities. Call option securities in particular are emphasized since the state of the field is well advanced in the analysis of those securities. The chapter begins with a discussion of basic properties of options and of some useful boundaries on their values. Next comes a discussion of simple option portfolio strategies that illustrates how their cash flows and the probability distributions of their cash flows relate to the underlying assets. Then arbitrage concepts are presented that are important in valuing derivative securities and analyzing strategies, followed by a development of two well-known models for option valuation. A brief empirical section presents results from the literature regarding the returns to put and call option portfolios and indicating how well the theoretical models work in practice. The applicability of option pricing principles to a variety of other types of securities will be discussed. Finally financial futures contracts are reviewed briefly.

BASIC PROPERTIES OF OPTION VALUES

Option contracts traded on the major options exchanges are of two primary types: calls and puts. A *call option* gives the owner of the contract the right to buy a fixed number of shares of the underlying security at a fixed price, called the *exercise*, or *strike*, *price*, within a fixed time period. A *put option* gives the owner of the contract the right to sell a fixed number of shares of the underlying security at a fixed price within a fixed time period.

Since an *option* is the right to buy or sell a given number of shares of the underlying stock at a given price on or before a specified date, options derive their values from the prices of the underlying assets and from the terms in the option contract. Since a call option is a right (rather than an obligation) to buy the underlying stock at the exercise price, only if the stock price at expiration is greater than the option exercise price will the holder of a call exercise the option and receive the difference between the stock price and the exercise price; if the stock price is equal to or less than the exercise price, the holder of the call will let the option expire rather than exercise it. Thus at the expiration date the call has zero value if the exercise price is greater than the underlying stock price. Hence we can express the value of a call at the expiration date *(T)* of the option as the stock minus the exercise price *(K)*, or zero, whichever is greater. This establishes the minimum value of a call. Since buying the underlying stock is obviously an alternative to buying a call on the stock, the maximum value of the call is the price of the stock itself.

Thus we can show the upper and lower boundaries of the price of a call as illustrated in Figure 5–1.

At expiration a call has zero value if the stock price is equal to or less than the exercise price, and the call option price increases a dollar for each dollar increase in the stock price if the stock price is greater than the exercise price. Therefore the possible value of a call option at expiration may be represented by a kinked line consisting of a horizontal line segment from the origin to the exercise price, *K*, and the upward sloping line from the

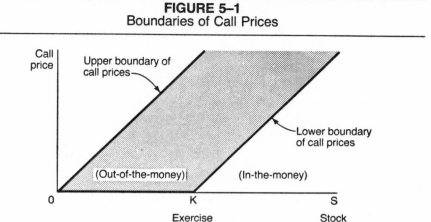

FIGURE 5-1
Boundaries of Call Prices

exercise price of a call. If a call option expires worthless at maturity, the call is said to expire *out of the money*. If it has a positive value at maturity, the call will be exercised and not allowed to expire, and the call is said to be *in the money*. These descriptions of the relationship between exercise price and underlying stock price at expiration are often loosely applied during the life of the option. A call option is said to be traded in the money, at the money, or out of the money whenever the current price of the underlying stock is greater than, close to, or less than the exercise price of the call, respectively.

The value of a call at expiration is referred to as its *intrinsic value*. At any time prior to expiration the call option should be worth at least its intrinsic value; otherwise investors who own the stock would sell stock and buy the call instead, profiting by the difference between the exercise price and the stock minus the call price. To the extent that the option may be further in the money at expiration than it currently is, it may be worth even more than its intrinsic value. However, it will not be worth more than the stock, since the investors would then sell the call and buy the stock. As we shall see, these *arbitrage* arguments are essential to an understanding of what determines option values.

Similarly a put option is a right and not an obligation to sell a given number of shares of the underlying stock at the exercise price. The value of a put at expiration is equal to either the exercise price minus the stock

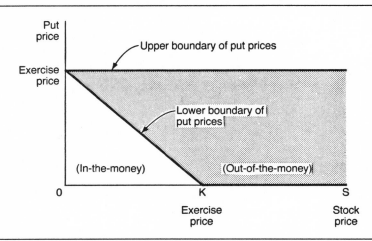

FIGURE 5–2
Boundaries of Put Prices

price at expiration or zero, whichever is greater. This gives the minimum value of a put price. Also note that the value of a put cannot exceed the exercise price, even if the stock price drops to zero. Thus we present the upper and lower boundaries of the put price as in Figure 5–2. A put is said to be traded in the money, at the money, or out of the money if the current stock price is less than, close to, or greater than the exercise price, respectively.

SIMPLE OPTIONS STRATEGIES

Many options strategies can be employed by investors in their portfolio management decisions. For instance an investor can purchase or sell short either a call option or a put option alone *(naked option strategy)*, trade the options with the underlying stocks at the same time *(hedging strategies)*, trade calls or puts with different exercise prices or different expiration dates *(spreading strategies)*, or combine calls and puts in one transaction *(combination strategies)*. We shall describe only a few simple naked and hedging strategies.

Long or Short Call Option

A call option is the right to buy the stock at the option exercise price. The price that an investor has to pay to acquire the right to buy the stock is referred to as the *call premium,* or *call price.* If an investor pays a call

FIGURE 5–3
Profit/Loss for Call Buyer and Call Writer

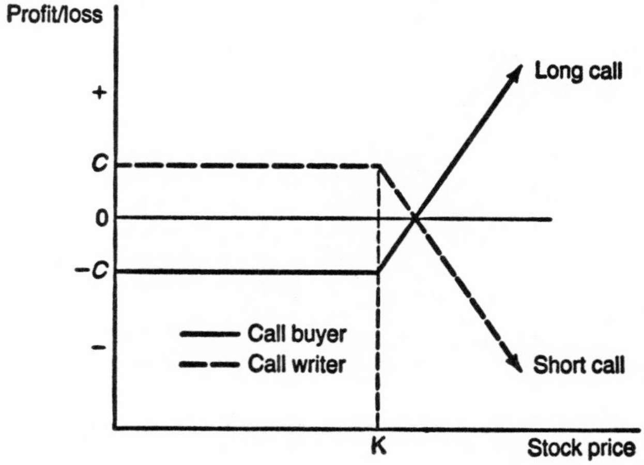

premium of C dollars today to obtain a call option, his profit or loss at the expiration date from buying the call can be easily determined. If the stock price is below the exercise price of K at expiration, the investor will let the option expire worthless and incur the loss of the initial investment, the call premium C. If the stock price at expiration is above the exercise price, then the investor gains the difference between the cost of buying the stock and the market price at which the stock can be sold. The profit/loss diagrams for the call buyer and call option writer are illustrated in Figure 5–3. The profit or loss to the call writer at expiration is just the opposite of that for the call buyer.

Long or Short Put Option

A put option is the right to sell the stock at the exercise price. If an investor pays put premium P today for the put option, his profit or loss at expiration can be determined easily. If the stock price at expiration is less than the exercise price, the investor can gain an amount equal to the exercise price minus the stock price; if the stock price is above the exercise price, the investor will let the option expire and incur a loss of the initial investment, which is equal to the put premium.

The profit/loss at expiration for a put buyer and put writer is illustrated

FIGURE 5–4
Profit/Loss for Put Buyer and Put Writer

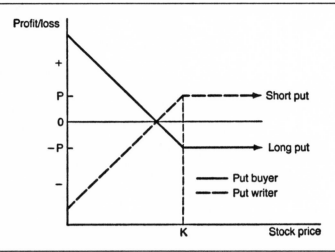

in Figure 5–4. For the writer of a put, the profit at expiration will be the put premium received if the stock price is greater than the exercise price and the option is allowed to expire worthless. However if the stock price at expiration is less than the exercise price, the net payoff to a put writer will be $P - (K - S)$.

Buying a Protective Put

A hedging strategy for buying stock and buying a put option is similar to buying insurance against unfavorable stock outcomes. The *protective put* avoids the downside risk faced by the investor. This strategy is referred to as buying a protective put. Figure 5–5 shows the profit/loss diagram for the strategy of buying a protective put. For simplicity we assume that the option was traded at the money and the put premium was P when the strategy was established. As illustrated in the figure, if the stock price at expiration is greater than the exercise price, the put has no value and the value of the hedged portfolio will be equal to the stock price minus the put premium. On the other hand, if the stock price at expiration is less than the exercise price, the investor can exercise the option and deliver the stock to the put writer for the payment of K (same as the stock purchase price) and thus incur

FIGURE 5–5
Profit/Loss for Protective Put

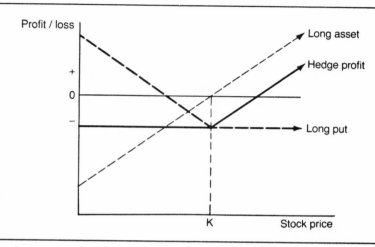

a loss of P. Therefore, with a protective put the maximum loss that an investor can incur is limited.

The protective put can also be illustrated using probability distributions that account for the probabilities of various outcomes. Suppose that a stock portfolio of $80,000 has a six-month distribution of returns that is normal with a mean return of .075 (7.5 percent) and a standard deviation of .30 (30 percent). Then the expected value of the portfolio in six months is also normal, and it has a mean of $86,000 (computed as $80,000 × 1.075) and a standard deviation of 24,000 (computed as 80,000 × .3).

The distribution of payoffs is illustrated in Figure 5–6. Since the distribution is normal in panel A it is symmetric around its mean value of $86,000. Panel B depicts the distribution of payoffs when a protective put is bought. Assume that the put costs $5,000 (or $3.125 × 1,600 shares). Its purchase shifts all portfolio values that were more than $80,000 down by $5,000. However, the put protects the portfolio from all stock price declines. Any stock price that would have led to a portfolio value of $80,000 or less now leads to a portfolio value of exactly $75,000. $75,000 then has a probability equal to the probability of all stock prices less than or equal to $50, and that probability can be shown to be .3235. The probability at $75,000 is known as a *probability mass* in contrast to the probability densities for payoffs above $75,000

FIGURE 5–6
Distribution of Payoffs

(Panel A: Distribution with stock only)

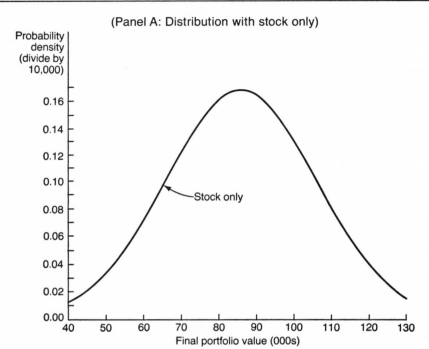

(Panel B: Distributions with and without put)

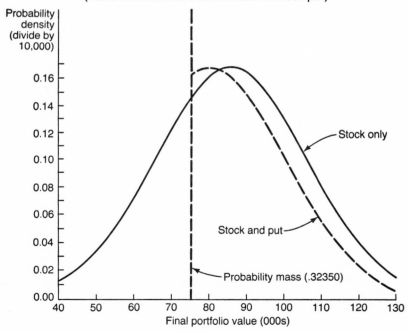

FIGURE 5–7
Profit/Loss for Writing Covered Call

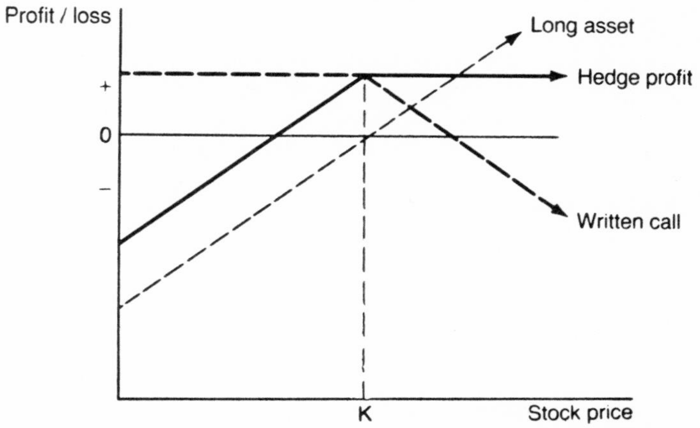

This example illustrates how an investor can change the opportunity set by combining options with other securities in a portfolio. As shown in Figure 5–6 the protective put transforms a symmetric, normal probability distribution into one in which the lower tail is removed, or *truncated*. The resulting *truncated distribution* is skewed to the right (that is, has positive skewness) and has a lower standard deviation. Whether its mean is lower or higher than the mean using only stock depends on the size of the total premium paid, but that effect may be offset by the truncation effect.

Writing a Covered Call

A strategy of writing a covered call involves buying the stock and shorting the call option. If the stock price at expiration is equal to or less than the exercise price, the call expires worthless, and the investor keeps the call premium (which will improve the value of the portfolio). On the other hand, if the stock price at expiration is greater than the exercise price, the investor can deliver the stock and receive the payment of K when the call option is exercised. The profit/loss diagram of writing a covered call is illustrated in Figure 5–7.

As in the case of the protective put, the effect of the covered call on the distribution of portfolio value can be obtained as illustrated in Figure 5–8. Assume that the call options sell for a premium of $3.75 for a total

FIGURE 5–8
Distribution of Portfolio Value

(Panel A: Distribution with stock only)

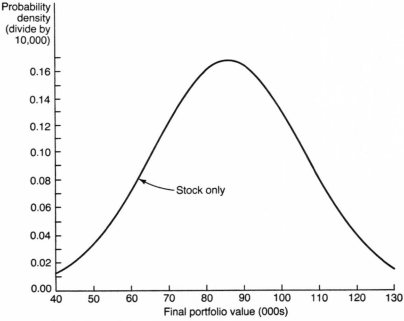

(Panel B: Distribution with and without written call)

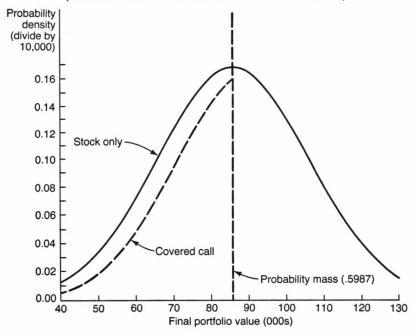

call premium income of $6,000 ($3.75 × 1,600 shares) and that the call has an exercise price of $50 per share. If the stock price declines, the call option premium income helps to offset the losses on the stock. However; if the stock price rises above $50, you cannot share in that increase because you are obligated to deliver the stock at $50. Nevertheless, in such cases the portfolio is worth $86,000. The premium income shifts the probability distribution of portfolio value to the right until $86,000 is reached. Since for all stock prices above $50 you receive a portfolio value of $86,000 the probability that the portfolio will be worth exactly $86,000 is the same as the probability that the stock price will exceed $50, which is .5987. In this case the probability distribution of payoffs has a higher mode than in the case of the protective put, and it has a somewhat lower standard deviation (and semiinterquartile range). But the distribution is left-skewed.

It should be apparent from these examples that skewness is an important factor in assessing option strategies. Skewness is generally less important in assessing common stock portfolios, since stock return distributions generally appear to be at least approximately symmetric. Option strategies generally impart skewness to a portfolio's distribution of returns.

Option Margins and Holding Period Returns

When an option is bought or sold or used in the context of a portfolio, it may be difficult to determine the holding period return. For example, if the strategy is simply to write a naked call, the option seller receives a payment of C per option transacted. But since the option writer is subject to the risk of having to deliver stock, a margin is required as well. The minimum margin requirement is

$$M = \text{Maximum of } [(1.3 \times S) - K, 2.50]$$

and the price of the option can cover a portion of the margin. As an example, if the stock price is $40, the exercise price is $50, and the price of the call is $4, then the investor must put up a margin of

$$\text{Maximum of } [52 - 50, 2.50]$$

which is $2.50. The margin is entirely covered by the price of the call itself, and rate of return for the position taken by itself is meaningless.

On the other hand a covered call position has a more complex set of requirements. If the call is out of the money, then margin is required on the stock but no additional margin is required on the option. If the call is in the money, then an additional margin is required; but again, the margin for the entire position is reduced by the price of the call itself.

It follows that options introduce some complexities to the task of finding the holding period return in a portfolio. Margin rules now in existence allow the investor to identify combinations of securities that minimize the overall margin requirement. John Cox and Mark Rubinstein provide details on the margin requirements for a variety of option positions and provide an algorithm for identifying the pairings of options and stocks that minimize margin requirements.[1]

ARBITRAGE AND OPTION VALUATION

Suppose the price of a stock is currently $60 and you could buy a call option on it with an exercise price of $50. If the call sold for, say, $5, then you could buy the call and immediately exercise it for a $10 gain, netting you $5 with no risk whatsoever. As noted before, this opportunity illustrates pure arbitrage: the gaining of certain profits at no net investment.

Since active traders follow market prices closely, constantly seeking opportunities for easy rewards, it is unlikely that significant arbitrage opportunities of this kind could persist for long. Consequently economists have developed many results to describe the relationships among the prices of various securities, and those results often depend on the absence of arbitrage.

The above example can be used by economists to argue that the price of an option must always equal or exceed the exercise value of the option— that is, the amount that could be earned by exercising the option. For put and call options, if the exercise price is K and the stock price is S, then the values of puts and calls must satisfy

$$C \geq S - K$$

and

$$P \geq K - S$$

where C and P denote the call price and put price, respectively. Also, an option gives the holder a right, not an obligation. The option holder can in the worst case merely throw the option away or ignore it, so the option would never have a negative value. Thus the option must have a value at least as large as zero or the exercise value, whichever is larger:

$$\text{Call value} \geq \text{Maximum of } [0, S - K]$$

---

[1]J. Cox and M. Rubinstein, *Options Markets* (Englewood Cliffs, N.J.: Prentice-Hall, 1985).

TABLE 5–1
Cash Flows to a Portfolio and to a Call

	Ending Price of Stock	
	$ST \leq K$	$ST > K$
Position A		
Stock value	ST	ST
Put value	$K - ST$	0
Pay off loan	$-K$	$-K$
Total cash flow	0	$ST - K$
Position B		
Call value	0	$ST - K$

---

and

$$\text{Put value} \geq \text{Maximum of } [0, K - S]$$

An additional result is that an investor with "perfect access" to the markets can create a portfolio consisting of a put, the stock, and a loan that has the same payoffs for all ending stock prices as the call has. By perfect access we mean that the investor pays no transaction costs and can borrow at the lowest rate available in the market, the riskless rate. The following two positions will have the same payoffs at all possible stock prices:

Position A: Buy one share of stock.
Buy one put option (exercisable at K).
Borrow $PV(K)$
Position B: Buy one call option (exercisable at K).

In position A, $PV(K)$ denotes the present value of the exercise price. Thus the position includes borrowing an amount that will require repayment of the amount K at the expiration date of the options.

Now consider the cash flows that will occur at the expiration of the two options, as shown in Table 5–1. As the results indicate, the portfolio (position A) has exactly the payoffs of the call regardless of the final value of the stock. In essence the purchase of stock along with a put contract and borrowing the present value of the exercise price of the option create an *equivalent* position to the call option. The position so obtained (position A) is referred to as a *synthetic call*.

Position A and position B have the same cash flows at the expiration date of the option. Unless the two positions cost the same amount to enter, there is an arbitrage opportunity. For example, if the call costs more than the synthetic call, then one could sell the call and carry out the transactions in the synthetic call. The result would be a positive cash flow now (that is, income) and no net cash flows later. On the other hand, if the call was underpriced relative to the synthetic call, then one could buy the call and reverse the transactions in the synthetic call. Again the result would be positive income now with no net cash flows later. The existence of active arbitrageurs in the market will prevent any such mispricing from persisting in the market.

The "no arbitrage" condition implied by the equivalence of the call to the synthetic call leads to the following relationship that must hold among the various securities:

$$\text{Call value} = S + \text{Put value} - PV(K)$$

The expression is usually rearranged to define a condition on the value of the put in terms of the call and written as

$$\text{Put value} = \text{Call value} - S + PV(K)$$

This relationship is known as *put-call parity*. It is the absence of perfect parity that gives rise to arbitrage opportunities in the market for options.

In using relationships such as put-call parity to look for possible mispricing of options, keep in mind that they may appear at times to be mispriced when in fact there is no mispricing. For example, the relationship requires that all prices are observed *contemporaneously*. Suppose we observe prices in the *The Wall Street Journal* for three such securities, and parity does not hold. If the prices are all closing prices they might reflect final trades at different times during the day, with the later price reflecting new information that came to the market. Then the earlier price might not be a price at which a trade could now be made. For example, the put might not have traded since 11 A.M., while the call and the stock both traded at 3 P.M. Then the observed put price might not be a price at which a trade could have been executed at 3 P.M. Powerful market forces act to take advantage of arbitrage opportunities and hence to eliminate mispricing, so one should not hastily conclude that the markets have missed something.

Dividends on the underlying stock also affect the parity relationship. If during the life of the put and call option contracts there will be dividends paid on the stock, the prices of the put and call will be affected. In fact the call may not be held to expiration if dividends are to be paid (that is, it may be optimal to exercise the call prematurely), and an American put may be exercised prematurely even if there are no dividends to be paid. The put-call parity relationship can be adjusted in an approximate way to accommodate dividends. If *PV(D)* represents the present value of dividends to be paid during the life of the options, then the relationship can be approximated by

Put value = Call value − S + $PV(K)$ − $PV(D)$

The no-arbitrage conditions illustrated in this section have been extended in the finance literature so that the value of an option can be computed under general conditions. Those extensions generally involve the use of options and stock to create a riskless hedge. Then, imposing the condition that a riskless investment must earn the riskless rate available in the market on alternative investments, a pricing relationship is obtained to value the option. Two models that apply this logic and that are important in practice are developed in the next section.

OPTION PRICING MODELS

Based on general arbitrage arguments, we have shown in previous sections that option values must lie within certain boundaries and that the following relationship between the option values and those of the underlying assets will hold only on the expiration dates (T) of the options:

Call value at T = Maximum of $[S_T − K, 0]$
Put value at T = Maximum of $[K − S_T, 0]$

At any time other than the expiration date the value of an option will be different from that given above. This section develops expressions that value the option at any time during its life.

On what variables do the values of options depend? How do those variables influence the values of the options? Answers to these questions can be given in broad terms without resorting to mathematical models. Values of call options are influenced by these variables: exercise price of the option, current price of the stock, time to maturity of the option, volatility of the underlying stock, and the level of interest rates over the life of the option. In addition many other variables (dividends, taxes, transactions costs, and so on) can influence option values, but we will confine our discussion to the above five key variables, taken one at a time.

The effects of the five variables on option values are intuitive. For example the exercise price is the price at which the owner of the option can buy the stock. The lower the exercise price, the more profitable the option will be at exercise as long as the stock price exceeds the exercise price. Thus the value of a call option is always greater, the lower the exercise price. (Similarly a put option is always worth more, the greater the exercise price.)

The effect of the current stock price is the reverse of the effect of the exercise price. All else being equal, the option is more valuable, the greater the current stock price. For one thing, the lower bound on the option's value is increased by raising S. Also, the likelihood that the option will be exercised profitably (or sold at a profit) is greater, the larger the current stock price. Increasing the stock price merely moves the probability distribution of gains to the right; positive gains are thus more likely, and the probability of larger gains is increased. (The opposite is true for puts.)

Time to maturity has several effects on the option value. First, because it delays the date of exercise, $PV(K)$ is reduced, raising the lower bound of the option's value. Also, an option with a long life has all of the features of an option with a shorter life except one: the owner is not forced to exercise at the earlier date if it is not advantageous to do so. Finally, by giving the share more time in which to experience a share price rise (or fall) there is more dispersion in the final share price. Thus the probability of larger gains is increased. In sum, the longer its time to maturity, the more valuable an option will be.[2]

The variance or volatility in the return of the stock is another important determinant of the value of an option. The higher the dispersion of the stock's returns, the greater the probability of larger gains from owning the option contract. Recall the probability distributions shown in Figures 5–6A and 5–8A. An increase in variance, all other things being equal, flattens the distribution of share prices, making both extremely small and extremely large stock prices more probable. On the downside there is no effect on the option buyer; as long as the stock price is below the striking price, the option expires worthless. Making the stock price even lower does not reduce the value of the option below zero. However on the upside the option holder is more likely to have larger gains as the variance rate increases; the option holder gains on the upside and is unaffected on the downside. The net effect is that an option is worth more the greater the volatility of the stock.

The final term to be considered is the riskless rate. Here it is important to reemphasize that we are examining these effects one at a time. If the riskless rate rises, the present value of the exercise price declines. As a result the lower bound of the option value rises, and in fact the option value also rises. An increase in interest rates may also have a negative effect on share prices (making S smaller), but here we are examining the effect of r while holding S constant. (This opposite is true for puts.)

The effects of each of these five variables will be made more explicit

---

[2]This effect can be ambiguous for put options that may be exercised only at maturity, so-called *European* puts. Reduction in $PV(K)$ reduces put value, but the dispersion increases value. However, for so-called *American* puts that can be exercised prior to maturity the effect is unambiguous since such options can be exercised early. For the American puts and calls that trade on U.S. exchanges, value increases with time to maturity.

in this section by developing models of option prices. In those models the effects of the variables can be observed directly. For the models to be regarded as reasonable they should agree with our intuition about the determinants of option values. Indeed they do.

The Black-Scholes Option Pricing Model

As shown earlier, the value of a call option at expiration is the larger of zero or the exercise value, and at any time prior to maturity the value is bounded below by the larger of zero or the excess of the stock price over the present value of the exercise price. Consider the two values S and $PV(K)$. S is the value of the stock now, and $PV(K)$ is the value now of the exercise price to be paid later. Intuitively it seems reasonable to think that the option value would be some weighted combination of S and $PV(K)$. In other words it is intuitive to postulate that there are weights w_s and w_k such that the option value is

$$\text{Call value} = (S \times w_s) - [PV(K) \times w_k]$$

What weights might be reasonable? At expiration either it is profitable to exercise or it is not profitable to exercise. If it is profitable, then the weights would both be one (1), that is,

$$\text{Call value} = S - K$$

and if not, the weights would both be zero, giving

$$\text{Call value} = 0$$

So one might postulate that the weights w_s and w_k have something to do with the probability that exercise is profitable. The *Black-Scholes option pricing model (BSOPM)* gives exact values to those weights. After developing the model below we will interpret it in terms of these weights w_s and w_k.

The Black-Scholes model was derived by Fischer Black and Myron Scholes in an article published in 1973.[3] The publication of the paper coincided with the opening of the Chicago Board Options Exchange, so that trading in options was stimulated simultaneously by the start-up of a new system for trading options and a new theory for valuing them.

Black and Scholes assumed that the continuously compounded (one plus) rate of return of the stock over some time interval T has a log normal

---

[3]F. Black and M. Scholes, "The Pricing of Options and Corporate Liabilities," *Journal of Political Economy*, May 1973, pp. 637–54.

distribution with a variance of V times T. Other assumptions of the model include:

1. No taxes or transactions costs.
2. No dividends paid on the stock over the life of the option.
3. No short sales restrictions.
4. Riskless borrowing and lending available at the continuous rate r.
5. Portfolio may be adjusted instantaneously.
6. Option can be exercised only at maturity.

With these assumptions Black and Scholes derived their famous call option pricing equation:

$$\text{Call value} = [S \times N(D1)] - [(K \times e^{-rt}) \times N(D2)]$$

where

S = Current stock price.
K = Exercise price of option.
T = Time to maturity of the option.
$N(.)$ = Standard normal distribution function.

$$D1 = \frac{\text{natural log}\left(\frac{S}{K}\right) + \left[\left(r + \frac{V}{2}\right) \times T\right]}{(V \times T)^{.5}}$$

$D2 = D1 - (V \times T)^{.5}$
V = Variance of return of the stock.
e = Exponential constant 2.71828 (See Chapter One, p. 14)

While the Black-Scholes formula appears formidable its components can be interpreted in terms of the probability model we proposed at the start of this section, with weights w_s and w_k. The model as shown above is of the general form discussed earlier, that is,

$$(S \times w_s) - [PV(K) \times w_k]$$

The weight w_s is given by $N(D1)$. The term $(K \times e^{-rt})$ is nothing more than the present value of the exercise price, $PV(K)$, at the continuously compounded rate r. Thus the weight w_k is given by $N(D2)$, which has the interpretation of being the probability of exercise at expiration. Thus,

$$(K \times e^{-rt}) \times N(D2)$$

can be interpreted as the expected present value of the outlay for exercising the option. Thus the BSOPM is the weighted sum of the stock price and present value of exercise price.

To illustrate the computations used in the model, suppose the input data are as follows:

$S = 45.$

$K = 50.$

$T = .75$ (nine months).

$V = .4^2 = .16.$

$r = .08$ (annual rate).

Then

$$D1 = \frac{\text{natural log } (45/50) + [(.08 + .16/2) \times .75]}{(.16 \times .75)^{.5}}$$

$$= \frac{\text{natural log } (45/50) + .12}{.3466} = \frac{-.10544 + .12}{.3466}$$

$$= .0423$$

$$D2 = D1 - (.16 \times .75)^{.5}$$

$$= .0423 - .3464 = -.3041$$

$$N(D1) = .51687$$

$$N(D2) = .38053$$

Finally

$$C = (45 \times .51687) - (50 \times 2.71828^{-.08 \times .75}) \times .38053$$

$$= 23.26 - 17.92 = \$5.34$$

The calculations illustrate the use of the model, given that the inputs are known. A later example will illustrate how to obtain the inputs from a set of historical security prices.

Properties of the BSOPM. The BSOPM serves as a basis for understanding how the key determinants of option values affect the value of the option. The value of the option predicted by the model is related to the other variables as follows:

Variable	Effect on Call Option Value
Stock price (S)	Positive
Exercise price (K)	Negative
Time to maturity (T)	Positive
Stock risk (V)	Positive
Riskless rate (r)	Positive

These effects are in agreement with intuition, which is the first test of a mathematical model and which was discussed at the beginning of this section.

Use of the Model with Real Data. To apply the BSOPM a number of input values must be estimated. The stock price itself is easily observed, and the exercise price and time to maturity of the option are known. Two inputs must be estimated: the riskless rate over the life of the option and the variance of the stock's rate of return. The riskless rate is obtained from the yield on Treasury bills with a maturity close to that of the option, and the stock's variance is most easily estimated from a series of historical prices of the stock.

We will apply the model to the valuation of Datapoint options. Datapoint is a stock that had never paid a cash dividend as of the date of the data, so the assumption was made that no dividends would be paid during the life of the option. The following data were obtained from March 19, 1982, trading:

Date: March 19, 1982.
Expiration: May 22, 1982.
T: $^{64}/_{365}$ days $= .17534$.
Stock price $= 23.125$.

In order to estimate the riskless rate, Treasury bill quotations were obtained from *The Wall Street Journal,* as shown in Table 5–2. The yield figure reported in the *Journal* is not appropriate for our purposes; it is a simple (that is, not compounded) yield figure based on the asked discount (although in fact it will generally be a reasonable approximation to the yield figure we will obtain). Our objective is to find the continuously compounded annual return on the T-bills.

To obtain the yield, the average of the bid and asked discounts are applied. (In some cases the bid discount itself will be appropriate; in others the ask discount will be appropriate.) The average discount is 11.20. That figure is converted into a yield:

$$\text{T-bill life} = 65 \text{ days}$$

$$\text{65-day discount} = \frac{11.2 \times 65}{360} = 2.0222 \text{ percent}$$

$$\text{65-day return} = \frac{2.0222}{100 - 2.0222} = 2.064 \text{ percent}$$

$$\text{Annual return} = 1.02064^{(365/65)} - 1 = 12.15 \text{ percent}$$

TABLE 5–2
U.S. Treasury Bills

Maturity Date	Discount		Yield
	Bid	Asked	
5–24–84	11.24	11.16	11.55

The annual return figure can be converted into a continuously compounded annual equivalent:

$$\text{Continuous } r = \text{Natural log } (1 + \text{return})$$
$$= \ln(1.1215) = .11467 = 11.467 \text{ percent}$$

As mentioned previously, the 11.55 percent yield figure reported in *The Wall Street Journal* is a bit off the mark.

The variance of the stock's continuous rate of return must also be estimated. This estimation can be done in a variety of ways, including a subjective assessment by the analyst, but the most common approach is to use historical stock prices for the stock in question. While daily data over perhaps a six-month interval are most commonly used, the ideas are well illustrated by using a few months of monthly data. On March 19 the historical data shown in Table 5–3 were observed. Those prices were used to calculate a variance estimate as illustrated by the table, resulting in an annualized variance estimate of .43064. With logarithmic returns as used here a monthly variance is converted into an annual one merely by multiplying it by 12. This variance corresponds to an annual standard deviation of .65623, which is relatively high among common stocks.

The rate of return, time to expiration, and variance must all be expressed in *equivalent time units*. What this means is simply that if the time to expiration is in years the return measure should be an annualized return, and the variance should also be annualized. If time is in months, then the rate of return and variance should correspond. The choice of time units is irrelevant as long as it is consistent for all three inputs. The figures above are all in annualized units since those are most familiar.

To compute the value of the option, the model is applied as in the previous numerical example. The inputs are:

$S = 23.12500.$
$K = 25.00000.$
$T = 0.17534.$

TABLE 5–3
Variance Calculations for Datapoint
(monthly data)

Month	End Price	Price Relative* (PR)	Natural log (PR)	Squared Error
1	54.750	NA	NA	NA
2	60.750	1.10959	0.10399	0.02946
3	65.500	1.07819	0.07528	0.02043
4	57.500	0.87786	−0.13027	0.00392
5	53.375	0.92826	−0.07444	0.00005
6	46.125	0.86417	−0.14599	0.00614
7	46.750	1.01355	0.01346	0.00658
8	48.250	1.03209	0.03158	0.00985
9	48.750	1.01036	0.01031	0.00608
10	51.250	1.05128	0.05001	0.01385
11	51.000	1.04615	−0.00488	0.00448
12	28.125	0.55147	−0.59517	0.27827
13	23.125	0.82222	−0.19574	0.01641

Average return† = −0.07182
Monthly variance‡ = 0.03589
Annualized variance§ = 0.43064
Annualized standard deviation = 0.65623

*The price relative is the month's price divided by the previous month's price. The natural log of the price relative, then, gives the (continuous) return over the month. The squared difference between the month's return and the average return is shown in the last column.
†Average return is computed as the mean of the 12 log price relatives.
‡Monthly variance is the sum of squared differences divided by 11, which is the number of returns minus one.
§Annualized variance is monthly variance times 12.

$r = 0.11467.$
$V = 0.43064.$

Those inputs lead to an estimated option value as shown in these calculations:

$$D1 = \frac{\text{natural log}\left(\frac{23.125}{25}\right) + \left[\left(.11467 + \frac{.43064}{2}\right) \times .17534\right]}{(.43064 \times .17534)^{.5}}$$

$$= -0.07315$$

$$D2 = D1 - (.43064 \times .17534)^{.5} = -0.34794$$

$$N(D1) = 0.47083$$

$$N(D2) = 0.36395$$

These values lead to a price estimate of $1.97, which corresponds to an option closing price of exactly $2

The numbers above were not contrived to give a result so close to the observed option value—they represent the actual data available for the estimation. The results are sensitive to the estimated inputs, however. For the example above, the estimate was also computed using the prior 13 weeks of data; and as it turned out, the estimated price exceeded $3. This illustrates the point that the results are sensitive to the inputs. In the Datapoint example the three-month period prior to March 19, 1982, was an unusually turbulent (high-volatility) time. In pricing the option at $2 the market seemed to convey the conviction that the volatile period was not indicative of the subsequent period of the life of the option.

One particularly interesting approach to estimating the option's variance is to let the Black-Scholes model determine the variance. That is, given the price of the option and given all other inputs except the option's variance there will be a unique variance (called the *implied variance*) such that the model price agrees with the observed price. Thus the option itself can provide evidence of the stock's underlying variability.

Given the sensitivity of the BSOPM price of the option to its inputs, caution must be used in interpreting the results of a price calculation. For example in the case of the Datapoint option a researcher using the mentioned weekly data might have concluded that the option's value was $3 and the option was therefore "underpriced" at $2. Such conclusions should only be reached with great care and attention to the inputs.

Sensitivity to Assumptions. As indicated in previous chapters all quantitative methods depend on sets of assumptions. The results from using such methods to ascertain value can best be thought of as approximations, the quality of which depend on the extent to which these assumptions approach reality. As also indicated earlier the BSOPM depends on a rather formidable-appearing set of assumptions. Fortunately only two are really crucial to the analysis.

The most serious assumption would appear to be the assumption that the option can be exercised only at expiration. Such options are referred to as *European options*. Options trading in the United States can be exercised prior to maturity. These are called *American options*.[4] While such options *may* be exercised prior to maturity it turns out that American options *will not* be exercised prior to maturity. However, this is not the case for options on stocks that pay dividends.

Early exercise is not optimal for stocks that do not pay dividends, because

---

[4]This terminology is somewhat misleading. Most options trading on European exchanges can be exercised prior to maturity.

of economic arguments that show the option is always worth more than its exercise value *(S − K)* prior to maturity. Those arguments are not valid for all options on dividend-paying stocks because the value of the stock declines on the ex-dividend date by the amount of the dividend. That price decline causes the ex-dividend value of the option to be the value based on the old stock price less the dividend, which can cause a discrete decline in the price of the option. In some cases the exercise value of the option prior to dividend payment may be greater than the market value of the option on the ex-dividend stock price. Thus the BSOPM must be adjusted for the possibility of premature exercise.

There are various ways of adjusting for dividends. One simple way is to assume the option can be exercised only on each of the various ex-dividend dates and to obtain values associated with each of the dates. For example imagine an option with one ex-dividend date prior to the maturity of the option. Compute the value of the option and compare the value so obtained to the value assuming the option is held to maturity (but using a stock price equal to the current price less the present value of the expected dividend payment). The larger of the two values would give the value of the option, assuming an "optimal exercise" strategy is followed. However, this approach tends to understate the value of the option.

Cox and Rubinstein refer to the value obtained by the procedure above as the pseudo-American call value since the procedure derives an anticipated optimal exercise date.[5] In reality the optimal exercise date will depend on the path the stock price takes after the computations are made. The stock price may subsequently fall, so that early exercise is no longer optimal, or rise, so that early exercise becomes optimal. Cox and Rubinstein demonstrate a procedure for determining call prices that fully accounts for the prospect of early exercise and recognizes that exercise policy is dynamic.

The BSOPM and Put Valuation. Earlier a parity between put and call prices was illustrated. If the parity relationship fails to hold, there will be opportunities for arbitrageurs to act and earn arbitrage profits, so market forces tend to maintain the put-call parity relationship.

Put-call parity was shown to imply

$$\text{Put value} = \text{Call value} − S + PV(K)$$

Substituting the BSOPM call value into the parity relationship, we can derive the value of a put, assuming both that the put is European (no early exercise) and that the underlying stock pays no dividends. It turns out that American

---

[5]Cox and Rubinstein, *Options Markets*.

puts may be exercised prematurely even if the underlying security pays no dividends, so the BSOPM value tends to understate the value of American puts even on non-dividend-paying stocks.

There are no closed-form solutions for the valuation of American puts. Michael Parkinson, a physicist, has developed numerical techniques for their valuation,[6] and Cox and Rubinstein present methods for such puts as well (with and without dividends). Such methods are available in computer software packages.

Two-State Option Pricing Model

The Black-Scholes model is an elegant model that has been important in the literature and in practice. A simpler approach called the *binomial option pricing model (BOPM)* is identical to the BSOPM under certain limiting conditions. The BOPM assumes that only two things can happen to the stock: it can go up or it can go down (it cannot, however, remain unchanged). The BOPM is rather intuitive, as will be evident in this discussion, and can be applied somewhat more generally than can the Black-Scholes model.

One-Period Model. A numerical example will be used to illustrate how a riskless hedged portfolio can be constructed and the value of a call option with one period to expiration can be derived under the assumption that the stock prices follow simple two-state movements.

Example: Suppose the current price of a stock is $S = \$100$, and at the end of a period the price will either be up to $S_1 = \$110$ with a probability of 80 percent or be down to $S_1 = \$90$ with a probability of 20 percent. A call on the stock is available with an exercise price of $K = \$100$, expiring at the end of the period. The risk-free rate of interest at which one can lend or borrow is assumed to be 5 percent. The question is "What should the value of this call be so that there will be no risk-free arbitrage opportunity?" Consider forming the following strategy of writing covered calls:

1. Buy one share of the stock at $100.
2. Write two calls.

---

[6]M. Parkinson, "Option Pricing: The American Put," *Journal of Business*, January 1977, pp. 21–36.

TABLE 5–4
Payoffs for Covered Call Strategy

| | | End-of-Period Position | | |
| | | | | Hedged |
Current Position	State	Stock	Call	Position
Long one share	Up	100	−20	90
Write two calls	Down	90	0	90

The initial investment for this strategy of writing covered calls is the price paid for a share of the stock minus the proceeds received from shorting two calls ($100 - 2C$). Table 5–4 below gives the payoffs to this strategy for each possible outcome for the stock price at expiration.

As shown in Table 5–4 the strategy described above is a riskless strategy; that is, the payoff is always the same regardless of the state. Thus, to prevent a profitable riskless arbitrage the cost of establishing the strategy of writing covered calls must be such that

$$(100 - 2C)(1 + .05) = 90$$

That is, the final certain payoff of $90 must reflect a riskless rate of return on the initial investment. Therefore the value of the call that assures no riskless arbitrage opportunity must be

$$\text{Call value} = \frac{100 - 85.71}{2} = \$7.14$$

If the call is not priced at $7.14, a sure arbitrage profit would be possible. For example, if $C = \$8$, the cost of establishing a riskless strategy of writing covered calls will be $84. Thus one can borrow $85.71 at 5 percent and promise to pay $90 back for the loan at the end of the period. Using $84 of the borrowed money to establish the writing-covered-calls strategy that will always result in a payoff of $90 for the repayment of the loan, the person has realized a sure profit of $1.71 at the beginning of the period.

This example might seem a little too neat. How general is this example? If the stock can only go up or down in price by certain, specified amounts, it is *always* possible to construct the riskless hedge. Intuitively, the *hedge ratio,* the number of stocks that have to be purchased to cover each call that is written, depends on how far the call price can move relative to the potential stock price move. Relatively straightforward algebra will verify that the hedge ratio *(h)* in this example will be given by

$$\text{Hedge ratio, } h = \frac{C_u - C_d}{uS - dS} = \frac{10 - 0}{110 - 90} = \frac{1}{2}$$

where

C_u = Value of the call in an "up" state.
C_d = Value of the call in the "down" state.
u = One plus the return on the stock in the up state.
d = One plus the return on the stock in the down state.

Therefore a riskless strategy of writing a covered call is to buy one share of the stock and to short two calls, as we have shown in Table 5–4. The above application of the formula for the risk-neutral hedge ratio indicates that the ratio is determined by the range of the call values and the stock prices at the end of the period.

Since we know that two options can be written for every stock held to establish a riskless hedge, we can use the above arithmetic to conclude that the option value is $7.14. In order to simplify the arithmetic, it is possible to use a little algebra to substitute the expression for the riskless hedge into the call value formula and solve for the call value *directly*.[7] If we define

$$p = \frac{(1 + r) - d}{u - d}$$

as an *implied probability* (where r is the riskless rate of interest), which is a function of the range of stock price movements and the risk-free rate of interest, then the expression for the value of a call can be simplified to

$$C = \frac{pC_u + (1 - p)C_d}{1 + r}$$

Thus the value of a call is simply the expected value of the call at the end of the period, weighted by the implied probabilities and discounted at the risk-free rate of interest.

This equation can be employed directly to obtain the values of the call in the example:

$$p = \frac{1.05 - .90}{1.10 - .90} = \frac{3}{4}$$

$$C = \frac{(3/4)10 + (1/4)0}{1.05} = \$7.14$$

---

[7]For details see Cox and Rubinstein, *Options Markets*, pp. 172–73.

Two-Period Model. Using the same arguments as in the one-period case, we can extend the analysis to a two-period case and obtain the value of a call with two periods to expiration.

Example: Given the same assumptions used in the earlier example except that the call has two periods to expiration, the question is how much the call should be worth today to prevent a riskless arbitrage opportunity, given that the current stock price is $100 and that it will go up or down 10 percent at the end of each period. Thus the stock price at the time when the call option has one period left will be $110 or $90, and at the expiration date of the option the stock price will be one of the following:

$$uuS = 100(1.1)(1.1) = \$121$$
$$udS = 100(1.1)(.9) = \$99$$
$$ddS = 100(.9)(.9) = \$81$$

The following diagram shows the movements of the stock price:

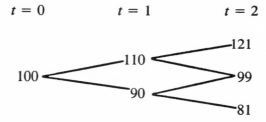

Since the call option at the expiration date must be the positive value of the stock price at expiration date minus the exercise price of $100, we know that the value of a call after two up movements (C_{uu} = 121 − 100 = 21) and the values after an up-down and a down-up movement (C_{ud} and C_{du}) are both zero. Working backward we can use the one-period option pricing formula to obtain the value of the call at time $t = 1$. If the stock price is at uS = $110 with one period left, then the value of the call at expiration will be C_{uu} = 21 or C_{ud} = 0. We know from the one-period example that

$$C_u = \frac{(3/4)21 + (1/4)0}{1.05} = \$15.00$$

If the stock price is at $dS = \$90$ with one period left, then the value of the call at expiration will be $C_{du} = 0$ or $C_{dd} = 0$. So we know that $C_d = 0$; that is, the call has no value.

Working backwards for one more period the current stock price is $100 with two periods left before the call option expires. Since the value of the call one period from now is either $C_u = \$15.00$ or $C_d = \$0$, we can obtain the value of the call today:

$$C = \frac{(3/4)15.00 + (1/4)0}{1.05} = \$10.71$$

The following diagram shows the values of the call at different points in time:

$$t = 0 \qquad\qquad t = 1 \qquad\qquad t = 2$$

Comparing the value of the call in the single-period example with the value of the call in the current example, which has two periods to expiration, we know that the longer the life of a call, other things being equal, the greater the value of the call will be.

The general two-state option pricing formula for the two-period case can also be obtained directly. After some algebra, it can be shown that the value of the call with two periods remaining is

$$C = \frac{p^2 C_{uu} + 2p(1 - p)C_{ud} + (1 - p)^2 C_{dd}}{(1 + r)^2}$$

The value of the call in the numerical example, with two periods before its expiration, can therefore be obtained:

$$C = \frac{(3/4)^2 21 + 2(3/4)(1/4)0 + (1/4)^2 0}{(1.05)^2} = \$10.71$$

Applying the same procedure that has been used to extend from the one-period case to the two-period case, we can extend from the two-period case to the three-period and the many-period cases. While the computational procedures in the three- and the many-period cases are complicated, the basic arbitrage argument in deriving the value of a call option is the same.

Cox and Rubinstein[8] and R. Jarrow and A. Rudd[9] include derivations of the BOPM for any number of time periods.

The two-period model is a very crude one; to approximate the continuous-time case would seem to require many time periods. Yet even the two-period model can approximate the Black-Scholes value of an option (albeit in many cases not very well). Consider the earlier example in which the BSOPM was applied to an option with this data:

$S = 45$
$K = 50$
$T = .75$
$V = .16$
$r = .08$

The terms u, d, and p can all be approximated in order to use the two-period BOPM for evaluating the option. Following the suggestions of Jarrow and Rudd in the context of a slightly different formulation of the model, we can approximate the parameters as follows:

$$u = 1 + \left[\left(r - \frac{V}{2} \right) \times \frac{T}{2} \right] + \sqrt{V \times \frac{T}{2}}$$

$$d = 1 + \left[\left(r - \frac{V}{2} \right) \times \frac{T}{2} \right] - \sqrt{V \times \frac{T}{2}}$$

These values give a value of the option of

$$C = \$5.86$$

The BSOPM value was $5.34. Although the two values differ appreciably the two-state model has done a good job, considering only two trading periods were assumed for an option with nine months' life remaining.

The error of approximation diminishes very considerably with the number of periods assumed. As the number of periods increases and the time interval (and u and d) between periods decreases, the result will lead to the many-period BOPM. In the limit, the model becomes the continuous-time Black-Scholes option pricing model. However, the value of this approach to valuing options does not lie in the extent to which option values do or do not approximate the Black-Scholes values. Rather the value is to be found in situations where Black-Scholes is either inappropriate or difficult to apply.

---

[8]Cox and Rubinstein, *Options Markets*, chap. 5.

[9]R. Jarrow and A. Rudd, *Option Pricing* (Homewood, Ill.: Richard D. Irwin, 1983).

Cox and Rubinstein show that it provides a relatively straightforward way of analyzing warrants, convertible and callable bonds, different compound options, and options on futures and other instruments.[10] In each case the rule is to trace out the cash flows to be received in each state, and work backwards to obtain the value today of the option under study.

EMPIRICAL ANALYSIS OF OPTIONS

There are no data bases of option prices available that are as rich and extensive as those available to describe the behavior of common stocks, bonds, and other securities. To the extent that security return patterns vary over time, then, we may be less confident of the behavior of option returns than we are about stock returns. However, since the opening of the options exchanges in 1973, data bases have been available that cover all transactions in common stock options, so we do have some knowledge of the historical pattern of returns from option strategies. This section will describe some of that available experience in two parts: historical returns to option strategies and the historical performance of option pricing models.

Historical Returns

It should be apparent from the probability distributions displayed in Figures 5–6 and 5–8 that skewness is an important attribute of the returns to buying or selling put or call options. In the empirical analysis of common stocks it was apparent that mean (or central tendency) and standard deviation (or dispersion) tell a large part of the story in describing the returns to common stock. Options, however, display a great deal of skewness. Thus, in judging the risk measures and expected returns of option strategies, conclusions must be drawn with special attention to the effects of skewness. Recalling the definition of skewness in Chapter One it should be apparent that a long position in a call or put has positive skewness (tails of the distribution to the right) and that a short position in a call or put has negative skewness (tails of the distribution to the left). To the extent that right skewness is desirable, then, one might expect to observe such "oddities" as negative mean returns from strategies of buying options. However, options are typically not used in isolation; they are used in conjunction with other securities. For example the put buyer who also holds the stock is holding a protective put that eliminates downside risk. The call writer's prospects depend both

---

[10]Cox and Rubinstein, *Options Markets,* chap. 7.

on the call and on other positions held; the call position may be naked or covered. In short the motives of option buyers and sellers are not easily inferred from their option positions alone, and our understanding of option returns must be tempered with that realization.

Only a relatively limited number of empirical studies are available depicting the historical return properties of option strategies. In studies of stock and bond returns, actual prices of the securities are used. Because of the relative paucity of data on options, however, authors in some of the best-known options studies have not used actual option prices but have computed returns assuming that the BSOPM or other theoretical models actually hold. Since empirical research has failed to confirm the validity of any specific model, returns computed "as if" the models held leave something to be desired. On the other hand, studies using actual option prices are limited by short data series, and they too leave something to be desired.

Gary Trennepohl and William Dukes studied returns from call option buying and from covered call writing strategies.[11] They assumed that the price of the call in call buying had to be put up as an initial payment and that the investor's net initial investment in covered call writing was the price of the stock less the price of the call. The options were calls listed on the Chicago Board Options Exchange in the period 1973 through 1976. The authors reached these general conclusions: Covered call writing had a positive weekly mean return, a relatively small standard deviation, and negative skewness. Call buying had negative mean returns, relatively high standard deviations (on the order of 25 percent per week), and right skewness.

Michael Gambola, Rodney Roenfeldt, and Philip Cooley examined returns from various option spreading strategies.[12] The strategies were either calendar (time) spreads or vertical (price) spreads. The time period examined was again 1973 through 1976. Spreads involve simultaneous transactions in options that have differing expiration dates (calendar spreads) or exercise prices (vertical spreads).

The idea is to take a long position in one option and a short position in another in order to profit from the relative movement of prices of the options. The BSOPM gives an indication of which of the two options would be affected more by price changes. In-the-money options tend to increase more in price than do out-of-the-money options for a given change in stock price.

---

[11]G. L. Trennepohl and W. P. Dukes, "Return and Risk from Listed Option Investments," *Journal of Financial Research*, Spring 1979, pp. 37–49.

[12]M. J. Gambola, R. L. Roenfeldt, and P. L. Cooley, "Spreading Strategies in CBOE Options: Evidence on Market Performance," *Journal of Financial Research*, Winter 1978, pp. 35–44.

Similarly options tend to be more sensitive to stock price changes the longer the time to maturity of the option.

Given these results, one can construct "bullish" and "bearish" spreads (that is, spreads that increase in value as the stock price rises or falls, respectively). A bullish calendar spread would involve buying a long call and selling a short call. A bullish vertical spread would involve buying a call with a low exercise price and selling a call with a high exercise price. Bullish spreads have favorable risk-return characteristics relative to single-option strategies. Calendar spreads in particular do well during periods in which stock prices move favorably, and the calendar spreads produce only small losses during unfavorable periods. After adjusting for the considerably higher commissions from spread transactions, however, it turns out that spreads compare unfavorably with option buying and writing strategies.

Empirical Analyses of Option Pricing Models

It is one matter to develop models of option pricing that are satisfactory on theoretical grounds; it is quite another to find models that predict actual market behavior. A large number of studies have examined the empirical validity of various option pricing models. The tests have generally demonstrated some limitations in the validity of the models; in some cases the tests have led to the development of models that attempt to depict reality more accurately. Dan Galai has recently surveyed many of the tests of option pricing models.[13] In his paper he concludes that:

1. The Black-Scholes model performs relatively well, especially for at-the-money options. Deviations from model prices are consistently observed for deep in-the-money and deep out-of-the-money options.
2. No alternative model consistently offers better predictions than the Black-Scholes model.
3. The major problem faced by the Black-Scholes model, or any other model suggested so far, is the nonstationarity of the risk estimator of the underlying stock.
4. No one model accounts for transaction costs and taxes, which may affect the prices of traded options.

Galai's survey summarizes a large body of empirical research that continues to evolve. Theoreticians continue to work toward better models to

---

[13]Dan Galai, "A Survey of Empirical Tests of Option Pricing Models" (Working paper no. 2–83, Graduate School of Management, University of California at Los Angeles, 1983).

describe the option pricing process, and empiricists continue to examine those models. At some point we will have perhaps developed the ideal model that captures all that is relevant to the option pricing process. That point has not yet been reached. Meanwhile the BSOPM, one of the earliest models of option pricing, has stood the test of time and remains a reasonable alternative.

OPTION PRICING THEORY APPLIED TO OTHER ASSETS

The concepts of option pricing theory are more generally concepts for the valuation of contingent claims. Such claims arise in a variety of seemingly unrelated contexts, including risky debt, convertible bonds, call provisions on debt, government insurance of bank and S&L deposits, government insurance of pension benefits, and others. Even the common stock of a firm may be viewed as an option on the assets of the firm: the shareholders (due to limited liability) have a claim worth zero if the value of the firm is less than the value of its debt, but it is worth the difference between the firm's value and the value of debt if the firm is worth more than the debt claim. In addition there are call and put options on many kinds of assets other than common stock, including options on stock indexes, commodities, debt securities (private and public), futures contracts, and others. Furthermore options and option-like portfolio investments can be used to insure the values of certain portfolios against loss below a certain level.

One simple example is the warrant on stocks. A *warrant* gives its holder the right to buy stock at a fixed price within a specified time period; in short it is a call option. Warrants are not written with the same standardized terms that apply to listed call options, but they are in other respects simply specialized options. All that has been said about the valuation of calls thus applies directly to warrants as well.

Option pricing analysis is far more widely applicable than the examples in the earlier sections indicate. Some additional applications will be considered in this section.

Valuing Risky Debt and Valuing the Firm

Imagine a firm financed entirely from equity and a simple debt contract. The debt must be paid off at the end of one period, and the amount due will be D. If the firm is not worth D at the end of the period, the equity holders can forfeit the firm—in essence, *put* the firm—to the debt holders in exchange for cancellation of the debt. The equity holders then face a set of payoffs:

$$\text{Payoff} = 0 \quad \text{if value} \leq D$$
$$= V - D \text{ if value} > D$$

where V is the value of the firm's assets at the end of the period. In this case the risky variable is V. The stock then has the same type of payoff patterns as a call option on the assets of the firm, with a striking price equal to the total debt obligation (principal and interest).

From the standpoint of the debt holders the payoff is D if the value of the firm exceeds D, and it is V if the value of the firm is less than D:

$$\text{Payoff} = D \text{ if value} \geq D$$
$$= V \text{ if value} < D$$

Their position is like that of a covered call writer who writes a call on the firm with an exercise price of D. The value of risky debt is thus the value of the firm less the value of a call option on the assets of the firm.

Other Debt Features

Two other debt features, convertibility and callability, can also be evaluated from the standpoint of option pricing theory. A convertible bond is one that can be exchanged for stock at a predetermined exchange rate, which implies an exercise price in terms of the bond price. The holder of the convertible bond then holds a call option on the stock of the firm. The debt holder's desire to avoid risk is then changed since the value of the debt holder's option is increased when the firm increases its stock price variability. The option pricing feature—an option is more valuable the greater the variability in return to the underlying asset—has a direct application to this case.

The callability feature gives the firm a call option on the debt. If the level of interest rates declines, for example, the value of the debt rises, and the firm could finance the same level of debt at a lower interest cost. The call feature gives the firm the right to call the bond at a schedule of prices, with the price generally declining as the date at which the call is exercised increases. In essence the call feature is similar to having a series of call options, with the later options being available only if the earlier calls have not been exercised. Again it follows that as the uncertainty in future interest rates increases, the value of the call feature increases and as a result the value of the bond is reduced.

Insurance Contracts: Deposit and ERISA

The Federal Deposit Insurance Corporation and the Federal Savings and Loan Insurance corporation insure deposit accounts in member institutions. For a fixed premium—that curiously does not vary with the risk of the institution—

the agency guarantees the deposits made in the institutions. From the standpoint of depositors it is as though they held a protective put on their deposits. The value of the put is obviously an increasing function of the risk associated with the deposit's value in the institution. Since a failing institution effectively "puts" the deposits to the insuring agency, the insurance contract actually gives the institution an incentive to bear greater risks than it might otherwise bear. The agency's failure to charge premiums that recognize the risk of fluctuations in deposit value—failure, in essence, to value the put, recognizing that the value increases with the risk of the underlying asset—creates an incentive perverse to the aims of the agency.

A virtually identical situation exists in the Pension Benefit Guarantee Corporation's insurance of pension accounts under the Employee Retirement Income Security Act. The corporation pays a premium for pension fund insurance, and the value of that insurance (or put option) increases as the risk of the pension fund increases. Since the PBGC does not discriminate on the basis of risk, it implicitly provides incentives to take on added risk. In insurance such effects are termed *moral hazards*.

Performance Fees

Portfolio managers can be compensated under a variety of schemes. One approach is to pay the manager a fixed fee or a fixed proportion of the value of the assets under management. Such an approach leaves management indifferent to the level of risk in the portfolio (ignoring issues such as the fear of losing the account altogether). An alternative is to reward the manager under a scheme in which the manager participates in the gains beyond some threshold level but does not share the risk on the downside. From the standpoint of option pricing theory, this approach gives the manager a call option. The call option is valuable at maturity—the end of the evaluation period— if the value of the portfolio exceeds the threshold level. See Chapter Seven for a more detailed discussion of this application.

Options on Other Assets

Competition in new-product development in securities has led to a bewildering array of new instruments in recent years. Many of them involve creating derivative securities such that the underlying asset is itself a derivative security. For example, consider an option to buy a futures contract for U.S. Treasury issues. From the standpoint of valuing the option, the underlying asset is the futures contract. To value the option, one needs to know the variability in the time series of futures prices, the level of interest rates *during the life of the option,* the life of the option itself, current futures prices, and the striking price. Finding the inputs may be more difficult than in the case of common stock options, but the principles are the same.

Recently options on stock market indexes have been introduced. These options allow the investor to alter the *market risk* component of a portfolio in fundamental ways. In this case the underlying asset is the portfolio against which the option is written. For example one may purchase a call option on the Value Line Stock Index or on other major stock indexes.

FINANCIAL FUTURES

Valuation

Another type of derivative instrument is a financial *futures contract.* These contracts obligate a seller to pay the value of the futures contract to the buyer at a specified date. Financial futures contracts typically have uniform terms with respect to quantity, expiration date, and underlying asset; hence there is a vast, well-organized secondary market for many of these instruments.

Just as with options, the fair value of a futures contract is based on the principle of arbitrage—that is, the notion that investors cannot earn riskless profits by exchanging assets with identical cash flows. For example consider a situation in which we purchase an asset valued at $100 by borrowing this amount at an interest cost of $2 for a period of three months. Suppose that at the end of three months we sell this asset for $110 for a total profit of $8 ($110 − $100 − $2). Now suppose that instead of purchasing the asset on margin we purchase a futures contract that expires in three months. The fair value of this contract should be the price that yields an $8 profit if we hold the futures contract to expiration. Since the contract's value at expiration will equal the price of the underlying asset at expiration, a price of $102 will return $8 to the purchaser of the futures contract. If the futures contract sold for less than $102, we could buy the futures contract and sell the underlying asset short, thereby earning a riskless profit. If on the other hand the contract sold for more than $102, we could buy the underlying asset and sell the futures contract, again earning a riskless profit.

Arbitrageurs monitor the relationship between the price of financial futures contracts and their underlying assets and engage in arbitrage activity whenever the opportunity exists. Such arbitrage prevents futures prices from drifting very far away from their fair values, unless it is difficult or costly to execute the arbitrage. For example some futures contracts are based on stock indexes such as the Standard & Poor's 500 (S&P 500). Arbitrage between the futures contract and the index is called index arbitrage. In order to arbitrage the mispricing between the S&P 500 Index and the futures contract exactly the arbitrageur would have to purchase or sell all 500 stocks. If some of these stocks are illiquid, the transaction costs may offset some of the arbitrage profits, thereby rendering the transaction less profitable.

In many instances an arbitrageur will trade a representative sample of the underlying index to minimize transaction costs. However, this trade would involve some risk that the specific portfolio that is traded will not track the futures contract exactly. In general the more expensive or uncertain it is to transact the underlying asset, the farther away from fair value the contract is likely to drift before arbitrageurs enter the market.

So far we have cited only the interest cost as determining the spread between the underlying asset and the futures contract. Investors who purchase a futures contract instead of the stock index, for example, forego any dividends that may be paid during the period in which the asset is held. Thus we must also factor this foregone income into our valuation of futures contracts. Suppose for example that the underlying asset in our earlier example paid $1 in dividends during the three-month period. This income, had we purchased the asset on margin, would partly offset our interest cost. Thus our profits would equal $9 instead of $8 ($110 − $100 − $2 + $1). If instead we purchased a futures contract for $101 and held it to expiration, then we would have received $110, and our profit would also equal $9. Within this context the interest cost associated with purchasing the asset on margin less the income it produces is called the *net cost of carry*, which in a frictionless market should equal the price difference between the underlying asset and the futures contract. The actual price difference between the asset and the contract is called the *basis*, and the variability of the basis as measured by its standard deviation is called *basis risk*.

We can estimate the fair value of a futures contract as

$$F = S + C$$

where

F = Fair value of financial future.
S = Price of underlying asset.
C = Net cost of carry.

Using Financial Futures to Control Risk

Suppose we have $10 million invested in an S&P 500 Index fund and we wish to protect it, in part, from the possibility that the S&P 500 Index will decline, by converting 30 percent of our assets to riskless instruments. One alternative would be to sell 30 percent of the fund and invest the proceeds in a short-term investment fund. A more efficient approach would be to sell short $3 million of S&P futures contracts. The combined $10 million investment in the S&P *index fund* and the $3 million of futures that are sold short are equivalent to a $7 million S&P position and a $3 million investment in a riskless asset.

Let us assume that an S&P 500 futures price is currently $300. The total price of an S&P 500 contract equals 500 times the futures price, which in this case is $150,000. Thus to sell short an amount equal to $3 million, we would need to sell 20 futures contracts ($3,000,000 ÷ $150,000).

The previous example is extremely straightforward but unfortunately not always realistic. We may have invested our $10 million in, instead of an S&P 500 Index fund, an actively managed portfolio that differs in several respects from the S&P 500 Index. For example the actively managed portfolio may be more or less exposed to systematic risk, and it is also exposed to *specific risk.* We may wish to control for systematic risk if it is not a discretionary investment management decision but rather a reflection of our appetite for risk. However, we should not worry about the fund's specific risk since this risk is the source of the fund's potential to add value to an index fund.

We can estimate the systematic risk of our portfolio by regressing its returns against the returns of the S&P Index. The slope of the regression line, called *beta,* represents the sensitivity of our fund's returns to the S&P's return. For example if the beta of our fund equals 1.1, we would expect our fund's return to equal 1.1 times the S&P's return. The extent to which our fund's return is above or below 1.1 times the S&P's return can be attributed to the contribution of discretionary management. We can adjust the number of contracts we need to trade in order to hedge 30 percent of our systematic risk as

$$N = \left(\frac{T}{P \times S} \right) \times \beta$$

where

    N = Number of contracts.
    T = Transaction amount.
    P = Price of stock index futures.
    S = Size of contract.
    β = Beta of portfolio.

Thus in our earlier example in which we wished to reduce our S&P exposure by $3 million, we would sell 22 futures contracts instead of 20 contracts:

$$22 = \left(\frac{3,000,000}{300 \times 500}\right) \times 1.1$$

For bonds a measure of systematic risk is given by a bond's sensitivity to changes in the level of interest rates. This sensitivity is measured by *adjusted duration* described on page 79. For example, if a bond's adjusted duration equals 5 and interest rates increase by 1 percentage point, the bond's price will decline approximately 5 percent.

We can use a similar adjustment to determine the number of bond futures contracts to trade given an underlying portfolio with a particular duration:

$$N = \left(\frac{T}{(P \times S)}\right) \times \frac{D_p}{D_t}$$

where

P = Price of Treasury bond financial futures.
D_p = Adjusted duration of bond portfolio.
D_t = Adjusted duration of Treasury bond that
underlies the futures contract.

Institutional Considerations in Using Financial Futures

When we buy or sell futures contracts, in effect we do so with borrowed funds. Thus we are required to deposit margin. In order to commence a transaction, we must deposit *initial margin* with a broker. The amount of margin varies from contract to contract and also through time. Moreover the amount of initial margin depends on whether we intend to use the futures contracts to hedge or to speculate. Since speculation is obviously riskier than hedging, the required initial margin is higher for speculators.

As the value of the contract changes each day, we either send funds to our broker or we receive funds from our broker to cover the variation in the contract's price. Appropriately this margin is called *variation margin*. Variation margin must be settled the business day after the market closes.

CONCLUSION

In this chapter, we have examined put and call options and financial futures as examples of a general class of securities known as derivative securities. Analysis of derivative securities depends importantly on the application of quantitative methods. Without quantitative tools it is virtually impossible to value these securities; and without a sound understanding of quantitative principles the impact of derivative securities on a portfolio's performance can be seriously misunderstood. Finally, the quantitative principles that underlie analysis of derivative securities can be extended to a wide variety of investment applications.

PROBLEMS

1. Suppose you observe that the variance of quarterly returns for the S&P 500 Index is significantly lower than three times the variance of monthly returns for the S&P 500 Index over the same measurement period. Assuming that options on the S&P 500 Index are priced according to the assumption that variances are linearly related to time, what strategy might you propose?

   Answer: Based on the fact that the observed variances are not related linearly to time, one might profit by buying one-month options and selling three-month options. The value of an option is related to the volatility of the underlying asset. In this example the S&P's variance does not increase linearly with time. It increases at a slower rate, consistent with mean reversion in the S&P's returns. Therefore, if the market is pricing these options according to the assumption that the S&P's variance changes linearly with time, either the one-month option is undervalued or the three-month option is overvalued.

2. Suppose that the S&P 500 Index is currently valued at $303.90 and that an S&P 500 futures contract expiring in 90 days is currently priced at $309.20. Also suppose that the interest rate to purchase the S&P 500 Index on margin or to sell short the S&P 500 Index is 2.10 percent unannualized for 90 days and that the S&P 500 stocks are expected to yield $2.95 in dividends 90 days from now. How might you profit by trading S&P 500 Index fund units and S&P 500 futures contracts, assuming that there are no transaction costs?

   Answer: By purchasing units in an S&P 500 Index fund on margin and simultaneously selling S&P 500 futures contracts, and then liquidating these positions in 90 days, one could lock in a profit of $935 for every futures contract sold (1.87 × 500).

	S&P Ending Price	
	$290.00	*$310.00*
Profit/loss on index	$290 − 303.9 − 6.38 + 2.95 = −17.33	$310 − 303.9 − 6.38 + 2.95 = 2.67
Profit/loss on futures	$309.20 − 290 = 19.20	$309.20 − 310 = −.80
Net profit	$1.87	$1.87

CHAPTER SIX

Quantitative Methods in Asset Allocation

Stephen J. Brown and Mark P. Kritzman

This chapter demonstrates the application of quantitative methods to asset allocation. It begins with a discussion of the calculation of expected return and standard deviation for a combination of assets, including foreign assets, and continues with a review of the estimating issues involved in asset allocation. The next section describes how an optimal portfolio can be identified from the efficient set, and the final section addresses dynamic strategies, including tactical asset allocation and portfolio insurance.

The application of quantitative methods to asset allocation is well established within the investment industry. With the recent advances in dynamic strategies, it appears that quantitative methods will continue as an integral part of the asset allocation process.

EXPECTED RETURN AND RISK

The *expected return* of a combination of asset classes is simply the weighted average of the expected returns of the component assets. If common stocks were expected to return 12 percent and long-term corporate bonds were expected to return 5.1 percent per year, a portfolio that consists of 60 percent common stocks and 40 percent bonds would have an expected return of 9.24 percent. To see this, note that 60 cents invested in stocks would be expected to grow to 67.2 cents [60 × (1 + .12)] and 40 cents invested in bonds would be expected to grow to 42.04 cents; a dollar in the portfolio would be expected to grow to $1.0924 in one year, an expected return of 9.24 percent. In other words,

$$\text{Expected return} = (.6 \times 12) + (.4 \times 5.1) = 9.24$$

and in general,

$$\text{Expected return} = (w_1 \times ER_1) + (w_2 \times ER_2) + (w_3 \times ER_3) + \cdots$$

where

w_1, w_2, w_3 = Proportion of the portfolio invested in assets 1, 2, and 3.

ER_1, ER_2, ER_3 = Expected return on assets 1, 2, and 3.

The weights w_1, w_2, and w_3, referred to as *portfolio weights,* are measured as of the beginning of the period in question.

The formula for the standard deviation of portfolio returns reflects the fact that returns can offset one another. Suppose the expected return of XYZ common is 20 percent and that of Hedge Securities Inc. is only 2 percent per year, while the standard deviation of each investment is about 20 percent. Hedge Securities appears an unattractive investment because it has low return and high risk. However, suppose that for every percentage point of return under expectation that XYZ earns, Hedge earns an equal amount over expectation. The returns of the two securities are said to have a perfect negative correlation. A portfolio with 50 percent invested in XYZ and 50 percent invested in Hedge will have a return of 11 percent per year regardless of what happens to XYZ; the expected return is 11 percent [(.5 × 20) + (.5 × 2)], and the standard deviation of the portfolio return is zero. This example explains why it is that positions in options and futures contracts that are considered high-risk investments can actually eliminate risk when held in a portfolio along with the assets on which those contracts are based.

In the other extreme the assets in question have a perfect positive correlation. Such a situation can arise where the portfolio consists of two classes of common stock issued by the same corporation under similar terms or, in the case of a pension fund, where the fund assets are allocated between two money managers with identical investment philosophies. In such an extreme case the standard deviation of the overall portfolio return is simply the portfolio weighted average of the standard deviations of the assets that compose the portfolio. In this case the formula for the standard deviation of portfolio returns is analogous to the above formula for the expected return.

In a typical case where the portfolio assets are less than perfectly correlated the standard deviation of the portfolio returns will be somewhat less than the weighted average of the component security standard deviations. This reflects the fact that security returns are less than perfectly correlated. The fact that the investor can reduce risk simply by holding securities within a larger portfolio is said to represent the *gains from diversification.* The magnitude of these potential gains will depend on the extent to which the security returns are correlated. The relationship between the portfolio standard deviation and correlations of component securities is given by the square root of the portfolio variance:

Portfolio variance $= \underbrace{w_1^2 s_1^2}_{\text{1 asset}} + 2w_1 w_2 r_{12} s_1 s_2 + 2w_1 w_3 r_{13} s_1 s_3 + \cdots$

$$\underbrace{+ w_2^2 s_2^2}_{\text{2 assets}} + 2w_2 w_3 r_{23} s_2 s_3 + \cdots$$

$$\underbrace{\qquad\qquad + w_3^2 s_3^2 \qquad\qquad}_{\text{3 assets}} + \cdots$$

$$\underbrace{\qquad\qquad\qquad\qquad\qquad\qquad}_{\text{More than 3 assets}} + \cdots$$

where

w_1, w_2, and w_3 = Proportion of the portfolio invested in assets 1, 2, 3.
s_1, s_2, and s_3 = Standard deviations of returns on assets 1, 2, 3.
r_{12}, r_{13}, and r_{23} = Correlations between returns on assets 1 and 2, 1 and 3, and 2 and 3, respectively.

To see how this formula works consider that the portfolio is invested 60 percent in common stocks and 40 percent in long-term corporate bonds. As mentioned before, such a portfolio will have an expected return of 9.24 percent. If the standard deviation of bond returns is 8.3 percent and the standard deviation of common stock returns is 21.2 percent, then the standard deviation of the portfolio returns can be calculated using the first two columns of the variance formula above. If the correlation between stock and bond returns is .18[1], the standard deviation *(SD)* is 13.71 percent, computed as

$$SD = \sqrt{(.6^2 \times 21.2^2) + (2 \times .6 \times .4 \times .18 \times 21.2 \times 8.3) + (.4^2 \times 8.3^2)}$$
$$= 13.71$$

---

[1]These and other numbers in this section are derived from Ibbotson Associates, *Stocks, Bonds, Bills and Inflation: 1985 Yearbook* (Chicago: Ibbotson Associates, Capital Management Research Center, 1986).

TABLE 6–1
Expected Return and Standard Deviation of Portfolios
of Stocks and Bonds

Portfolio	Stock Portfolio Weight	Bond Portfolio Weight	Expected Return	Standard Deviation (r = .18)	Standard Deviation (r = +1.00)	Standard Deviation (r = −1.00)
0	0.00	1.00	5.10%	8.30%	8.30%	8.30%
1	0.05	0.95	5.45	8.14	8.95	6.83
2	0.10	0.90	5.79	8.12	9.59	5.35
3	0.15	0.85	6.14	8.24	10.24	3.88
4	0.20	0.80	6.48	8.50	10.88	2.40
5	0.25	0.75	6.83	8.87	11.53	0.93
6	0.28	0.72	7.04	9.16	11.93	.00
7	0.30	0.70	7.17	9.35	12.17	0.55
8	0.35	0.65	7.52	9.93	12.82	2.03
9	0.40	0.60	7.86	10.58	13.46	3.50
10	0.45	0.55	8.21	11.29	14.11	4.98
11	0.50	0.50	8.55	12.06	14.75	6.45
12	0.55	0.45	8.90	12.87	15.40	7.93
13	0.60	0.40	9.24	13.71	16.04	9.40
14	0.65	0.35	9.59	14.59	16.69	10.88
15	0.70	0.30	9.93	15.48	17.33	12.35
16	0.75	0.25	10.28	16.40	17.98	13.83
17	0.80	0.20	10.62	17.34	18.62	15.30
18	0.85	0.15	10.97	18.29	19.27	16.78
19	0.90	0.10	11.31	19.25	19.91	18.25
20	0.95	0.05	11.66	20.22	20.56	19.73
21	1.00	0.00	12.00	21.20	21.20	21.20

To gain some further insight the expected return and standard deviation of returns for a variety of portfolios is given in Table 6–1. There portfolios 0 and 21 correspond to all-bond and all-stock portfolios, respectively. The all-bond portfolio has an expected return of 5.10 percent and a standard deviation of 8.30 percent, and the all-stock portfolio has an expected return of 12.0 percent and a standard deviation of 21.2 percent. A portfolio consisting of 60 percent stocks and 40 percent bonds would have an expected return of 9.24 percent and a standard deviation of 13.71 percent if the correlation between bond and stock returns is 18 percent ($r = .18$). If bond and stock returns were perfectly correlated ($r = 1.00$), then the expected return would be the same but the standard deviation would be 60 percent of the distance between the bond standard deviation and the higher stock return standard deviation, or 16.04 percent. The fact that bond and stock returns are not perfectly correlated implies a reduction in the standard deviation of portfolio

FIGURE 6–1
Mean and Standard Deviation of Risky Portfolios

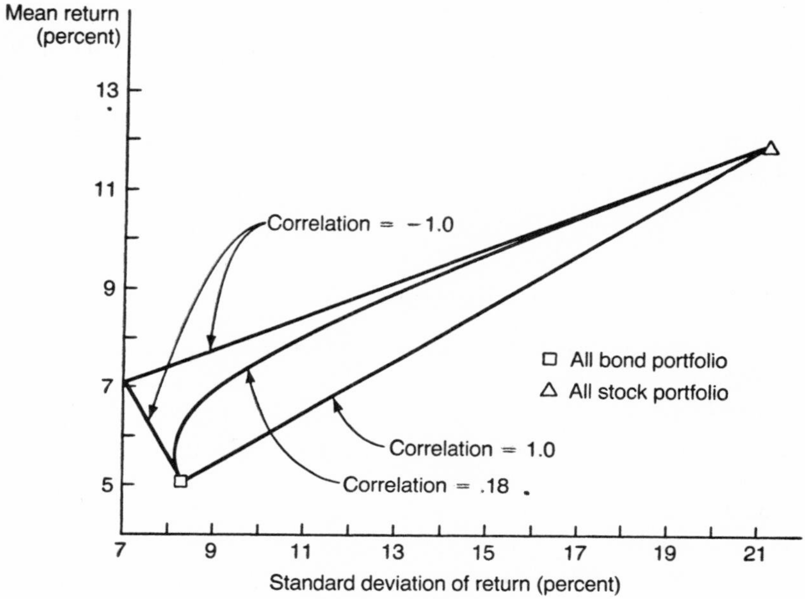

returns. If the bonds represented a perfect hedge to the stock investment or in other words were perfectly *negatively* correlated ($r = -1.00$), the standard deviation would be only 9.40 percent. In that case, in fact, there exists a portfolio consisting of 28 percent stocks and 72 percent bonds (portfolio 6) that has a zero standard deviation of returns. Such a portfolio would return 7.04 percent with certainty.

It is common to plot expected return against standard deviation in a figure similar to that presented as Figure 6–1. The center line gives the set of choices between portfolios that are completely invested in bonds and those that are completely invested in stocks if the correlation between returns on the two asset classes is .18. The other lines give the set of choices if the assets were perfectly correlated, as well as if they were perfectly negatively correlated in their returns. Such a figure can be drawn where there are more than two asset classes; each point on the line then has the interpretation of being the standard deviation and expected return of a portfolio chosen to minimize standard deviation for that level of expected return, given the correlations and other parameter values input to the analysis. Thus it is referred to as the *minimum standard deviation* (or *variance*) *frontier.*

From this figure it is apparent that an all-bond portfolio does not have desirable risk and return attributes; portfolios exist that have the same or lower risk, as measured by the standard deviation of returns, but a higher expected return. Portfolio 3 in Table 6–1 has an expected return of 6.14 percent but a standard deviation of only 8.24 percent, dominating the all-bond portfolio. The extent of this gain would be even higher if the two asset returns were less correlated. However, it is not possible to rule out an all-stock portfolio on this basis.

Currency Risk in Asset Allocation

Those who invest in foreign markets are exposed to currency risk. Although foreign investment is generally beneficial since foreign assets usually have a low correlation with domestic assets, an important issue for quantitative analysis is how to measure and control for currency fluctuations. Obviously, if a currency's return is sufficient to compensate for its contribution to portfolio risk, currency exposure helps. However over the long run most currencies have produced average returns close to zero, although with substantial volatility. Thus the net effect of currency exposure often depends on the diversification properties of the currency.

In order to focus on these issues suppose the following:

1. We divide our portfolio equally between a domestic asset and a foreign asset.
2. Both assets have expected returns equal to 10 percent and standard deviations equal to 20 percent. (The foreign asset's return is denominated in the domestic currency.)
3. The currency in which the foreign asset is denominated has an expected return of zero with a standard deviation of 20 percent. (Currency return and risk pertain to the futures or forward contract on the currency.)
4. The domestic asset and the foreign asset are uncorrelated with each other, while the currency is uncorrelated with the domestic asset and 75 percent correlated with the foreign asset.

We can estimate the risk of a portfolio that is allocated to a domestic asset and a foreign asset assuming various degrees of currency hedging using the formula given on page 169 for the standard deviation of a portfolio with three assets. In the present application, the first asset is the domestic asset. The second asset is the foreign asset denominated in domestic currency. The third asset is the amount invested in a futures or forward contract on the foreign currency.

In the table below we compare the expected return and risk of both assets and our portfolio, assuming we hedge the currency risk completely and do not hedge the currency risk at all.

	Expected Return	Standard Deviation
Domestic asset	10.00%	20.00%
Foreign asset	10.00	20.00
Unhedged portfolio	10.00	14.14
Hedged portfolio	10.00	12.25

As we should expect, diversification into the foreign asset reduces risk, evidenced by the fact that the unhedged portfolio's standard deviation is lower than the standard deviation of each asset. However if we hedge the currency exposure, we lower portfolio risk even further, evidenced by the lower standard deviation of the hedged portolio relative to the unhedged portfolio. In this example it seems fairly clear that we should hedge the currency exposure. However we have not demonstrated that hedging it entirely is necessarily optimal or that we should always hedge it. If we were to hedge only 75 percent of our currency exposure (an amount equal to 37.5 percent of the portfolio value), we could reduce the portfolio's risk even further to a standard deviation of 11.99 percent. (By hedging 37.5 percent of the portfolio value, we set the fraction of the portfolio allocated to the futures or forward contract on the foreign currency equal to $-.375$.) The intuition is as follows. Part of the foreign asset's return denominated in the domestic currency is due to the currency's return. Therefore, to the extent that the foreign asset and the currency are not perfectly correlated with each other, the currency must be hedging some of the foreign asset's local return.

Thus it is not always optimal to eliminate the currency exposure completely. In a situation in which there is only a single foreign asset and the currency has an expected return of 0 percent the optimal percent of the currency exposure to hedge is equal to the currency's beta. In the above example the currency's beta relative to the foreign asset was 75 percent (its correlation coefficient with the foreign asset times the ratio of its beta to the foreign asset's beta). Thus the optimal percent to hedge is equal to 75 percent of the foreign asset value.

If our portfolio contains investments in several foreign countries, the currency's beta relative to the foreign asset will not yield the appropriate hedge ratio unless we assume that the correlations are constant between all pairs of currencies. Unfortunately this assumption is probably not very realistic. For example it is unlikely that the correlation between the Swiss franc and the German mark is the same as the correlation between the Swiss franc and the Canadian dollar. Thus, in a situation in which we are exposed to several foreign assets, we must explicitly account for all of the correlations between the currencies and solve for the optimal hedging strategy. One approach is to use the multiple regression analysis described in Chapter One in which the dependent variable is the portfolio return and the currency returns represent the independent variables. The optimal hedging strategy would be based on the coefficients estimated using such an analysis. In general the optimal currency exposure is positively related to the expected return of the currency, while it is inversely related to the currency's risk, its correlation with other currencies and assets, and our aversion toward risk.

ESTIMATION ISSUES

Asset allocation procedures generally assume a limited number of asset classes because of the great demands such procedures make on data that is limited in both quality and availability. To estimate the variance of portfolio returns, the analyst needs to know the values of many correlation parameters. Asset allocation procedures require estimates of all such correlations as well as estimates of standard deviations and expected returns. Moreover these parameter values are assumed to be known with certainty. If the portfolio manager recommends a particular portfolio of assets based on parameter inputs that are estimated, the fact that such estimates can differ from the true underlying parameters subjects the portfolio to *estimation risk.*

There are at least three approaches to this particular problem. The first and most obvious approach is to use the highest-quality transactions data for returns to estimate the various parameters. This will minimize but not eliminate the problem. The second approach is to account for estimation risk explicitly in the asset allocation process as just another source of risk. The third approach is to simplify the problem in order to reduce the number of parameter values that need to be estimated.

With sufficient high-quality data and using the formulas given in Chapter One, one should be able to estimate the value of relevant parameter inputs with such precision that estimation risk is not an issue. Unfortunately the parameter values tend to change over extended periods of data; there is a finite limit to the amount of useful data. For the purpose of portfolio analysis, returns should be measured on the basis of transaction prices.

The use of appraisal data is unsatisfactory for at least two reasons. Even where these data provide a satisfactory measure of expected return the appraisal process artificially smooths prices, leading to low estimates of the standard deviation of return. Measured real estate returns have a much lower standard deviation than do returns to real estate investment trust (REIT) securities backed by real estate assets (even after accounting for the leverage associated with such securities). Real estate is one area where appraisal values are virtually all the analyst has to work with. In addition, real estate returns have an artificially low correlation with other assets whose returns are based on transactions data. This illustrates another problem: both the quality and quantity of data can vary across asset classes.

Even where data is readily available and is of high quality, as is usually the case with equity portfolios, there is a practical limit to the number of assets that can be studied. Suppose the portfolio under study is large and well diversified, comprising over 500 equities. If the very large correlation matrix is estimated on the basis of less than 500 periods of returns, a portfolio can always be found that appears to have a standard deviation of zero. The data correspond to a maximum of only 500 scenarios of returns; a portfolio can be constructed out of the 500 securities to match exactly every historical scenario. The correlation matrix estimated on the basis of fewer periods of data than there are securities is said to be *singular*. Obviously the results of such analysis are misleading; with 500 assets the number of possible return scenarios is far in excess of that number.

This example illustrates that the acquisition of high-quality data is alone not sufficient to eliminate the effects of estimation risk. One approach is to account for this risk directly. Suppose the standard deviations and correlations are known values, but expected returns are estimated on the basis of T periods of returns. The uncertainty facing the investor arises not only from the variance of returns but also from uncertainty that results from using estimates of expected returns. Thus the standard deviations should be augmented by a factor equal to the square root of the sum $1 + 1/T$, where the $1/T$ factor accounts for the fact that expected returns are not known with certainty. Where the standard deviations and correlations also have to be estimated and historical data represent the sole source of information for the analyst, a similar form of reasoning follows,[2] and estimates of the standard deviation parameters should be augmented by a factor equal to

$$\sqrt{\frac{(T + 1)(T - 1)}{T(T - n - 2)}}$$

where n represents the number of securities under study. This formula assumes that there are at least three more periods of returns that there are securities under study $(T > n + 2)$.

Fortunately the available data does not necesssarily represent the sole source of information for the analyst. Returns on assets within specific asset classes and within particular industries tend to move together in systematic ways. This suggests that simple one-factor and multifactor models of a type discussed in Chapter One and Chapter Two might lead to simplified models with fewer parameters to be estimated. Recall that in such models asset returns were correlated with each other only to the extent that they were correlated to factors of uncertainty common across all assets. In the case of a single-factor model,

$$R_i = a_i + (b_i \times R_m) + e_i$$

where

R_i and R_m represent the return on asset i and on the market factor.
e_i represents the return idiosyncratic to security i.

The correlation between the return on security i and security j, r_{ij}, is given by

$$r_{ij} = b_i \times b_j \times \frac{\text{variance of } R_m}{s_i \times s_j}$$

where s_i and s_j represent the standard deviation of returns on assets i and j, respectively.

This leads to a substantial reduction in the number of parameters to be estimated. In the case of 100 assets the number of parameters falls from 100 expected returns, 100 standard deviations, and 4,950 [$100 \times (99 \div 2)$] correlations—a total of 5,150 parameters—to only 100 expected returns, 100 standard deviations, 100 betas $(b_i s)$, and one factor variance parameter, a total of 301 parameters all told.

---

[2]For the development of this concept, see V. S. Bawa, S. J. Brown, and R. W. Klein, *Estimation Risk and Optimal Portfolio Choice* (Amsterdam: Elsevier–North Holland Publishing, 1979).

However, this reduction in the number of parameters to be estimated comes at the cost of assuming that the single-factor model is in fact correct. The restrictiveness of this model can be relaxed by assuming that a multifactor model explains security returns. If so, then a somewhat more complicated formula applies[3] although the number of parameters to be estimated is still substantially reduced. Another approach is to estimate the correlation coefficients directly through use of the single- or multifactor models and to average the coefficients so obtained over industry groups.[4] This procedure assumes that the underlying or true correlation coefficients are in fact the same within industry groups; returns within broad industry categories tend to move in similar ways. The fact that individual correlation coefficients differ within such categories may be just a manifestation of the random error associated with trying to estimate these numbers precisely. As a consequence the average correlation coefficient may be a better estimate of the underlying correlation between the returns of the assets in question than are the individual correlation estimates.

These simple models are a response to the difficulties associated with estimating the large number of correlations required as inputs to any asset allocation problem of reasonable scale. To the extent that they are useful they introduce information above and beyond what is available in the return data themselves. This information may not be exactly and literally correct; approximations are involved. There is thus a necessary trade-off. The correctly specified model that estimates every correlation directly from the sample data of rates of return implies an estimation risk that may be unacceptable to the analyst. The model that is easier to estimate precisely but is slightly misspecified may be the more acceptable choice.

---

[3]In the case where the common factors of variation are themselves uncorrelated (the assumption of factor analysis) the formula is given by

$$r_{ij} = b_{1i}b_{1j}s_{f1}^2 + 2b_{1i}b_{2j}s_{f1}s_{f2} + 2b_{1i}b_{3i}s_{f1}s_{f3} + \cdots$$
$$+ b_{2i}b_{2j}s_{f2}^2 + 2b_{2i}b_{3j}s_{f2}s_{f3} + \cdots$$
$$+ b_{3i}b_{3j}s_{f3}^2 +$$

where

b_{1i}, b_{2i}, and b_{3i} = Factor exposures of security i to factors 1, 2, and 3.
b_{1j}, b_{2j}, and b_{3j} = Factor exposures of security j to factors 1, 2, and 3.
s_{f1}, s_{f2} and s_{f3} = Standard deviations of factors 1, 2, and 3.

[4]This approach was suggested by E. Elton and M. Gruber, "Estimating the Dependence Structure of Share Prices—Implications for Portfolio Selection," *Journal of Finance*, December 1973, pp. 1265–73.

FIGURE 6–2
Hypothetical Efficient Frontier

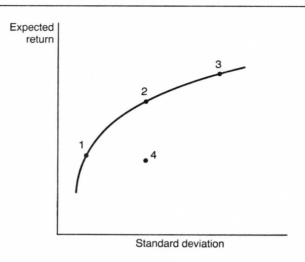

THE OPTIMAL PORTFOLIO

Figure 6–1 illustrates that asset classes can be combined to produce portfolios that offer the highest expected return for a given level of risk. They also minimize risk for every level of expected return. Portfolios that accomplish these objectives are termed *efficient*, and the set of all such portfolios is referred to as the *efficient frontier*. A hypothetical efficient frontier is shown in Figure 6–2. Portfolios 1, 2, and 3 represent efficient asset mixes whereas portfolio 4 represents an inefficient asset mix. At the risk level associated with portfolio 4 a higher expected return is available from portfolio 2; and given its expected return, risk can be reduced by selecting portfolio 1.

Based on the long-term historical performance of the capital markets, portfolio 1 might reflect a heavy commitment to short-term securities, while portfolio 3 would probably include a substantial position in common stocks.

Although the efficient frontier isolates those portfolios that offer the highest expected return for a given level of risk, it does not by itself indicate which of these portfolios is most appropriate for the client. A conservative client for example would be willing to sacrifice high expected return in exchange for a greater degree of certainty in the outcome, whereas an aggressive client would be more willing to incur uncertainty in exchange for a higher expected return. In theory an investor's willingness to exchange

FIGURE 6–3
The Optimal Portfolio

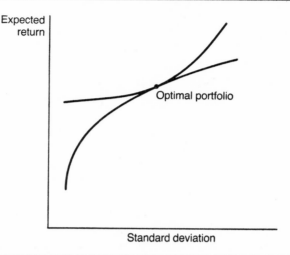

Expected return

Optimal portfolio

Standard deviation

expected return for risk reduction is called an investor *preference curve* or a utility function.

If a utility function were plotted with expected return on the vertical axis and standard deviation on the horizontal axis (as in Figure 6–3), it would typically be convex. That is, at low levels of expected return an investor is more willing to incur risk in exchange for additional units of expected return than he or she is at high levels of expected return. The point along the utility function that is tangent to the efficient frontier represents the optimal trade-off between expected return and risk for the investor, given that he or she is limited to portfolios along the efficient frontier. Those portfolios below the efficient frontier are undesirable and those above the frontier are unobtainable, given the assumptions about each asset class's expected return, standard deviation, and correlation with the other asset classes.

William Sharpe suggests that an appropriate measure of utility for an asset mix is expected return less a *risk penalty,* and he defines risk penalty as risk squared divided by risk tolerance.[5] This definition is consistent with the notion that risk aversion is convex. For example, if an asset mix has a 10.5 percent standard deviation and the investor has a risk tolerance of 50,

[5]W. Sharpe, *Asset Allocation Tools* (Palo Alto, Calif.: Scientific Press, 1985), p. 74.

then the appropriate risk penalty is 110.25 percent divided by 50, which equals 2.2 percent. If the portfolio has an expected return of 12 percent, its utility equals 12 percent minus 2.2 percent, which is 9.8 percent. This utility is then compared to the utility of other asset mixes to determine which one has the highest utility, given the investor's risk tolerance. The asset mix with the highest utility is the investor's optimal asset mix. The chief obstacle to implementation of this approach is that risk-return trade-offs defined in these terms are unintuitive to most investors.

An alternative approach is to restate a portfolio's expected return and standard deviation in terms of such a portfolio's likelihood of achieving some objective. On this basis an investor may feel more comfortable in choosing among portfolios with different asset mixes. For example, a conservative investor may be very sensitive to negative returns. Given a choice between a portfolio with an expected return of 8 percent with a standard deviation of 4 percent versus a portfolio with an expected return of 15 percent with a standard deviation of 15 percent, he or she can base the selection on the likelihood each portfolio has of exceeding a zero return. Since zero is two standard deviations below the expected return of the conservative portfolio (expected return = 8 percent, standard deviation = 4 percent) there is a 98 percent chance that the portfolio will generate a positive return.

Zero percent is only one standard deviation below the expected return of the more aggressive portfolio; hence we have less confidence (84 percent) that the portfolio will produce a positive return.

In general we can estimate a portfolio's probability of exceeding a target in terms of the number of standard deviations of return the expected return is away from the target. This number of standard deviations (z) is given by the formula

$$\text{Number of standard deviations} = \frac{x - ER}{s} = z$$

where

$$x = \text{Target return.}$$
$$ER = \text{Expected return.}$$
$$s = \text{Standard deviation.}$$

In the case of the conservative asset mix, the mean is 8 percent and the standard deviation is 4 percent. If the target were 12 percent it would be one standard deviation above mean return, or

$$z = \frac{12 - 8}{4} = 1$$

For the aggressive mix, the mean and standard deviation equal 15, and the target is now .2 standard deviations below the mean:

$$z = \frac{12 - 15}{15} = -.2$$

These numbers can be translated into the probability of meeting a target, using the standard normal distribution function available in most elementary statistics textbooks:

$$\text{Probability of meeting target} = 1 - N[z]$$

where $N[z]$ is the probability that returns are more than z standard deviations below the mean return. In the conservative asset mix case,

$$\begin{aligned}
\text{Probability of meeting 12 percent target} &= 1 - N[1] \\
&= 1 - .84 \\
&= 16 \text{ percent}
\end{aligned}$$

In the aggressive asset mix case,

$$\begin{aligned}
\text{Probability of meeting 12 percent target} &= 1 - N[-.2] \\
&= 1 - .42 \\
&= 58 \text{ percent}
\end{aligned}$$

This analysis would argue in favor of the aggressive mix, given the 12 percent target.

If our investment horizon were four years rather than one year and our annual assumptions about risk and return were assumed to be valid for the entire four years, then we could estimate the probability of achieving a return on average over the four-year horizon for the aggressive asset mix as 66 percent:

$$z = \frac{12 - 15}{\dfrac{15}{\sqrt{4}}} = -.4$$

$$\begin{aligned}
\text{Probability of meeting target} &= 1 - N[-.4] \\
&= 1 - .33 = 66 \text{ percent}
\end{aligned}$$

In general if we assume that our annual risk and return assumptions apply over T years we can estimate the probability of achieving a result on average over T years, using

$$z = \frac{x - ER}{\dfrac{s}{\sqrt{T}}}$$

This approach is an approximation that loses accuracy as T increases, because it does not account for the compounding of returns.[6]

The probability of achieving a return on average that is lower than the expected return increases as the number of years in the investment horizon increases, because returns are smoothed over time (low returns in certain years are offset by high returns in other years). Specifically, if returns from year to year are independent the annualized variance of returns decreases roughly with time, and the annualized standard deviation therefore decreases approximately with the square root of time.

What if we had a multiple-year investment horizon and we were concerned about never experiencing a year in which the portfolio generated a negative return? If our investment horizon was five years our objective would be to achieve a positive return in five consecutive years. If an asset mix has only a 1 in 10 chance of producing a negative return in any one year, it has a 90 percent chance of producing a positive return in any one year. Again, if we assume that returns are serially independent, then the probability of this asset mix achieving a positive return in two consecutive years is $.90^2$, or 81 percent. The probability of experiencing a positive return in five consecutive years is $.90^5$, which equals 59 percent. Thus although this asset mix has only a 1 in 10 chance of generating a negative return in any one year, its chance of generating a negative return in one or more of the next five years is 41 percent $(1.0 - .59)$.

As shown above, it is fairly easy to restate expected return and standard deviation in terms of the probability of achieving a particular objective, thus rendering comparison among alternative asset mixes reasonably intuitive.

Selection of the appropriate return objective is also an important issue, and it sometimes can be dealt with through quantitative techniques. Consider for example a pension fund with an objective of funding current and future benefits. A reasonable objective may be to achieve an asset value in the pension fund equal to the future value of the pension liabilities, thus ensuring benefit security for the plan participants.

If we can anticipate contributions and disbursements to and from the pension fund and if we can project the growth in liabilities, then by using the present value formula we can solve for the rate of return required on the pension assets to achieve full funding of liabilities within a given time frame.

Assume an initial asset value of $100 million for the pension fund, a

---

[6]An alternative is to recast the analysis, substituting for the rate of return R the *logarithm* of $(1 + R)$. This automatically accounts for the compounding effect.

present value of $115 million growing at 5 percent annually for the liabilities, and the following contributions and disbursements:

Year	Contributions ($ millions)	Disbursements ($ millions)
1	6	3
2	6	4
3	5	5
4	5	6
5	4	6

We can solve for the internal rate of return required to achieve full funding within five years as follows:

$$100 = \frac{(-6 + 3)}{(1 + r)} + \frac{(-6 + 4)}{(1 + r)^2} + \frac{(-5 + 5)}{(1 + r)^3}$$
$$+ \frac{(-5 + 6)}{(1 + r)^4} + \frac{(-4 + 6) + 115(1 + .05)^5}{(1 + r)^5}$$

$$r = .073$$

The contributions can be thought of as negative payments from the pension fund; hence their negative sign.

The next step would of course be to estimate the likelihood of each asset mix achieving an average annual rate of return of 7.32 percent over the next five years[7] and to weigh these results with the probability estimates of other objectives.

This example oversimplifies asset/liability analysis, but it demonstrates (conceptually at least) the applicability of the present value formula.

DYNAMIC STRATEGIES

Thus far in our discussion of asset allocation we have assumed implicitly that the asset positions were bought and held. As an alternative to a buy/hold asset allocation strategy, dynamic strategies are often employed.

Tactical Asset Allocation

A popular dynamic strategy for asset allocation is called *tactical asset allocation*. This strategy requires that we revise our fund's asset mix peri-

---

[7]To be precise a 7.32 percent return is required each year, not just an average over the five years.

odically to capture transitory misvaluations among asset classes. For example suppose we determine that a 60 percent allocation to stocks and a 40 percent allocation to bonds is the optimal asset mix for our portfolio in the sense that this mix offers the greatest probability of satisfying our investment objectives. However, we currently believe that stock prices have been bid up beyond their fair value relative to bonds and we expect that this misvaluation is likely to be corrected soon. Despite the fact that our long-term asset mix strategy calls for us to start out with a 60 percent allocation to stocks, we may wish to temper this allocation to exploit our perception that stock prices are currently overvalued.

A common approach to tactical asset allocation is to determine the near-term expected return of an asset class by estimating an equilibrium valuation level and computing the return that would occur should the asset class move from its current price to its equilibrium value, taking into account the cash flows that it is expected to generate in the meantime. The notion that asset class prices fluctuate around an equilibrium or fair value is based on a principle called *mean reversion*. In its simplest form mean reversion refers to the phenomenon in which prices fluctuate around some fair value that serves as an anchor or central tendency. The further from fair value an asset price drifts, the more likely it is to revert to fair value, and the greater the return from the reversion to the mean. Implicit in mean reversion is the view that asset markets temporarily overcompensate for any change in fundamental value. Hence the purpose of tactical asset allocation is to shift a fund toward an asset class that has temporarily fallen below its fair value and away from an asset class that has temporarily risen above its fair value.

The success of tactical asset allocation, as we have just described it, depends of course on the degree to which asset prices do fluctuate around some equilibrium value. One way to test for the presence of a mean-reverting process is to study the times-series property of the net returns between asset classes. Suppose we believe that the prices of stocks and bonds fluctuate around some equilibrium relationship. We may wish to examine the pattern of their net returns (stock return–bond return).

For example a pertinent issue is the extent to which the prior period's returns are related to the subsequent period's returns. We can measure this serial correlation by performing a regression in which the dependent variable equals the current period's net return and the independent variable equals the prior period's net return. If the net returns are positively related, as evidenced by positive serial correlation, then they tend to follow trends rather than a mean-reverting process. If, however, the net returns are negatively serially correlated, then they likely follow a pattern of reversal that is consistent with a mean-reverting process.

We can also test for serial dependence with a *variance ratio test*. First we estimate the variance from a time series of, say, monthly net returns. Then we estimate the variance from the same sample but based instead on quarterly returns. We compute the ratio of the variance estimated from quarterly returns to the variance estimated from monthly returns and normalize this value by dividing by three (since a quarter is three times as long as a month). If the time series of net returns is random, the normalized variance ratio should be close to one since variances are linear with respect to time. If the normalized variance ratio is greater than one, the times series is positively serially correlated and inclined toward trends. A normalized variance ratio of less than one is evidence of negative serial correlation, which again is consistent with a mean-reverting process. We can extend the intervals used to estimate the variance in the numerator to whatever periodicity we like.

Finally, we can test for serial dependence, using a nonparametric technique called a *runs test*. In this test we simply examine the pattern of positive net returns and negative net returns, ignoring their magnitude. A *run* is an uninterrupted sequence of positive or negative values. For example if we observed the series $+ + + +$, this series would constitute a single run. If on the other hand we observed the series $+ - + -$, this series would constitute four runs. Based on the number of positive and negative values, we can estimate the expected number of runs from a random series and the standard deviation of runs in a times series of net returns. If we observe fewer runs than we would expect from a random series, we have evidence that the series tends to follow trends, since the average run is longer than we would expect from a random series. If, however, we observe more runs than expected, we have evidence of reversals, again suggesting a mean-reverting process.

If our times-series analysis indicates that the net returns between the asset classes to which we allocate our fund follow a mean-reverting process, we may be able to add value to a buy and hold strategy by following a tactical asset allocation strategy designed to exploit this mean reversion.

Portfolio Insurance: Risky versus Riskless Assets

Another popular dynamic strategy is *portfolio insurance*. This strategy calls for the continual rebalancing of a portfolio between a risky and a riskless component so as to ensure that the total fund's terminal value will not fall below a prespecified minimum level. This protection is accomplished by gradually shifting funds from the risky to the riskless component as the portfolio value decreases and from the riskless to the risky component as the portfolio value increases. This type of dynamic strategy produces essentially the same result as purchasing a protective put option on a portfolio. However, it does not require investment in options; it simply requires the continual rebalancing of a portfolio between a risky and a riskless component.

A put option on a risky asset can be replicated by selling the risky asset short and lending at the risk-free rate.[8] The amount to sell short and to lend can be determined from the binomial model or the Black-Scholes model, both of which are described in Chapter Five.

Suppose we wish to invest $100 so that it will capture the performance of a risky asset if it does well and at the same time lose no more than 5 percent should the risky asset perform poorly. We could achieve this outcome by investing in the risky asset along with a protective put option with a strike price of $95. We begin by deriving the value of a put option with a strike price of $95 on a risky asset that is valued at $100. For convenience we will assume that this asset can either increase to $120 or decrease to $90. We will also assume that the riskless rate of interest is 8 percent. Below we show these possible outcomes in the familiar form of a binomial tree. The numbers in parentheses are the value of the put option, given the possible prices for the risky asset. The possible values for the put option at expiration are obvious. They equal the maximum of zero or the strike price less the risky asset price. The value of the put option at the start of the tree is not as obvious.

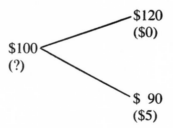

We can replicate the payoff for a put option by selling short some fraction of the risky asset and by lending some amount at the riskless rate of interest. This equivalence (which we will demonstrate shortly) can be used to form two equations, which when solved simultaneously yield the specific amounts to sell short and to lend:

---

[8]For a demonstration of this strategy, see Mark Rubinstein and Hayne Leland, "Replicating Options with Positions in Stock and Cash," *Financial Analysts Journal*, July –August 1981, pp. 63–72.

TABLE 6–2
Option Replication

In Order to Replicate:	Amount to Invest in Risky Asset	Amount to lend
Put option	$– 16.67	$18.52
Risky asset	100.00	0.00
Protective put		
Option strategy	$ 83.33	$18.52

$$(N \times 120.00) + (1.08 \times L) = 0.00$$
$$(N \times 90.00) + (1.08 \times L) = 5.00$$

In the above equations N equals the amount of the risky asset to sell short, while L equals the amount of money to lend at the riskless rate. It turns out that we can replicate the put option by selling short 16.67 percent of the risky asset and lending $18.52 at 8 percent. Again, by virtue of the fact that we can replicate a put option by selling short the risky asset and lending at the riskless rate, we can determine the put option's value at the start of the period by summing our short position and the amount we lend:

$$P = (-.1667 \times 100) + 18.52 = 1.85$$

We can easily verify that selling short and lending in these amounts provides the same outcome as investment in a put option. For example suppose the risky asset increases to $120. The put option will expire worthless for a net loss of $1.85, the cost of the option. If instead we had sold short $16.67 of the risky asset, we would have lost $3.33. However, this loss would have been partly offset by lending $18.52 at 8 percent, which would have generated $1.48 in income, for a net loss of $1.85, the same outcome as the put option strategy. Now suppose that the risky asset decreases to $90. The option would return $5, which after subtracting its cost of $1.85 leaves a net gain of $3.15. The short position of $16.67 would return $1.67, which when added to the proceeds of lending $18.52 at 8 percent also leaves a net gain of $3.15.

Portfolio insurance, however, is not equivalent to a put option alone. Rather it is intended to replicate investment in a risky asset together with a put option. Thus, to replicate a protective put option strategy, we simply add the investment in the risky asset to our short position, resulting in a net exposure of $83.33 in the risky asset, as shown in Table 6–2.

The strategy we have just described presents only one problem. In order

TABLE 6–3
Strategy Payoffs

	Risky Asset Return	
	20 Percent	–10 Percent
Put payoff	$ 0.00	95 – (.9 × 97.22) = $7.50
Less put cost	2.78	2.78
Profit	$–2.78	$4.72
Risky asset payoff	–25 × .2 = $–5.00	–25 × –.1 = $2.50
Lending payoff	27.79 × .08 = 2.22	27.79 × .08 = 2.22
Profit	$–2.78	$4.72

to implement this strategy we need $101.85 ($83.33 + $18.52), but we only have $100 to invest. If we intend to limit our potential loss to 5 percent by actually purchasing the risky asset along with the put option, we would have to scale back the amount of the risky asset that we purchase, such that when we add it to the cost of the put option we would have spent exactly $100. Otherwise the potential loss of $5 on the strategy combined with the cost of the option could result in a total loss of more than 5 percent. In order to replicate this strategy by selling the risky asset short and lending at the riskless rate, we must first determine the precise combination of the risky asset and the put option that we wish to replicate. If we repeat the process described above, iteratively substituting various amounts for the risky asset, we will eventually find that we are able to purchase a put option valued at $2.78 to protect $97.22 of the risky asset. We can replicate the put option part of this strategy by selling 25.72 percent of the risky asset short (which equals $25) and lending $27.79 at the riskless rate. In Table 6–3 we again demonstrate that this strategy is equivalent to a put option.

In order to replicate a protective put option strategy we add the $97.22 to the positions we established to replicate the put option, resulting in a $72.21 exposure to the risky asset and a $27.79 exposure to the riskless asset (which of course is tantamount to lending at the riskless rate).

The foregoing example is extremely oversimplified in the sense that it assumes the risky asset can only increase by 20 percent or decrease by 10 percent. We can overcome this simplification by including a greater number of intervals in our binomial tree. Alternatively we can solve for the risky asset and riskless asset exposures by employing the Black-Scholes continuous-time model.

As we mentioned earlier, portfolio insurance is a dynamic hedging strategy that replicates either investment in a risky asset along with a put option (which we just demonstrated) or investment in a riskless asset along with a call option. In this section we will draw upon its correspondence with investment in a riskless asset plus a call option to show how the strategy can be implemented with the continuous-time Black-Scholes model.

Again suppose we have $100 to invest and we want to be reasonably certain that we will have no less than $95 one year from now. Moreover, should the risky asset increase in value over the course of the year, we want to participate in this performance to the fullest extent possible. Assume that we can purchase a riskless asset to yield 8 percent and that the risky asset's standard deviation equals 20 percent. Let us start by computing the value of a call option on the risky asset. From the above information we have all of the inputs required by the Black-Scholes model:

Risky asset value = $100
Strike price = $95
Risky asset standard deviation = .20
Riskless rate of return = .08
Time to expiration = 1

Recall from Chapter 5 that according to the Black-Scholes model the value of a call option equals

$$[S \times N(D1)] - [(K \times e^{-rt}) \times N(D2)]$$

where

S = Current stock price.
K = Exercise price of option.
T = Time to maturity of the option.
$N(.)$ = Standard normal distribution function.

$$D1 = \frac{\text{natural log}\left(\dfrac{S}{K}\right) + \left[\left(r + \dfrac{V}{2}\right) \times T\right]}{(V \times T)^{.5}}$$

$D2 = D1 - (V \times T)^{.5}$
V = Variance of return of the stock.
e = Exponential constant 2.71828.

First let us compute the value for $D1$ and $D2$, as shown below:

$$D1 = \frac{\text{natural log}\left(\dfrac{100}{95}\right) + .08 + \dfrac{.2^2}{2}}{.2} = .7565$$

$D2 = D1 - .2 = .5565$

Next we substitute these values into the Black-Scholes model:

$$C = [100 \times N(.7565)] - [87.6961 \times N(.5565)]$$

If we look up the area under the normal distribution curve that corresponds to .7565 and .5565 we find that the value for this call option equals \$15.17 [(\$100 × .7753) − (\$87.6961 × .7111)]. We can easily convert this call option value into a value for a put option by invoking the well-known relationship of *put-call parity* condition given on page 138. Expressed in terms of the notation given above, we have:

$$P = C - S + Ke^{-rT}$$

From put-call parity the value of a put option, given the above parameters, equals \$2.87 (\$15.17 − \$100 + \$87.70). However, we are faced with the same problem that we encountered with the binomial model approach to portfolio insurance. The total cost of a protective put option strategy is greater than our available funds. We only have \$100 to invest, but we need \$100 to purchase the risky asset plus an additional \$2.87 to purchase the put option. Hence we do not wish to replicate this particular strategy. Instead we wish to replicate a protective put option strategy whereby we spend exactly \$100. So, just as before, we must iteratively change the amount of the risky asset until its value plus the cost of the shadow put option equals \$100 exactly. Suppose we are lucky and on our next try we select \$96.15 for our risky asset value. The value for D1 equals .5602:

$$D1 = \frac{\text{natural log}\left(\dfrac{96.15}{95}\right) + .08 + \dfrac{.2^2}{2}}{.2}$$

and the value for the call option equals \$12.30:

$$C = [96.15 \times N(.5602)] - [87.6961 \times N(.3602)]$$
$$C = (96.15 \times .7123) - (87.6961 \times .6406) = 12.60$$

Again, using the put-call parity relationship the value for a corresponding put option equals \$3.85:

$$P = 12.60 - 96.15 + 87.70 = 3.85$$

Conveniently the cost of a \$3.85 put option used to protect a risky asset valued at \$96.15 from declining below \$95 exactly uses up our total available funds of \$100. Therefore our next task is to determine how to replicate this option strategy by investment in a risky and a riskless asset.

Remember that in theory a portfolio insurance strategy is equivalent to investment in a risky asset along with a put option or investment in a riskless asset along with a call option. We will draw upon the latter correspondence to determine the initial positions for the risky and riskless assets. The letter D was not chosen arbitrarily in the Black-Scholes formula. The expression $N(D1)$ refers to delta, the fraction of the risky asset that hedges an investment in a call option on the risky asset. Therefore, in order to replicate a call option plus investment in a riskless asset (which is equivalent to replicating investment in a risky asset plus a put option) we simply invest an amount equal to delta times the risky asset in the risky asset, with the remainder of the fund allocated to the riskless asset. In the above example we would invest $68.48 (.7123 × $96.15) in the risky asset and the balance, $31.52, in the riskless asset.

Portfolio Insurance: Assets versus Liabilities

In the above analysis we have assumed that we can only choose between a risky and a riskless asset. What if we are not as concerned with the absolute value of our portfolio at some future date as we are with its relative value? For example it may make sense to protect a pension fund's value in relation to the value of the pension liabilities. It is possible to adapt the portfolio insurance methodology described above to ensure that a prespecified ratio of pension assets to pension liabilities will be met or exceeded. To accomplish this type of protection we need to replace the riskless component with a portfolio that mimics the changes in value of the pension liabilities. With this substitution we need to modify the Black-Scholes model by redefining risk and return as *net* risk and *net* return. Therefore net variance is calculated as

$$V_N = V_A + V_L - 2 \times r_{AL} \times V_A^{.5} \times V_L^{.5}$$

where

V_N = Net variance of the pension assets and liabilities.
V_A = Variance of the assets.
V_L = Variance of the liabilities.
r_{AL} = Correlation between the pension assets and liabilities.

Within this context the risk-free return equals 0 percent since it represents the *net* return of the portfolio that mimics the liabilities relative to the return of the liabilities. With these two modifications we can rewrite the Black-Scholes formula:

$$C = [A \times N(D1)] - [L \times N(D2)]$$

where

C = Value of an option to exchange one risky asset for another.
A = Value of the pension assets.
L = Value of the pension liabilities.
$N(.)$ = Standard normal distribution function.
$D1 = \dfrac{\text{natural log } (A/L) + (V_N/2) \times T}{(V_N \times T)^{.5}}$
$D2 = D1 - (V_N \times T)^{.5}$
V_N = Net variance as defined earlier.
T = Investment horizon.

This formula is identical to William Margrabe's model of an option to exchange one asset for another.[9] It can be used just as the Black-Scholes model was used earlier to replicate a protective put strategy. In this application we are replicating a protective put strategy whereby the put has a variable exercise price that is indexed to the value of the pension liabilities and whereby the strategy calls for continually rebalancing a portfolio between a risky component and a liability-mimicking component.

Replicating Dynamic Strategies with Linear Investment Rules

In order to understand the essence of dynamic strategies for asset allocation, we can examine the payoff functions of simple linear investment rules that are designed to replicate more complex dynamic strategies. Most of the insights presented in this section were introduced in a paper by André Perold and William Sharpe entitled "Dynamic Strategies for Asset Allocation."[10]

Consider for example a stock index and a bond index that are both valued at $100, so that the relative value of stocks to bonds equals one. In Figure 6–4 the horizontal axis represents the relative value of the stock index to the bond index, and the vertical axis represents the incremental return relative to the bond index. In the context of this graph, which is called a *payoff diagram*, a 100 percent allocation to stocks is represented by a straight line

---

[9]W. Margrabe, "The Value of an Option to Exchange One Asset for Another," *Journal of Finance*, March 1978, pp. 117–86.

[10]A. Perold and W. Sharpe, "Dynamic Strategies for Asset Allocation," *Financial Analysts Journal*, January–February 1988, pp. 16–27.

FIGURE 6–4
Equal Allocation to Stocks and Bonds

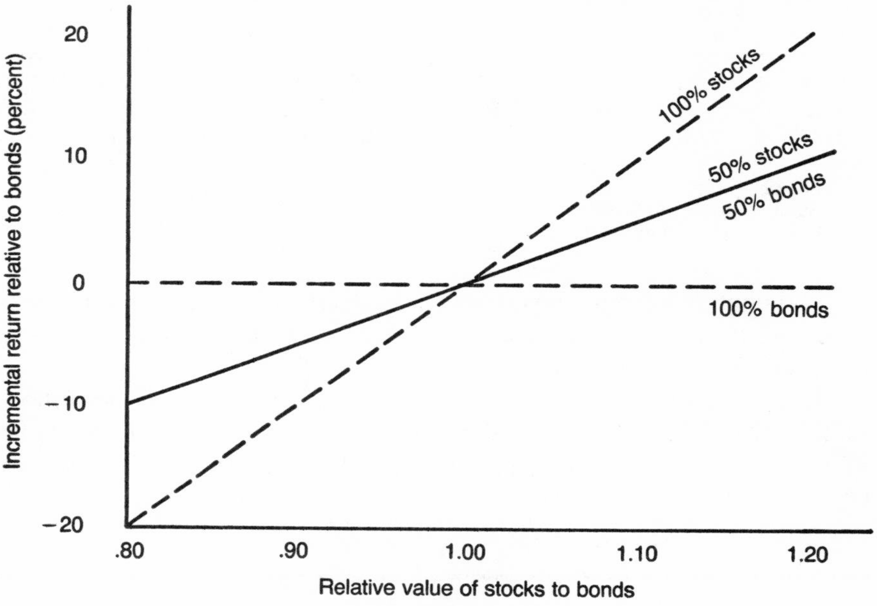

emanating from the origin and proceeding at a 45-degree angle. A 100 percent allocation to bonds, on the other hand, is represented by a horizontal straight line located at 0 percent incremental return on the vertical axis, since the incremental return of the bond index relative to itself is 0 percent. A 50/50 buy and hold allocation between stocks and bonds is represented by a line halfway between the two lines that represent 100 percent allocations to the two assets. These lines are called *payoff functions*. The payoff functions for buy and hold strategies always take the form of a straight line.

In tactical asset allocation strategies based upon the presumption of mean reversion a fund is shifted toward the asset class that has fallen in price and away from the asset class that has risen in price. We can replicate such a strategy with a simple linear investment rule. We multiply the change in an asset's percentage allocation due to that asset's relative performance by some factor less than one and add this value to the asset's percentage allocation before the return-induced change. In Table 6–4 we demonstrate this rule for stocks and bonds:

TABLE 6–4
Linear Investment Rule for Tactical Asset Allocation

	Initial Value	Initial Percent	Return	New Value	New Percent	Revised Percent	Revised Value
Stocks	$ 50.00	50.00%	5.0%	$ 52.50	51.22%	43.90%	$ 45.00
Bonds	50.00	50.00	0.0	50.00	48.78	56.10	57.50
Total	$100.00	100.00%		$102.50	100.00%	100.00%	$102.50

Factor = −5.
Stock return = 5 percent.
Bond return = 0 percent.

Although this simple investment rule clearly would not capture the nuances of all tactical asset allocation strategies, it does capture the essence of mean reversion–based strategies.

In order to replicate *dynamic hedging* strategies such as portfolio insurance we could follow a similar rule in which we chose a factor greater than one to determine the change in mix. We demonstrate this rule in the table below:

TABLE 6–5
Linear Investment Rule for Dynamic Hedging Strategies

	Initial Value	Initial Percent	Return	New Value	New Percent	Revised Percent	Revised Value
Stocks	$ 50.00	50.00%	5.0%	$ 52.50	51.22%	56.10%	$ 57.50
Bonds	50.00	50.00	0.0	50.00	48.78	43.90	45.00
Total	$100.00	100.00%		$102.50	100.00%	100.00%	$102.50

Factor = 5.
Stock return = 5 percent.
Bond return = 0 percent.

The payoff function for a strategy that buys the asset that has fallen in price and sells the asset that has risen in price is not a straight line but rather is *concave* (it increases at a decreasing rate). A payoff function that buys the asset that has risen in price and sells the asset that has fallen in price is *convex* (it increases at an increasing rate). These payoff functions are illustrated in Figure 6–5.

When is it preferable to follow a concave strategy versus a convex strategy? The answer to this question is apparent from the payoff diagram.

FIGURE 6–5
Buy and Hold versus Dynamic Strategies

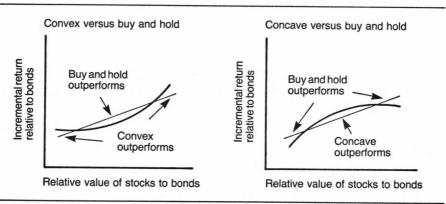

The concave payoff function produces a higher incremental return when the relative value of stocks to bonds is close to one. In other words, a concave strategy will add value if the prices of stocks and bonds vibrate within a relatively narrow interval (again, the notion of a mean-reverting process). Conversely a convex strategy will add value when the relative value of stocks to bonds diverges away from its initial value; as is apparent from Figure 6–5B the convex line is above the buy and hold line at extreme values in either direction.

In general, strategies with concave payoff functions, such as tactical asset allocation, add value to buy and hold strategies when the net returns of the assets between which the fund is allocated are negatively serially correlated (reversals), resulting in similar holding period returns. Strategies with convex payoff functions add value to buy and hold strategies when the net returns of the assets between which the fund is allocated are positively serially correlated (trends), leading to divergent holding period returns. In fact, tactical asset allocation can be thought of as selling portfolio insurance.

CONCLUSION

As this chapter demonstrates, quantitative methods are widely applied in support of asset allocation decisions. In fact the level of complexity of the quantitative techniques used in asset allocation is relatively advanced and increasing at a rapid pace. To compete effectively in this arena the serious financial analyst should be conversant with the quantitative techniques described in this chapter

PROBLEMS

1. Suppose you must choose between two funds. Fund A is allocated 75 percent to stocks and 25 percent to bonds. Fund B is allocated 25 percent to stocks and 75 percent to bonds. Further suppose that your investment objective is to maximize your expected return, subject to the condition that you have at least a 75 percent change of achieving a positive return in a given year. Based on the information shown below and the cumulative normal distribution table included in the Appendix to this book, would you choose fund A or fund B?

	Expected Return	Standard Deviation	Correlation
Stocks	13%	20%	
Bonds	9	10	50%

Answer: Based on the stated objectives fund A is the superior choice. It has a higher expected return than fund B and a 77 percent probability of achieving a positive return, which exceeds the required confidence level of 75 percent.

Fund A:

Expected return $= (.13 \times .75) + (.09 \times .25) = .12$

Standard deviation $= \sqrt{(.20^2 \times .75^2) + (.10^2 \times .25^2) + (2 \times .5 \times .20 \times .75 \times .10 \times .25)} = .1639$

$$\frac{\text{Probability of}}{\text{positive return}} = \frac{0 - .12}{.1639} = -.7321 = >76.7\%$$

Fund B:

Expected return $= (.13 \times .25) + (.09 \times .75) = .10$

Standard deviation $= \sqrt{(.2^2 \times .25^2) + (.1^2 \times .75^2) + (2 \times .5 \times .2 \times .25 \times .1 \times .75)} = .1090$

$$\frac{\text{Probability of}}{\text{positive return}} = \frac{0 - .10}{.1098} = -.9174 = >82.1\%$$

2. Suppose your fund is currently allocated equally between stocks and bonds. You have no conviction about whether stocks will outperform bonds in the next 12 months or whether bonds will outperform stocks. You are convinced, however, that their returns will gradually but significantly diverge during this period. What dynamic strategy should you follow in order to add value to a buy and hold strategy in which you let the markets determine the asset mix of your fund?

Answer: If stock returns and bond returns diverge, a strategy that generates a convex payoff function will add value to a buy and hold strategy during this period of divergence. A convex strategy is one in which a fund is continually shifted to the asset class with the better relative performance. In the chart below, note that a convex strategy beats a buy and hold strategy as relative values diverge:

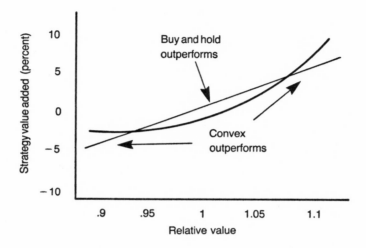

CHAPTER SEVEN

Quantitative Methods in Performance Measurement

Mark P. Kritzman

The five preceding chapters demonstrate how the quantitative principles described in Chapter One can be applied to improve the investment process. This chapter extends the same quantitative principles to investment performance measurement.

The purpose of performance measurement is neither to reward nor to penalize managers for past performance but rather to identify managers who are likely to add value to a portfolio going forward. Hence past performance is relevant only to the extent it reveals something about a manager's likelihood of future success. Unfortunately past performance is influenced heavily by the randomness of security returns. Thus such performance by itself may tell us little about the likelihood of future success. Within this context performance measurement should be viewed as a means of uncovering evidence of manager conduct. This evidence should be used in conjunction with one's qualitative appraisal of the manager to determine if the manager is indeed likely to add value to the portfolio.

This chapter begins with a discussion of rates of return and proceeds with a review of the conventional techniques for ranking returns and risk-adjusting returns. This review is followed by a discussion of some important limitations to performance measurement, such as benchmark error and the ambiguity between skill and chance. Next are introduced some more-advanced techniques designed to overcome these limitations, including performance attribution, normal portfolios, and nonparametric performance measurement. The next section demonstrates how the quantitative framework of option pricing theory can be applied to analyze performance-based fees. The chapter concludes with a discussion of how managers adapt their behavior in order to circumvent various performance measurement techniques.

As will become apparent, performance measurement is highly dependent upon the application of quantitative tools. The limitation of quantitative tools, though, is also very apparent when applied to performance measurement.

RATE OF RETURN

Rate of return is a straightforward concept. It is equal to the income generated by an investment plus or minus the investment's change in price during the measurement period, all divided by the beginning price, controlling the contributions and disbursements. For *common stock*, therefore:

$$\text{Rate of return} = \frac{\text{Dividends} + (\text{Ending price} - \text{Beginning price})}{\text{Beginning price}}$$

For *bonds* we simply substitute coupons for dividends:

$$\text{Rate of return} = \frac{\text{Coupons} + (\text{Ending price} - \text{Beginning price})}{\text{Beginning price}}$$

For *real estate* the income component is net operating income:

$$\text{Rate of return} =$$
$$\frac{\text{Net operating income} + (\text{Ending price} - \text{Beginning price})}{\text{Beginning price}}$$

Although rate of return is conceptually simple it is sometimes obscured by measurement problems. For example, real estate prices are often not readily available, since properties are turned over infrequently. Values based on appraisals are used instead of actual transaction-based prices, and an appraised value can differ significantly from the price at which a property could be sold.

The rate of return on discount instruments such as Treasury bills can also be potentially misleading. These instruments are purchased at a discount from their redemption price. A Treasury bill, for example, may be purchased for $9,500 and redeemed 26 weeks later for $10,000. Its rate of return therefore is not 5 percent but rather $500 divided by $9,500, which equals 5.26 percent for one-half year.

So although the concept of rate of return is simple, one should apply it carefully, recognizing the unique features of the various investment media.

TIME–WEIGHTED AND DOLLAR–WEIGHTED RATES OF RETURN

As indicated in Chapter One, the *time-weighted rate of return* is the standard by which investment performance is measured. It is used as the basis of comparison with competing portfolio managers and with benchmarks such as the S&P 500 Stock Index. Although the dollar-weighted rate of return measures the actual internal growth rate of the portfolio, it does not measure a portfolio manager's performance accurately. It is influenced by portfolio contributions and disbursements that are beyond the control of the portfolio manager.

Example: An investment management firm, Brownian Management, is given $10 million to invest on January 1, 1981. It is given additional contributions of $2 million on January 1, 1982, $4 million on January 1, 1983, and $6 million on January 1, 1984. On January 1, 1985, the company is required to disburse $5 million from the portfolio. By December 31, 1985, the portfolio grows to $34 million. What rate of return should be used to measure Brownian Management's performance?

The *dollar-weighted rate of return* of the portfolio, or its internal growth rate, is simply the rate of return that discounts the final market value of $34 million and the interim cash flows back to the initial market value of $10 million. It is derived directly from the present value formula described in Chapter One:

$$PV = \frac{-2}{1 + r} + \frac{-4}{(1 + r)^2} + \frac{-6}{(1 + r)^3} + \frac{5}{(1 + r)^4} + \frac{34}{(1 + r)^5} = 10$$

$$r = .167$$

Thus the dollar-weighted rate of return equals 16.7 percent.

The actual returns generated by Brownian Management on the assets under their management were −7.9 percent in 1981, 24.3 percent in 1982, 25.6 percent in 1983, 8.5 percent in 1984, and 31.0 percent in 1985. The $34 million figure represents the future value of contributions less disbursements given these returns. If we link the returns we find that the cumulative return over the entire period was 104.4 percent:

$$r = (1 - .079)(1 + .243)(1 + .256)(1 + .085)(1 + .310) - 1 = 1.044$$

To annualize the five-year cumulative return of 104.4 percent, we simply add 1, raise this value to the 1/5 power, and subtract 1. Hence the annualized return equals 15.4 percent:

$$(1 + 1.044)^{1/5} - 1 = .154$$

In general the formula for annualizing a return (whether it is less than or greater than one year) is

$$AR = (1 + R)^{1/n} - 1$$

where

AR = Annualized return.
R = Return over entire measurement period.
n = Number of years in measurement period.

If the client had switched the timing of the $5 million disbursement with the $6 million contribution, the ending market value would have been $32.8 million rather than $34 million, given the same returns on funds invested. The dollar-weighted rate of return would have been 17.5 percent instead of 16.7 percent:

$$PV = \frac{-2}{1 + r} + \frac{-4}{(1 + r)^2} + \frac{5}{(1 + r)^3} + \frac{-6}{(1 + r)^4} + \frac{32.8}{(1 + r)^5} = 10$$
$$r = .175$$

Nonetheless the return generated by Brownian Management on the assets under its control each year would not have changed. Clearly therefore the time-weighted rate of return controls for the impact that contributions and disbursements have on the portfolio and isolates the return due to investment management.

The time-weighted rate of return, although different from the dollar-weighted rate of return over a measurement period with cash flows, can be reconciled quite easily with the present value framework. It is equivalent to the linked dollar-weighted rates of return between cash flows.

Again consider the example. Although the dollar-weighted rate of return over the entire five years is 16.7 percent, the dollar-weighted rate of return for each individual year is different.

In 1981 the dollar-weighted rate of return can be found by discounting the market value at the end of the year back to the initial market value:

$$\frac{9.21}{1 + r} = 10$$
$$r = -.079$$

The same procedure can be used to find the dollar-weighted rate of return in the second year. That is, the market value at the end of the second year is discounted back to the market value at the beginning of the second year (note that the market value at the beginning of the second year includes the $2 million contribution made on January 1, 1982):

$$\frac{13.93}{1 + r} = 11.21$$
$$r = .243$$

If we repeat this procedure for years 1983 through 1985, we find that the dollar-weighted rates of return are 25.6 percent, 8.5 percent, and 31 percent, respectively.

These annual dollar-weighted rates of return are exactly equivalent to the returns generated by Brownian Management each year. Hence the present value framework described in Chapter One can be applied to measure investment performance, given the simple modification of discounting the market value before each cash flow back to the market value subsequent to each prior cash flow and linking these returns. This procedure will yield the portfolio's time-weighted rate of return over the entire measurement period, after we annualize the cumulative return.

Universe Comparisons

In the foregoing example Brownian Management generated an annualized time-weighted rate of return of 15.4 percent for the five years ending in 1985. How good is this result?

One way to answer this question is to compare its rate of return to the returns achieved by other portfolio managers with whom it competes. In fact, *universe comparisons* are the most common approach for evaluating portfolio managers. The procedure is quite simple. The returns of a representative sample of portfolio managers are collected and assembled into a universe. The universe is then segmented into *percentile* groupings, and each manager is evaluated by the grouping in which he or she appears. For example, if 100 managers are included in the universe and only 10 of them have a

FIGURE 7–1
Universe Comparison: Overlapping Periods

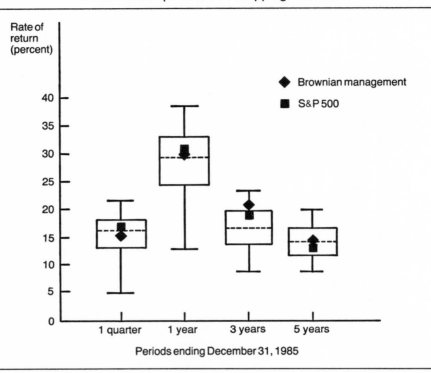

Periods ending December 31, 1985

return equal to or greater than 15.4 percent, then a manager whose return exceeds 15.4 percent is a top-decile performer for the five years ending in 1985. If 25 managers produced returns equal to or in excess of 15.4 percent, then a manager with a 15.4 percent return or greater would rank within the top quartile.

The universe comparison approach simply ranks each participant's return and divides the absolute ranking by the number of managers in the sample to determine the percentile ranking.

A typical universe comparison exhibit is shown in Figure 7–1, which ranks managers over four periods: one quarter, one year, three years, and five years ending on December 31, 1985. The boxplots (see Chapter One) for each period span the returns ranging from the 95th to the 5th percentile of the universe. Within each plot is shown the percentile ranking of Brownian Management as well as a relevant benchmark. Although performance during four periods is shown, these periods all end on the same date; they overlap

FIGURE 7–2
Universe Comparison: Discrete Periods

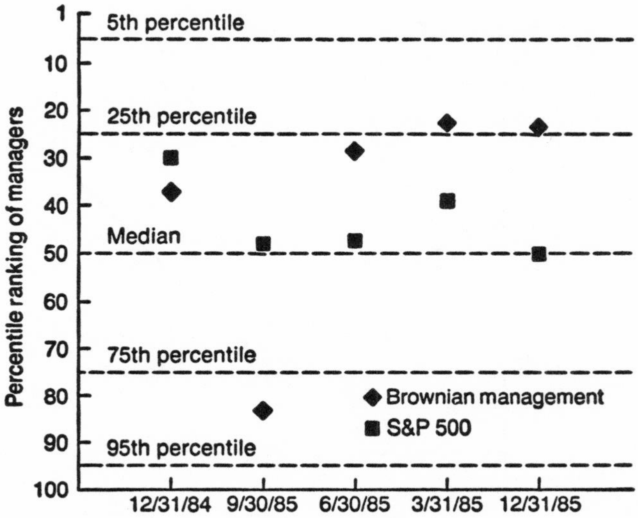

each other. Therefore, a manager's ranking in all of the periods can be largely affected by the manager's performance in the most recent quarter. By using overlapping periods to compare managers, relative performance may appear to be more consistent than it really is.

Figure 7–2 shows the percentile ranking of Brownian Management over five independent quarters. It is more apparent from this exhibit that Brownian Management's percentile rankings are rather unstable from quarter to quarter. The use of discrete measurement periods is a more reliable indicator of consistency.

The appeal of the universe comparison approach is its simplicity. Nonetheless it has several limitations. First, there should be uniformity of style across managers within a given universe or the ranking may be specious. For example, it would not be very informative to include equity and fixed-income managers in the same universe, since their performance will be influenced largely by the performance of the markets in which they operate. More subtle variations of this problem can also jeopardize the integrity of a universe comparison. Some equity managers concentrate their selection of securities among large companies, while other managers focus on small companies. This difference in style will affect the results so that the ranking

FIGURE 7–3
Perfect Positive Relationship

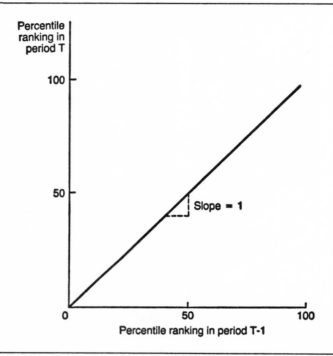

may reflect not the managers' discretionary investment judgments but rather their investment style. This issue is addressed in some depth later in this chapter.

Another shortcoming of universe comparisons is that most empirical evidence suggests there is no correlation between a manager's ranking in one period and his ranking in the subsequent period.

The implicit expectation of those who rely on universe comparisons to evaluate money managers is that relative performance will persist from period to period, that it is serially correlated. Regression analysis allows us to test this belief. For example the percentile rankings of a group of managers over a particular measurement period can be regressed on their pecentile rankings over the previous measurement period. In the extreme, if relative performance in the first period corresponded perfectly with relative performance in the subsequent period, the scatter plot would form a straight line emanating from the origin at 45 degrees, as shown in Figure 7–3. The intercept of the line would be zero while its slope would be one. The *R*-squared of such a relationship would also be 1. This relationship would indicate that a manager's percentile ranking in one period is repeated exactly in the next period.

Obviously it is quite unlikely that relative performance among portfolio managers is perfectly correlated from period to period. Nonetheless most members of the investment industry believe that past relative performance foretells something about subsequent relative performance. For example a common view is that top-quartile managers are more likely to generate superior results in the next period than are bottom-quartile managers.

A study of the Bell System managers covering the period 1972 through 1981 showed that virtually no relationship existed between relative performance in the first five-year period and the second five-year period.[1] A perfect serial relationship would have produced an intercept of zero, a slope of one, and an *R*-squared of one. If relative performance were perfectly uncorrelated the intercept would equal 50 (the 50th percentile would be the best guess for next period's ranking), while the slope and *R*-squared would both equal zero (Figure 7–4). The actual results of the Bell System study are:

	Intercept	Slope	R-Squared
Equity managers	51	−0.05	0.00
Fixed-income managers	46	.10	0.00

These results show that relative performance is almost perfectly independent from period to period and that regardless of whether a manager appears in the top or bottom quartile in one period the best guess of the manager's ranking in the future is the 50th percentile!

RISK ADJUSTMENT

A fundamental principle of finance is that investors require compensation for bearing risk; hence riskier assets have higher expected returns than less risky assets. Moreover historical precedent has demonstrated that investors' expectations have been realized over most extended time periods. Figure 1– 3 in Chapter One shows that over the period 1926–1984 small stocks provided higher returns and higher variability of returns than large stocks and that the

---

[1]See Mark Kritzman, "Can Bond Managers Perform Consistently?" *Journal of Portfolio Management*, Summer 1983, pp. 54–56. The equity results are from an unpublished portion of the same study.

FIGURE 7–4
No Relationship

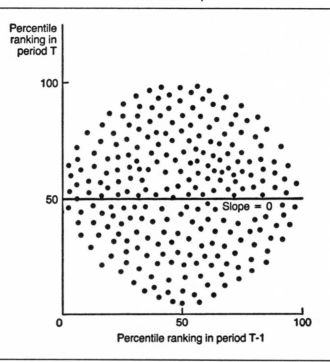

same relationship holds between large stocks and bonds. Without exerting any skill whatsoever, a portfolio manager could therefore increase a portfolio's expected return and, over most extended horizons, its realized return simply by increasing the portfolio's risk. Thus it is argued that portfolio managers should be evaluated according to their risk-adjusted returns, not their total returns.

As a first approximation for portfolio risk, one might consider the standard deviation of returns. The Sharpe measure[2] adjusts returns by dividing a portfolio's excess return (portfolio return less Treasury bill return) by the standard deviation of total return. This measure implicitly assumes that there is only one manager for the entire portfolio; hence total risk is relevant.

The *capital asset pricing model (CAPM)* assumes two separate sources of portfolio risk: systemwide influences and company-specific influences.

---

[2]See William Sharpe, "Mutual Fund Performance," *Journal of Business*, January 1966, pp. 119–38.

Since the risk associated with company-specific influences can be eliminated by diversification, investors are not compensated for bearing specific risk. They are compensated only for bearing systematic risk that cannot be diversified away.

The Treynor measure[3] relates return to systematic risk only and therefore can be applied to a situation where there are multiple managers. It is calculated by dividing a portfolio's excess return by its beta. Beta can be estimated by regressing the portfolio excess returns on the excess returns of the market portfolio over some representative time period. The coefficient from such a regression is beta. It measures the portfolio's expected change in excess return, given a one-unit change in the market's excess return. For example, if Brownian Management had a beta of 1.25 the company would be expected to generate 5.0 percent excess return when the market portfolio generates a 4.0 percent excess return.

The intercept from a regression of the portfolio excess return on the market's excess return is referred to as *alpha,* and it measures the value added by the portfolio manager, given the level of risk *(beta)* chosen for the portfolio. For example, since Brownian Management generated a 4.8 percent excess return with a 1.25 beta while the market's excess return was 4.0 percent, their alpha (value added) was -0.2 percent:

$$\text{Alpha} = (\text{Portfolio return} - \text{Risk-free return})$$
$$- [\text{Beta} \times (\text{Market return} - \text{Risk-free return})]$$
$$= (15.4 - 10.6) - [1.25 \times (14.6 - 10.6)] = -0.2 \text{ percent}$$

Thus although Brownian Management generated a higher return than the market, their value added was slightly negative after accounting for the risk they incurred.

Alpha is also referred to as the Jensen measure,[4] and it too is suitable for a multiple-manager situation since it is based on systematic risk rather than total risk.

BENCHMARK ERROR

Performance measurement techniques that are based on the CAPM or that compare performance to the market assume implicitly that the market is observable. Of course if we acknowledge that the market includes the entire wealth of the world, it cannot be observed, so indexes such as the S&P 500

---

[3]See Jack Treynor, "How to Rate Management of Investment Funds," *Harvard Business Review,* January–February 1965, pp. 63–75.

[4]See Michael Jensen, "The Performance of Mutual Funds in the Period 1945–1964," *Journal of Finance,* May 1968, pp. 389–416.

Stock Index are used as a surrogate for the market and as a benchmark for performance.

The substitution of an index such as the S&P 500 for the market leads to theoretical as well as practical problems. For example the CAPM assumption that the market is observable is obviously false. Therefore some argue that the validity of the CAPM cannot be tested—that any proposed test of the CAPM is in effect a joint test of the CAPM and the appropriateness of the particular benchmark chosen to represent the market. Therefore we have no way of judging whether or not performance measurement techniques based on the CAPM are theoretically sound.

Of a more practical nature is the problem that a manager's risk-adjusted performance is partly determined by the benchmark chosen for risk adjustment. Richard Roll demonstrated that manager rankings based on the CAPM are inconclusive except when alpha is negative, because the benchmark may not be an optimal portfolio.[5] When alpha is negative, switching to an optimal benchmark will only make alpha more negative. When alpha is positive, however, it is not clear whether it represents superior performance or measurement error resulting from the application of a suboptimal benchmark. Moreover Roll demonstrated that manager rankings can be exactly reversed simply by choosing a different benchmark to represent the market. Therefore what we perceive as superior manager performance may be nothing more than benchmark error.

Philip Dybvig and Stephen Ross argue further that even a negative alpha is inconclusive,[6] asserting that a manager with superior information can produce a negative alpha if the manager's information set differs from the information set of the evaluator. Therefore a negative alpha produced within the context of a particular information set might actually be a positive alpha within the context of a different information set.

These problems can be ameliorated to a large extent by using normal portfolios to measure performance, an approach discussed in some detail later in this chapter.

AMBIGUITY BETWEEN SKILL AND CHANCE

Perhaps a more serious problem with performance measurement is the ambiguity between skill and chance. This arises because investment returns

---

[5]R. Roll, "Performance Evaluation and Benchmark Errors," *Journal of Portfolio Management*, Summer 1980, pp. 5–12.

[6]P. Dybvig and S. Ross, "Differential Information and Performance Measurement Using a Security Market Line," *Journal of Finance*, June 1985, pp. 383–99.

over a short time period, even if they are risk adjusted, are mostly random. Therefore it is extremely difficult to infer skill or lack of skill from a summary statistic such as total return or risk-adjusted return.

The uncertainty about whether or not a portfolio's performance reflects manager conduct can be addressed using the same methodology described in the section on hypothesis testing in Chapter One. In this particular situation the null hypothesis is that the value added by the manager does not differ significantly from zero.[7] The alternative hypothesis is that the manager has added significant value. If we divide the estimate of mean value added by the standard error of the estimate,[8] we can compute a *t-statistic* to measure the significance of the value added by the manager.

For example if the value added in a particular year equaled 4 percent and the standard error was 3 percent, the *t*-statistic would equal 4 ÷ 3, or 1.33.[9] Therefore we would accept the null hypothesis that the value added by the manager does not differ significantly from zero.

If the manager's performance persisted for five years on average, we would compute the *t*-statistic as 4 ÷ (3 ÷ $\sqrt{5}$). In this case the *t*-statistic equals 2.98; hence we would reject the null hypothesis and instead assert that value added is significantly different from zero or more prosaically that the manager is skillful rather than lucky.

By rearranging terms in the *t*-statistic computation we can estimate how long a result must persist on average in order to assert confidently that it was caused by a manager's investment skill. Since

$$t = \frac{\text{Value added} \times \text{Time}}{\text{Risk} \times \sqrt{\text{Time}}}$$

therefore,

$$\text{Time} = \text{Risk}^2 \times t^2 \times (\text{Value added})^{-2}$$

For example if we want to be 95 percent confident that the value added by the manager is significantly greater than zero, we would require a *t*-statistic of 1.65. In the above example, where the manager's mean value added was

---

[7] Value added can be thought of as that part of the return caused by a manager's investment decisions. In the context of the CAPM it would be alpha. In the context of a normal portfolio it would equal the return differential between the managed portfolio and the normal portfolio.

[8] Recall from Chapter One that the standard error is given by the standard deviation (in this case, of value added) divided by the square root of the number of observations used to estimate the sample mean.

[9] As is typical in this type of application involving a one-tailed test, we are assuming that a *t*-statistic of 1.65 is required for significance.

TABLE 7–1
Years Required for 95 Percent
Confidence that Result Reflects Skill and
Not Chance Return

Risk	Return (percent)				
	.5	.75	1.0	2.0	5.0
2%	44	19	11	3	0
3	98	44	25	6	1
4	174	77	44	11	2
6	392	174	98	25	4
8	697	310	174	44	7

4 percent with a standard error of 3 percent, the result would have to persist on average for 1.53 years:

$$\text{Time} = 3^2 \times 1.65^2 \times 4^{-2} = 1.53$$

Table 7–1 shows the number of years required to distinguish a result from chance with 95 percent confidence, given various combinations of value added and the standard error of value added. It should be clear from this table that unless the mean value added is fairly large relative to its standard error, a very long measurement period is required to reject the null hypothesis that it does not differ significantly from zero.

PERFORMANCE ATTRIBUTION

An insignificant t-statistic does not necessarily imply an absence of skill. It simply indicates that skill is not apparent from the summary statistics used to describe the manager's performance.

It may be true for some managers, even given a low t-statistic, that skill exists at a particular type of decision. For example a manager may be skillful in forecasting the relative performance of industries, yet he incurs risk in his market timing decisions, where he has no skill. Or a manager may possess insight about the behavior of a particular economic factor or security attribute that is associated with differences in return, yet risk incurred from other portfolio exposures may obscure his insights. Performance attribution partitions a portfolio's return and attributes it to the various decisions made by the portfolio manager or to the portfolio's factor exposures incurred either intentionally or unintentionally.

Regression analysis enables us to test whether or not an attribute is correlated with return by regressing differences in the attribute's value across securities with differences in return across securities. This type of regression, referred to as a cross-sectional regression, appears as

$$R_i = \text{Constant} + (g_i \times b_{1i}) + (g_2 \times b_{2i}) + \cdots + e_i$$

where

$$R_i = \text{Return to asset } i.$$

$b_1, b_2, \ldots$ = Observed exposure of security i to attributes 1, 2, . . .

$g_1, g_2, \ldots$ = Marginal returns to attributes 1, 2, . . . that are to be estimated using the cross section of security returns.

$$e_i = \text{Idiosyncratic component of returns.}$$

This cross-sectional regression analysis is repeated for as many periods (usually months) as data is available in order to generate a history of attribute returns.

The t-statistic can be used to determine if differences in return are significantly correlated with differences in attribute value. If we establish 95 percent as our significance threshold, which is typical, then we expect to observe a t-statistic of greater than 1.96 in more than 5 percent of the regressions. If such is the case, then we can assert with 95 percent confidence that differences in the attribute value help to explain differences in return across our sample of securities.

William Sharpe has followed roughly this approach to identify security attributes that correspond with security returns.[10]

Although performance attribution provides greater detail about portfolio performance, this refinement may actually lead to even less reliable results than a summary measure of performance. Both factors and a company's sensitivity to factors shift over time, such that attempts to measure them with statistical tools may result in more noise than information.

NORMAL PORTFOLIO

Since the measurement of return and risk is determined in part by the chosen benchmark, it is important to choose a benchmark that isolates the return

---

[10]See W. Sharpe, "Factors in New York Stock Exchange Security Returns—1931–1979," *Journal of Portfolio Management*, Summer 1982, pp. 5–19.

and risk due to discretionary investment management decisions. For example a manager should not be evaluated according to the return and risk attributable to the manager's style, since almost any style can be mimicked mechanically. The choice of a style is the responsibility of the client who selects the manager.

A *normal portfolio* is designed to control for management style and to provide a benchmark against which the manager's discretionary investment decisions can be evaluated. It can be viewed as a default portfolio or those securities a manager would hold in the absence of any information or judgment about their relative attractiveness.

The first step in constructing a normal portfolio is the same initial step required in performance attribution, which is to identify relevant attributes. As shown above, relevant attributes can be identified by regressing differences in return across a sample of securities with differences in various attributes among those securities. To determine if the hypothesized attributes are indeed relevant in explaining differences in return, each attribute's t-statistic should exceed 1.96 in more than 5 percent of the regressions. It is important to observe the t-statistic in a multiple regression context, since the attributes are likely to be partly correlated with each other.[11] In such a case their t-statistic would be overstated if they were derived independently from a series of simple regressions.

The next step in constructing a normal portfolio is to distinguish those attributes that reflect management style from those that reflect discretionary investment decisions. This task can be accomplished by examining the historical attribute exposures of the portfolio under consideration.

If the exposure of a portfolio to a particular attribute is fairly stable over time, the exposure probably reflects a manager's style. If the exposure to a particular attribute is highly variable over time, the changes in exposure probably reflect discretionary investment judgments. Whether a portfolio's attribute exposure is stable or variable can be determined by the ratio of the mean attribute exposure to the standard deviation of exposures.

Again we can perform a significance test. In this application the null hypothesis is that the average exposure to the attribute is zero; hence exposure to the attribute is part of the manager's discretionary investment decision. The alternative hypothesis is that exposure to the attribute differs significantly from zero and therefore reflects the manager's style. If the ratio exceeds 1.96 we reject the null hypothesis and explain the attribute exposure by management style.

The final step in the normal portfolio construction process is to identify

---

[11]This phenomenon is called *multicollinearity*.

the security holdings that make up the normal portfolio. The names in the normal portfolio should be capitalization weighted so that passive investment in this portfolio would not require frequent rebalancing and the names in aggregate should exhibit approximately the same attributes as those identified with the manager's style.

The process described above normalizes a portfolio so as to isolate a manager's selection decisions. It may also be desirable to normalize a portfolio to isolate a manager's timing decisions. The impact of timing can be measured simply by applying the managed portfolio's ongoing asset mix to representative benchmark (normal) portfolios for each asset class. The return of this hypothetical portfolio can then be compared to an alternative hypothetical portfolio invested in the normal portfolios in accordance with the manager's normal asset mix. This approach controls for that part of return due to investment decisions within each asset class.

NONPARAMETRIC PERFORMANCE MEASUREMENT

The performance measurement procedures described thus far depend on the estimation of parameters such as mean and variance and, in the more elaborate procedures, the validity of a model such as the CAPM or a particular multiple-factor model. The principal advantage of these procedures is that they provide a specific quantitative measure of value added. Nonetheless they have several important disadvantages:

- They usually require extensive data.
- They often depend on complex statistical techniques.
- The parameters are estimated with error.
- They depend on models that cannot be tested adequately.

Hence the resultant measure of value added, although specific, is not always correct.

The application of nonparametric techniques to measure performance circumvents the aforementioned problems because these techniques do not involve parameters nor do they depend on the validity of a particular asset pricing model. Moreover nonparametric techniques are relatively simple. They do suffer from a serious limitation, however; *nonparametric performance measurement* does not yield a precise quantification of value added.

To illustrate the advantages and disadvantages of using nonparametric procedures to measure performance, suppose we wish to evaluate a portfolio manager's ability to time the market. A straightforward approach would be to observe when the manager favored equities over short-term securities and when he favored short-term securities over equities. We could then compare these decisions to the subsequent performance of equities and short-term securities and compute the percentage of times he was correct in assessing their relative attractiveness.

If we define P_e as the percentage of times that the manager favors equities when they subsequently outperform short-term securities and P_{st} as the percentage of times that the manager favors short-term securities when they subsequently outperform equities, then $P_e + P_{st}$ provides a measure of a manager's forecasting ability, as demonstrated by Robert Merton.[12]

Moreover Merton shows that if we limit predictive ability to correct forecasts, then a manager has timing skill if $P_e + P_{st}$ is greater than one, because for his timing skill to be of value to others, his beliefs about the relative attractiveness of equities and short-term securities must not be commonly known or this information would be redundant. For example if it is commonly known that stocks outperform short-term securities more than half the time, it requires no skill to forecast that stocks will always outperform short-term securities even though such a forecast would be correct more than half the time. It should also be apparent that $P_e + P_{st}$ will equal two if a market timer has perfect predictive ability.

The important limitation of this approach is that the forecasts are qualitative—they do not include information about the magnitude of the predicted differential in return. Therefore it is possible for a market timer with a score of one (no timing ability) to generate a higher return through his timing decisions than, for example, a market timer with a score of 1.5. This result could occur if the market timer with no skill correctly favored equities when they outperformed short-term securities by a substantial margin while the market timer with significant skill favored equities when they only marginally outperformed short-term securities.

Hence nonparametric techniques can yield useful insights about a portfolio manager's forecasting ability but not necessarily information sufficient to evaluate his investment skill.

INCENTIVE FEES

Quantitative methods can also be applied to evaluate compensation for managers whose fees are based on performance. Performance-based fees or incentive fees are typically structured with two components: a base component

---

[12]R. C. Merton, "On Market Timing and Investment Performance: 1. An Equilibrium Theory of Value for Market Forecasts," *Journal of Business* 54, no. 3 (1981), pp. 303–405.

FIGURE 7–5
Performance-Based Fee Arrangement

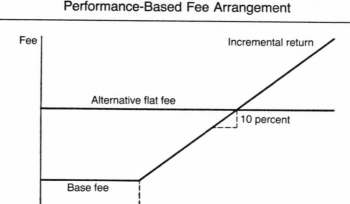

that is a flat percentage of assets under management and an incentive component that is a percentage of the incremental return of the portfolio relative to the benchmark. This fee arrangement is illustrated in Figure 7–5.

If the portfolio returns less than or as much as the benchmark, such that incremental return is less than or equal to 0 percent, the manager collects a base fee that is equal to some constant percentage of assets under management. If the portfolio's return exceeds the return of the benchmark such that incremental return is positive the manager collects the base fee plus some percentage of incremental return. Under an alternative flat-fee arrangement the fee would equal some constant percentage of assets regardless of the portfolio's incremental return.

The *payoff diagram* for an incentive fee is the same as the payoff diagram for a call option (see Chapter Five). With an incentive fee the manager in effect has a call option on superior performance. He can collect a fee indexed to his performance if it is favorable, or he can collect a flat fee if performance is unfavorable. Moreover he can arbitrage away his risk by taking opposite positions in his other client's portfolios or in his own personal portfolio.

Performance is defined in this context in terms of incremental return relative to a benchmark. Because performance is defined as a relative value the relevant measure of risk is net risk, or the uncertainty of incremental return. Net risk is affected by the covariance between the benchmark and the managed portfolio as well as by the individual risk of the two portfolios. It is equivalent to the standard deviation of a hypothetical portfolio consisting of a long position in the managed portfolio and a short position in the benchmark portfolio, and it is calculated as follows:

$$s = \sqrt{s_P^2 + s_B^2 - 2\,r_{PB}s_Ps_B}$$

where

s = Net risk.
s_P = Portfolio standard deviation.
s_B = Benchmark standard deviation.
r_{PB} = Correlation coefficient.

Moreover the risk-free return in this context is 0 percent rather than the risk-free rate of interest, since the incremental return of the benchmark is 0 percent by definition.

With these two modifications we can apply option theory to value an incentive fee. Recall from Chapter Five that the value of a call option equals

$$\text{Call value} = S \times N(D1) - (K \times e^{-rt}) \times N(D2)$$
$$D1 = \frac{\text{natural log } (S/K) + (r + V/2) \times T}{(V \times T)^{.5}}$$
$$D2 = D1 - (V \times T)^{.5}$$

where

C = Call value.
S = Stock price.
K = Exercise price.
r = Risk-free interest rate.
T = Time to expiration.
V = Variance.
$N(.)$ = Normal cumulative density function.

Therefore the value of an incentive fee (a call option on superior performance) equals[13]

---

[13]William Margrabe, "The Value of an Option to Exchange One Risky Asset for Another," *Journal of Finance*, March 1978, pp. 177–86, shows that this formula is equivalent to the valuation of an option to exchange one risky asset for another.

$$V = d\{[P \times N(D1)] - [B \times N(D2)]\}$$

$$D1 = \frac{\text{natural log } (P/B) + [\frac{1}{2}(s_P^2 + s_B^2 - 2r_{PB}s_Ps_B) \times T]}{(s_P^2 + s_B^2 - 2r_{PB}s_Ps_B)^{.5} \times \sqrt{T}}$$

$$D2 = D1 - (s_P^2 + s_B^2 - 2r_{PB}s_Ps_B)^{.5} \times \sqrt{T}$$

where

V = Incentive free value.
d = Participation in incremental return.
P = Portfolio price.
B = Benchmark price.
s_P = Portfolio standard deviation.
s_B = Benchmark standard deviation.
r_{PB} = Correlation.
T = Measurement period.
$N(.)$ = Normal cumulative density function.

The differences between the formula used to value an incentive fee and the standard Black-Scholes formula are:

- d is added to reflect the degree of participation in incremental return.
- The stock price is replaced by the price of the portfolio.
- The exercise price is replaced by the value of the benchmark portfolio.
- e^{-rt} drops out since r equals zero.
- The standard deviation of the stock return is replaced by the standard deviation of the portfolio's net return relative to the benchmark.

To demonstrate how this formula can be used to value an incentive fee consider the following situation:

Assets under management: $10 million.
Participation in incremental return: 10 percent.
Portfolio standard deviation: 15 percent.
Benchmark standard deviation: 15 percent.
Correlation: 95 percent.
Measurement period: one year.

In this situation the incentive component is worth $18,900 to the manager, as shown on the following page.

$$D1 = \frac{\text{natural log}\left(\dfrac{10}{10}\right) + \left\{\dfrac{1}{2}[.15^2 + .15^2 - (2 \times .95 \times .15 \times .15)] \times 1\right\}}{[.15^2 + .15^2 - (2 \times .95 \times .15 \times .15)^{1/2}] \times 1}$$

$$= .0237$$
$$D2 = .0237 - .0474 = -.0237$$
$$N(D1) = .5094$$
$$N(D2) = .4905$$
$$V = .1(.5094 - .4905) \times \$10 \text{ million} = \$18,900$$

GAMING PERFORMANCE MEASUREMENT

Quantitative tools have certainly enhanced our ability to measure investment performance, but we are a long way from developing a foolproof, purely quantitative approach for identifying superior portfolio managers. Regardless of complexity, quantitative performance measurement techniques are inexact because they depend on noisy data. Moreover performance measurement techniques can be gamed easily by those who are familiar with the statistical tools that are used or the asset pricing models upon which the techniques are based. In this section we discuss three common ways managers can adapt their behavior in order to circumvent performance measurement techniques.

Closet Indexing

Perhaps the most common practice for gaming performance measurement is *closet indexing*. Index funds are portfolios designed to mimic a particular index, such as the S&P 500 Stock Index. They are constructed mechanically and involve no judgment about the investment merits of the component securities. The purpose of an index fund is to provide cost-effective diversification. Index funds are relatively inexpensive because they obviate the need for investment research and minimize transaction costs since securities are traded only to reinvest income or to rebalance the portfolio when there are contributions or disbursements.

Closet indexing refers to the practice of managing a portfolio such that its performance does not depart significantly from the performance of an index, yet charging clients active management fees for what is essentially passive management. The client may not perceive the similarity between the so-called actively managed portfolio and the index because the portfolio may hold many securities that are not in common with the index. Nonetheless, close tracking with the index is guaranteed because the securities in aggregate are highly correlated with the index. Portfolio managers might pursue such a strategy either intentionally or unintentionally because they do not wish to risk the chance of underperforming the index by a significant margin. Of course they also sacrifice the opportunity to outperform the index significantly. Managers who substantially underperform the index are highly vulnerable to termination. If they only marginally underperform the index, the clients may be inclined to tolerate another year or two of mediocre performance before taking action. The clients unfortunately end up paying active management fees and transaction costs for results that could be achieved mechanically at a substantially lower cost. A client with several active managers, all of whom overdiversify to track the index, is almost assured of underperforming an index fund after accounting for transaction costs and fees.

Skewness

Most performance measurement techniques assume implicitly that investment returns are approximately normally distributed. This assumption implies that the mean and variance of the return distribution are sufficient statistics to measure performance. Not all investment strategies, however, produce normal or even symmetric return distributions. By using derivative securities such as options or by using dynamic hedging strategies it is possible to produce return distributions that are skewed. When only mean and variance are used to compute measures of performance for these strategies the results can be misleading.

For example, alpha assumes that the returns of a portfolio are linearly related to the returns of the benchmark. A protective put option strategy, however, will produce a kinked relationship between the returns of a portfolio and the benchmark. The portfolio's return will be flat at the exercise price and linearly related to the benchmark returns above the exercise price. Beta will be estimated as the average of these two slopes, which *could* understate the true risk and thus overstate alpha.

This same result can be achieved without using options. A portfolio manager can replicate a protective put strategy by continually adjusting a portfolio's cash position in accordance with the hedge ratio from the option pricing formula. In general the portfolio manager would increase the cash position as the portfolio's price declined and decrease it as the portfolio's price increased. (See Chapter Six for a more detailed description of this strategy, which is referred to as *dynamic hedging*.)

Strategies such as these produce kinked payoff patterns that result in asymmetric (skewed) return distributions (see Chapter Five). These strategies can be used to game the traditional performance measurement techniques, since these techniques ignore the effect of skewness.

Risk Modification

Incentive fees also can be gamed easily. Consider the incentive fee described earlier, where the manager received a base fee when underperforming the benchmark and a base fee plus an incentive component when outperforming the benchmark. It was shown earlier that this particular incentive structure is tantamount to granting the portfolio manager a call option that could be valued by using a variation of the Black-Scholes option pricing model.

Since the value of the incentive component is determined in part by the net risk of the benchmark and the managed portfolio, portfolio managers can increase the value of their incentive components and the expected value of their fee income merely by increasing the net risk between the benchmark and the managed portfolio. They can increase risk in three ways: increase the standard deviation of a managed portfolio if it is above the benchmark's standard deviation, decrease it if it is below, or reduce the managed portfolio's correlation with the benchmark. At the same time, they can hedge away their risk by taking opposite positions in their other clients' portfolios or in their personal portfolios.

The gaming situations described above are intended to illustrate the vulnerability of performance measurement techniques that depend strictly on quantitative tools. Obviously there are many other ways by which performance measurement can be gamed; and even without gaming, performance measurement is a tenuous science at best.

CONCLUSION

Quantitative tools are a necessary component of performance measurement but by no means sufficient. The better we understand quantitative tools, including their limitations, the more effectively we will be able to apply them. Combined in proper balance with sound judgment, quantitative tools should enhance our ability to distinguish skillful managers from lucky managers.

PROBLEMS

1. Pension plan sponsors rely heavily on universe rankings to evaluate money managers. In fact it appears that sponsors implicitly assume

that managers who rank in the top quartile of a representative sample of peer managers are more likely to generate superior relative performance in the future than managers who rank in the bottom quartile. The validity of this assumption can be tested by regressing percentile rankings of managers in one period on their percentile rankings in the prior period.

If the implicit assumption of plan sponsors is true to the extent that there is perfect correlation in percentile rankings from one period to the next, what values would you expect to observe for the intercept, slope, and R-squared of the regression?

If there were no correlation in percentile rankings from period to period, what values would you expect to observe for the intercept, slope, and R-squared of the regression?

Upon performing such a regression, you determine the intercept to equal .51 and the slope to equal -0.05. Based on this regression, what is the best estimate of a manager's percentile ranking next period if this manager ranked at the 15th percentile (.15) this period?

	Intercept	Slope	R-Squared
Perfect correlation	0.0	1.0	1.0
No correlation	0.5	0.0	0.0

Best estimate of next period's ranking: .5025

$$.5025 = .51 - 0.05 \times .15$$

2. Suppose an index fund vendor at a presentation to the investment committee argues that a group of active managers is unlikely to add value to an index fund even if each individual active manager has a 65 percent chance of adding value. He reasons that the likelihood of two managers adding value equals 65 percent squared and that the likelihood of three managers adding value equals 65 percent raised to the third power, which is only 27 percent. Comment on this reasoning.

Answer: The index fund vendor is very confused. He is referring to the likelihood that every one of the managers will add value in his calculation. The relevant issue is whether or not the managers collectively will add value. Given that each individual manager has a greater than 50 percent chance of adding value and that their value added is mutually independent (based on the index fund vendor's implicit assumption) the probability that the group of managers will add value increases as more managers are added, rather than decreasing as suggested by the confused index fund manager.

A Statistical Primer

In this appendix we provide a nontechnical introduction to some of the more difficult statistical concepts used in the text: probability distributions, means and variances, special cases of normal and lognormal probability distributions, and applications to hypothesis tests. We illustrate how to read tables for the normal distribution and provide a useful numerical approximation. In addition we provide an introduction to logarithms and some simple applications in financial analysis.

PROBABILITY DISTRIBUTIONS

Much of the task of the quantitative analyst is to make the best possible decision in the context of uncertain or incomplete information. In many circumstances, a stock price move can be thought of as a flip of a coin. The analyst may conceive of scenarios in which XYZ common stock, currently trading at $100, could go up 30 percent or down 10 percent in the coming year. Because the analyst may not know with certainty which scenario will eventuate, the holding period return on his or her investment is referred to as a *random variable*. Suppose for argument's sake that the up or down move is equally likely. Then we say that the *probability* of an up move is .5. The collection of possible events, resulting random variables, and as-

TABLE A–1
Probability Distribution of Annual Holding Period Returns, Based on Scenarios of Terminal Value

Event	Terminal Value	Return	Probability
Up	$130	0.30	.50
Down	90	−.10	.50

sociated probabilities is referred to as a *probability distribution*. The probability distribution of holding period returns on XYZ common is given in Table A–1.

Of course the chance is fairly remote that XYZ common will trade at precisely $130 or $90 one year hence. But this may be the best that an analyst can accomplish, given the quality of available information. XYZ Corporation is in the petrochemical industry, so the scenarios for XYZ will depend on what happens to the price of oil. If we consider unexpected rises and falls in the price of oil in the coming year we can generate quite a large number of possible scenarios for XYZ. The probabilities associated with an up or down movement conditional on an unexpected rise in the price of oil are referred to as *conditional probabilities*. By multiplying the conditional probabilities with the probabilities of the conditioning variables (in this case, movements in the price of oil) we obtain the probability distribution for returns, considering the many possible oil price and stock market scenarios. In general the probability of an up movement will depend on what happens to the price of oil. In the special case where the probability of an up movement is unaffected by the conditioning variable (the price of oil), the two sources of uncertainty—oil prices and stock market factors—are said to be *independent*.

The assumption of independence is particularly useful in the context of option analysis (Chapter Five). Suppose that successive movements in the price of XYZ common are independent. Instead of considering annual changes in the value of XYZ, the analyst may consider an increase of 15 percent or a decline of 5 percent to be equally likely within any given six-month interval. By the end of the year, the stock may rise as high as $132.25 with two successive rises of 15 percent, or it could fall as low as $90.25 with two consecutive falls. Alternatively it could rise and fall, or first fall and then rise to $109.25 ($100 × 0.95 × 1.15). Each of these four scenarios is equally likely to occur. This gives rise to the probability distribution of returns given in Table A–2.

TABLE A–2
Probability Distribution of Annual Holding Period Returns, Based on Semiannual Return Scenarios

Event	Terminal Value	Return	Probability
Up, up	$132.25	0.3225	.25
Up, down or down, up	109.25	0.0925	.50
Down, down	90.25	− .0975	.25

Finally, we can extend the possible scenarios by considering hypothetical month-to-month moves. Suppose we allow XYZ common to rise one 12th of 30 percent, or 2.5 percent in any month, or to fall by .8333 percent. After some calculation the probability distribution of annual holding period returns will be as given in Table A–3.

TABLE A–3
Probability Distribution of Annual Holding Period Returns, Based on Monthly Return Scenarios

Terminal Value	Return	Probability
$134.49	0.3449	0.000244
130.12	0.3012	0.002929
125.88	0.2588	0.016113
121.79	0.2179	0.053710
117.82	0.1783	0.120849
114.00	0.1400	0.193359
110.29	0.1029	0.225585
106.70	0.0670	0.193359
103.23	0.0323	0.120849
99.88	− .0012	0.053710
96.63	− .0337	0.016113
93.49	− .0651	0.002929
90.45	− .0955	0.000244

Such probability distributions are represented graphically by plotting probability on the vertical axis and returns (realizations of the random variable) on the horizontal axis, as in Figure A–1.

The probability distributions dealt with so far and depicted in Tables A–

FIGURE A–1
Discrete Probability Distribution
(holding period return after one year)

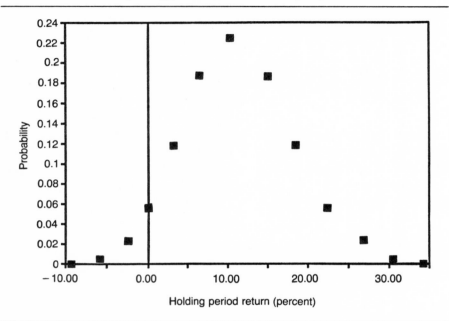

1 through A–3 and Figure A–1 are referred to as *discrete probability distributions,* since they consider only a finite, or discrete, number of possible scenarios. In the particular case considered here, where the scenarios are assumed to evolve much as a sequence of flips of a coin, the resulting discrete distribution is called a *binomial distribution.* As pointed out in Chapter Five and later chapters, this distribution has particular relevance in the context of pricing options and other contingent claims.

Of course it is possible to consider arbitrary increases in the number of possible scenarios by finer divisions of the return interval. With month-by-month return intervals we have 13 possible scenarios. Consideration of week-to-week returns yields 53 scenarios, and daily returns give rise to 366 scenarios of annual holding period return. The calculations reported in Table A–3 ignore the salient point that XYZ common trades only in eighths. This constraint imposes an obvious limit on the number of terminal value scenarios we may consider. However in many practical circumstances it is convenient to approximate the discrete distribution by another distribution obtained on the assumption that the number of possible scenarios is potentially infinite.

FIGURE A–2
Discrete and Continuous Probability Distributions
(holding period return after one year)

Such distributions are referred to as *continuous probability distributions.*
Figure A–2 shows how a continuous probability distribution of annual holding
period returns approximates the distribution obtained by considering month-
by-month return scenarios.

How does the introduction of infinitely many possible scenarios simplify
analysis? The answer is that we can use simpler calculations and tables to
obtain more precise answers to questions of interest. Figure A–3 illustrates
the problem that arises from the use of too few terminal value scenarios.
Suppose the analyst needs to know the probability that XYZ will yield a
zero or negative return over the annual holding period. It might seem that
all we have to do to answer this question is to refer to Table A–3 and add
up the probabilities associated with terminal values of $99.88, $96.63,
$93.49, and $90.45. This calculation, which yields 0.073 as the probability
of zero or negative return, is depicted graphically in Figure A–3. The shaded
area represents the sum of the four probabilities. However this figure also
reveals that using the discrete distribution to approximate the many possible
returns on XYZ common will overstate the probability of return less than
or equal to zero, since the probability associated with the $99.88 scenario

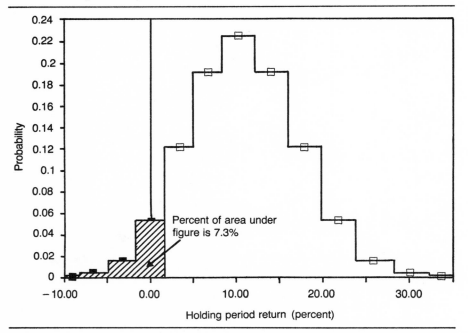

FIGURE A–3
Discrete Probability Distribution
(probability of return less than or equal to zero = .073)

in fact applies to returns in the range of − 1.7 percent to 1.5 percent. This picture, which associates probabilities with *ranges* of return, is referred to as a *histogram*.

A more precise answer to the question can be given by inspection of the associated continuous probability distribution given in Figure A–4, where the shaded area represents the sum of probabilities associated with very many small return intervals. This calculation yields the result that the probability of return less than or equal to zero is .044. The remaining questions are how to obtain the continuous distribution approximation and how to do the calculations that give rise to the .044 number. The two continuous distributions of greatest application in financial analysis, the *normal* and *lognormal* distributions are easy to obtain, since they require knowledge of at most two parameters, the *mean* and *variance* of returns. The calculations in question are in fact straightforward, since they are available in the form of tables or numerical approximations. The remainder of this appendix will review these concepts and discuss the two continuous distributions and how they are applied.

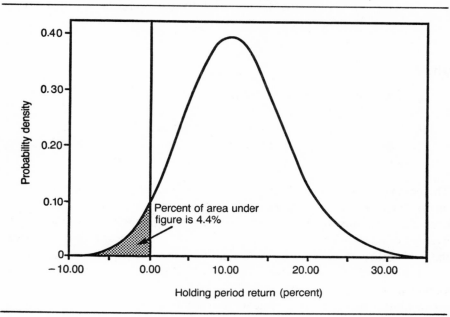

FIGURE A–4
Continuous Probability Distribution
(probability of return less than or equal to zero = .044)

Percent of area under figure is 4.4%

Holding period return (percent)

MEANS AND VARIANCES

A major characteristic of all probability distributions is the measure of central tendency referred to as the *mean*, or *expected value*. That single number represents all possible values of the random variable of interest. In the present example it would represent the best single measure of return over the annual holding period of the investment. The *variance* represents a measure of the extent to which returns can deviate from this measure of central tendency. As noted above, several important probability distributions are completely characterized once we know these two parameters.

The *mean*, or *expected value*, of a random variable is simply the weighted average of the variable taken over all possible scenarios. The weights are the probabilities of the different scenarios. In the Table A–3 example the mean annual holding period return is 10.47 percent, computed as follows:

$$\text{Mean return} = E(R) = (Pr_1 \times R_1) + (Pr_2 \times R_2) + \cdots$$
$$= (0.000244 \times 0.3449) + (0.002929 \times 0.3012)$$
$$+ (0.016113 \times 0.2588) + (0.053710 \times 0.2179)$$

$$+ (0.120849 \times 0.1783) + (0.193359 \times 0.1400)$$
$$+ (0.225585 \times 0.1029) + (0.193359 \times 0.0670)$$
$$+ (0.120849 \times 0.0323) + (0.053710 \times -.0012)$$
$$+ (0.016113 \times -.0337) + (0.002929 \times -.0651)$$
$$+ (0.000244 \times -.0955)$$
$$= 0.1047$$

where

R = Annual holding period return.

$E(R)$ = Expected value of return.

Pr_1 and Pr_2 = Probabilities of scenarios 1 and 2, respectively.

R_1 and R_2 = Annual holding period returns in the first and second scenarios.

The mean can be estimated on the basis of historical data, using the *sample mean*. Each past data point is considered a separate scenario, and each is considered equally likely. For that reason the sample mean is the simple average of past data values (by analogy with the mean return formula above, the probability of having observed each data point is equal).

The second important characteristic of any probability distribution is the *variance*, a measure of the dispersion of the random variable around the mean value. The mean value of deviations from the mean is zero by definition:

Mean deviation = $E[R - E(R)]$
$$= \{Pr_1 \times [R_1 - E(R)]\} + \{Pr_2 \times [R_2 - E(R)]\} + \cdots\cdot = 0$$

as can be verified from the formula itself or by numerical calculation using the previous example. A more meaningful measure is the mean deviation *squared*, which represents the measure of variance:

Variance = $E[R - E(R)]^2 = \{Pr_1 \times [R_1 - E(R)]^2\}$
$$+ \{Pr_2 \times [R_2 - E(R)]^2\} + \cdots\cdot$$
$$= [0.000244 \times (0.3449 - 0.1047)^2]$$
$$+ [0.002929 \times (0.3012 - 0.1047)^2]$$
$$+ [0.016113 \times (0.2588 - 0.1047)^2]$$
$$+ [0.053710 \times (0.2179 - 0.1047)^2]$$
$$+ [0.120849 \times (0.1783 - 0.1047)^2]$$
$$+ [0.193359 \times (0.1400 - 0.1047)^2]$$
$$+ [0.225585 \times (0.1029 - 0.1047)^2]$$
$$+ [0.193359 \times (0.0670 - 0.1047)^2]$$
$$+ [0.120849 \times (0.0323 - 0.1047)^2]$$

$$+ [0.053710 \times (-.0012 - 0.1047)^2]$$
$$+ [0.016113 \times (-.0337 - 0.1047)^2]$$
$$+ [0.002929 \times (-.0651 - 0.1047)^2]$$
$$+ [0.000244 \times (-.0955 - 0.1047)^2]$$
$$= 0.004007$$

Since variance is measured in units of the square of the random variable, it is common to take the square root of variance as the measure of dispersion. The square root of the variance of returns, referred to as the *standard deviation*, is thus measured in units of return:

$$\text{Standard deviation of return} = \sqrt{\text{Variance}} = \sqrt{.004007} = .0633$$

As was the case with the mean, the variance can be estimated using historical data. To compute the *sample variance*, first compute deviations by subtracting the sample mean from each data value; then square the deviation and take a simple average of those squared deviations.[1]

NORMAL AND LOGNORMAL DISTRIBUTIONS.

As noted before, the most generally useful of continuous distributions are the *normal* and *lognormal* distributions, which require knowledge of only two parameters, the mean and variance. The normal distribution arises naturally as the probability distribution of a cumulation or average of nearly independent random variables. In the context of financial analysis it represents the probability distribution of financial statement items that are themselves summaries of a large collection of data. It is also the probability distribution of return on a large portfolio of common stock after extraction of common or market factors of return. However, it is best thought of as a first approximation to any continuous probability distribution that is said to be symmetric. By *symmetry* we mean that any data value less than the mean value is as likely to occur as a data value the same amount greater than the mean. In graphical terms probability distributions such as those depicted in Figures A–1 through A–3 would be symmetric around a vertical line drawn through the highest point in the figure. This point is known as the *mode*.

---

[1]As noted in the text, purists take this average squared deviation by first computing the sum of squared deviations and dividing by a number that is one less than the number of deviations. The reason for this is that in subtracting off the sample mean, we are passing through the data once and for this reason lose one *degree of freedom*. The resulting correction yields an estimate of the variance that in a statistical sense is an *unbiased estimator*. Fortunately this correction is of little practical consequence and, as a result, is ignored in many popular business statistics software products.

For distributions that are symmetric in this fashion the mode is also the mean value.

From this discussion it is clear that the mean has a central role in defining this distribution. The mean is referred to as a *measure of location*. In addition to location, scale is also important: Do we measure returns as decimals or percents? The probability distribution should not be affected by how we choose to scale the random variable. One very natural scaling is the standard deviation mentioned above. To further explore the XYZ example we can ask the question "How far below the mean return does a return of zero percent lie?" The mean return is 10.47 percent, and the standard deviation is 6.33 percent. Thus zero return lies 1.65 standard deviations less than the mean.

Standardizing the random variable by subtracting the mean and expressing the resulting quantity in units of the standard deviation is a very basic statistical calculation. If the holding period return R has a normal distribution, the *standardized variable*

$$z = \frac{R - E(R)}{\text{Standard deviation of } R}$$

also has a normal distribution, but with mean zero and standard deviation one. The probability that the holding period return will be less than or equal to zero is the same as the probability that the standardized variable z will be less than or equal to -1.65. It would be very difficult to calculate this number directly, but fortunately the answer is available in many published tables. In the most common notation used in such tables,

$$N(-1.65) = \text{Probability } (z \leq 1.65) = .05$$

so that we say that there is a 5 percent probability that returns will be less than or equal to zero. Later in this Appendix we will discuss how to construct and read such tables.

The careful reader will note that this application presents a small difficulty. The probability distribution of returns depicted in Table A–3 is *not* symmetric. The largest possible return is 34.49 percent, realized with probability .000244. The difference between this value and the mean of 10.47 percent is 24.02 percent. The difference between the mean and the smallest return, realized with the same probability, is 20.02 percent. Extremely large values are more likely than extremely small values. In the language of statistics the probability distribution of returns is said to be *skewed*. The skewness becomes more marked as we move from 1 year to 5, 10, and longer holding periods of return. The normal probability distribution assumption, strictly speaking, does not apply to this example.

A Digression on Logarithms

To motivate the source of this skewness and to propose a practical remedy, we must introduce the concept of a *logarithm*. Before the advent of pocket calculators and personal computers the analyst had to be extremely comfortable with the concept and application of logarithms, either directly, through the use of tables, or indirectly, through the use of a slide rule calculator, which allowed difficult multiplication problems to be performed using simple addition. Compound interest calculations, if they were not tabulated directly, required the use of logarithms.

The basic idea of a logarithm is very simple. Suppose that one wished to multiply the number 10 by the number 100. Now we know that the answer is 1,000. We can write this calculation in two equivalent ways:

$$\text{Answer} = 10 \times 100 = 1,000$$

or

$$\text{Answer} = 10^1 \times 10^2 = 10^3 = 1,000$$

The answer 1,000 is equal to the number 10 raised to the power three. This power represents the sum of the powers of 10 that are being mulltiplied together. Take another example. Multiply two times four:

$$\text{Answer} = 2 \times 4 = 8$$

or

$$\text{Answer} = 10^{.3010} \times 10^{.6021} = 10^{.9031}$$

Again, the answer is equal to the number 10 raised to a power equal to the sum of the powers of 10 that are being multiplied together. The only difference now is that the powers are fractional powers (and can be computed using the y^x key available on most pocket calculators). If we tabulate a correspondence between any number and its corresponding power of 10, we have a way of performing multiplications and divisions using simple additions and subtractions. These tabulations are widely available and are referred to as *logarithms*. The number .3010 is said to be the *logarithm* to the base 10 of 2. The number .6021 is the logarithm to the base 10 of the number 4.

What might be a little mysterious in this example is the role of the number 10. Actually the choice of number to take the power of is somewhat arbitrary.

For general numerical work prior to the era of pocket calculators, the base 10 was most popular, since the logarithm to the base 10 of 10 is one, of 100 is two, of 1,000 is three, and so forth. It was easy to keep track of the units of 10, 100 and 1,000. However, since the advent of pocket calculators this type of logarithm is seldom used. In computer science the base 2 is often used. However, in financial mathematics the exponential constant e (2.718282) is most frequently used as a base because of its intimate relationship with continuous compounding. Powers of the exponential constant are available on most pocket calculators (look for e^x), and logarithms to the base e are often referred to as *natural logarithms*. So frequently is this type of logarithm used that the important qualifier "to the base of" is often omitted. Thus, when we read that "the logarithm of one plus return of 12.15 percent equals .11467" we understand this statement to mean

$$\text{One plus return} = 1.1215 = e^{.11467} = 2.718282^{.11467}$$

In technical reports one may also see this statement written:

$$\text{Natural logarithm of one plus return} = \ln(1.1215) = .11467$$

where the abbreviation ln refers to taking the natural logarithm of the quantity in parentheses.

To illustrate how the use of natural logarithms may be useful in financial analysis consider Figure A–5, which shows the growth (in yen) of the value of equities trading on the first section of the Tokyo stock exchange, from 1968 through 1989. In that figure we plot the natural logarithm of the value-weighted index TOPIX as a function of time. The natural logarithms are given on the right axis, while values of TOPIX itself can be found on the left.

Figures such as Figure A–5 are sometimes referred to as *ratio charts*, since a given percentage change is represented by a constant vertical difference in the figure.[2] Note that TOPIX doubles in value from 250 to 500 and from 500 to 1,000. Both differences are represented by the same vertical distance in the figure. A straight line in such a figure denotes a constant rate of growth in value. Thus we conclude from this figure that the recent strong performance of the Japanese equity markets is part of a steady pattern of growth over at least the past 20 years.

The compounding of value in TOPIX can be represented as a simple

---

[2]In fact this is the principle on which slide rule calculators are based. By lining up two ratio scales one can perform multiplications. Effectively one is adding together the logarithms on which the ratio scales are based.

FIGURE A–5
Tokyo Stock Market Performance
(January 4, 1968–April 20, 1989)

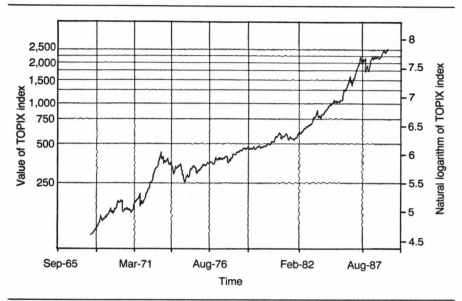

cumulation when expressed in terms of logarithms. This insight explains why the normal probability distribution may be a poor approximation of the probability distribution of holding period returns given in Table A–3. Recall that the normal probability distribution applies to cumulations or averages of nearly independent random variables. By assumption the month-to-month percentage changes in value may indeed be nearly independent. The problem arises because we are *compounding* rather than *cumulating* the month-to-month changes. To understand what difference this makes consider the one-year holding period value $134.49, calculated as follows:

$$\text{Holding period value} = \$100 \times (1 + .025) \times (1 + .025) \times \ldots$$
$$= \$100 \times (1 + .025)^{12}$$
$$= \$100 \times (1 + .3449) = \$134.49$$

and the quantity .3449 is the annual holding period return. One plus this number represents the *product* of one plus the monthly holding period returns. The logarithm of one plus .3449 is the *sum* of the logarithms of one plus the monthly holding period returns. Since this is the sum of independent random variables, it is the *logarithm* of one plus the annual holding period return that has a normal probability distribution.

From Table A–3 the mean and variance of the logarithm of one plus the annual holding period return are .0979 and .003279, respectively. The standard deviation is .0573. The logarithm of one plus zero return is itself zero, so the standardized variable is

$$\text{Standardized variable} = z = \frac{0.0 - .0979}{.0573} = -1.71$$

With this result we conclude that the probability that returns are less than or equal to zero is given by

$$N(-1.71) = \text{Probability} \, (z \le -1.71) = .044$$

which is slightly less than before. When as in this case the logarithm of a random variable follows a normal probability distribution, the random variable itself follows a *lognormal* probability distribution. It is actually this continuous probability distribution that is plotted in Figures A–2 and A–4.

It is very common to assume that one plus holding period returns follows a lognormal probability distribution, particularly in the context of option analysis. However, as this example illustrates, the practical significance of the difference between the lognormal and normal probability distributions is typically fairly slight for holding periods of less than one year. For holding periods of greater than one year the difference can be substantial. It is precisely this difference that motivates the use of geometric over arithmetic return measurements for performance measurement purposes.

Tables of the Normal Distribution

This discussion focuses attention on the need to obtain accurate numbers for the normal probability distribution. To continue the example above, suppose that the logarithm of one plus the holding period return is normal, with mean .0979 and standard deviation .0573. If the target return is zero, then the standardized variable is equal to -1.71, as above.

In order to find the probability that the realized return will be less than or equal to a return of zero we look up the value -1.71, in the normal distribution table (Table A–4). We read down the left column to -1.7 and across to the column under $-.01$. This value, .0436, equals the probability that the realized return will be less than or equal to the target return. One minus this value, .9564, equals the probability that the return will equal or exceed the target return.

TABLE A-4
Normal Distribution Table
(probability that standardized variable is less than z)

z	-.00	-.01	-.02	-.03	-.04	-.05	-.06	-.07	-.08	-.09
-3.0	.0013	.0013	.0013	.0012	.0012	.0011	.0011	.0011	.0010	.0010
-2.9	.0019	.0018	.0018	.0017	.0017	.0016	.0015	.0015	.0014	.0014
-2.8	.0026	.0025	.0024	.0023	.0023	.0022	.0021	.0021	.0020	.0019
-2.7	.0035	.0034	.0033	.0032	.0031	.0030	.0029	.0028	.0027	.0026
-2.6	.0047	.0045	.0044	.0043	.0041	.0040	.0039	.0038	.0037	.0036
-2.5	.0062	.0060	.0059	.0057	.0055	.0054	.0052	.0051	.0049	.0048
-2.4	.0082	.0080	.0078	.0075	.0073	.0071	.0069	.0068	.0066	.0064
-2.3	.0107	.0104	.0102	.0099	.0096	.0094	.0091	.0089	.0087	.0084
-2.2	.0139	.0136	.0132	.0129	.0125	.0122	.0119	.0116	.0113	.0110
-2.1	.0179	.0174	.0170	.0166	.0162	.0158	.0154	.0150	.0146	.0143
-2.0	.0228	.0222	.0217	.0212	.0207	.0202	.0197	.0192	.0188	.0183
-1.9	.0287	.0281	.0275	.0268	.0262	.0256	.0250	.0244	.0239	.0233
-1.8	.0359	.0351	.0344	.0336	.0329	.0322	.0314	.0307	.0300	.0294
-1.7	.0446	.0436	.0427	.0418	.0409	.0401	.0392	.0384	.0375	.0367
-1.6	.0548	.0537	.0526	.0516	.0505	.0495	.0485	.0475	.0465	.0455
-1.5	.0668	.0655	.0643	.0630	.0618	.0606	.0594	.0582	.0571	.0560
-1.4	.0808	.0793	.0778	.0764	.0750	.0735	.0721	.0708	.0694	.0681
-1.3	.0968	.0951	.0934	.0918	.0901	.0885	.0869	.0853	.0838	.0823
-1.2	.1151	.1131	.1112	.1093	.1075	.1056	.1038	.1020	.1003	.0985
-1.1	.1357	.1335	.1314	.1292	.1271	.1251	.1230	.1210	.1190	.1170
-1.0	.1587	.1562	.1539	.1515	.1492	.1469	.1446	.1423	.1401	.1379
-0.9	.1841	.1814	.1788	.1762	.1736	.1711	.1685	.1660	.1635	.1611
-0.8	.2119	.2090	.2061	.2033	.2005	.1977	.1949	.1921	.1894	.1867
-0.7	.2420	.2389	.2358	.2327	.2296	.2266	.2236	.2206	.2177	.2148
-0.6	.2743	.2709	.2676	.2643	.2611	.2578	.2546	.2514	.2483	.2451
-0.5	.3085	.3050	.3015	.2981	.2946	.2912	.2877	.2843	.2810	.2776
-0.4	.3446	.3400	.3372	.3336	.3300	.3264	.3228	.3192	.3156	.3121
-0.3	.3821	.3783	.3745	.3707	.3669	.3632	.3594	.3557	.3520	.3483
-0.2	.4207	.4168	.4129	.4090	.4052	.4013	.3974	.3936	.3897	.3859
-0.1	.4602	.4562	.4522	.4483	.4443	.4404	.4364	.4325	.4286	.4247
-0.0	.5000	.4960	.4920	.4880	.4840	.4801	.4761	.4721	.4681	.4641

TABLE A–4 (Continued)
Normal Distribution Table
(probability that standardized variable is less than z)

z	-.00	-.01	-.02	-.03	-.04	-.05	-.06	-.07	-.08	-.09
0.0	.5000	.5040	.5080	.5120	.5160	.5199	.5239	.5279	.5319	.5359
0.1	.5398	.5438	.5478	.5517	.5557	.5596	.5636	.5675	.5714	.5753
0.2	.5793	.5832	.5871	.5910	.5948	.5897	.6026	.6064	.6103	.6141
0.3	.6179	.6217	.6255	.6293	.6331	.6368	.6406	.6443	.6480	.6517
0.4	.6554	.6592	.6628	.6664	.6700	.6736	.6772	.6808	.6844	.6880
0.5	.6915	.6950	.6985	.7019	.7054	.7088	.7123	.7157	.7190	.7224
0.6	.7257	.7291	.7324	.7357	.7389	.7422	.7454	.7486	.7517	.7549
0.7	.7580	.7611	.7642	.7673	.7704	.7734	.7764	.7794	.7823	.7852
0.8	.7881	.7910	.7939	.7967	.7995	.8023	.8051	.8078	.8106	.8133
0.9	.8159	.8186	.8212	.8238	.8264	.8289	.8315	.8340	.8365	.8389
1.0	.8413	.8438	.8461	.8485	.8508	.8531	.8554	.8577	.8599	.8621
1.1	.8643	.8665	.8686	.8708	.8729	.8749	.8770	.8790	.8810	.8830
1.2	.8849	.8870	.8888	.8907	.8925	.8944	.8962	.8980	.8997	.9015
1.3	.9032	.9049	.9066	.9082	.9099	.9115	.9131	.9147	.9162	.9177
1.4	.9192	.9207	.9222	.9236	.9251	.9265	.9279	.9292	.9306	.9319
1.5	.9332	.9345	.9357	.9370	.9382	.9394	.9406	.9418	.9429	.9441
1.6	.9452	.9463	.9474	.9484	.9495	.9505	.9515	.9525	.9535	.9545
1.7	.9554	.9564	.9573	.9582	.9591	.9599	.9608	.9616	.9625	.9633
1.8	.9641	.9649	.9656	.9664	.9671	.9678	.9686	.9693	.9700	.9706
1.9	.9713	.9719	.9726	.9732	.9738	.9744	.9750	.9756	.9761	.9767
2.0	.9772	.9778	.9783	.9788	.9793	.9798	.9803	.9808	.9812	.9817
2.1	.9821	.9826	.9830	.9834	.9838	.9842	.9846	.9850	.9854	.9857
2.2	.9861	.9864	.9868	.9871	.9875	.9878	.9881	.9884	.9887	.9890
2.3	.9893	.9896	.9898	.9901	.9904	.9906	.9909	.9911	.9913	.9916
2.4	.9918	.9920	.9922	.9925	.9927	.9929	.9931	.9932	.9934	.9936
2.5	.9938	.9940	.9941	.9943	.9945	.9946	.9948	.9949	.9951	.9952
2.6	.9953	.9955	.9956	.9957	.9959	.9960	.9961	.9962	.9963	.9964
2.7	.9965	.9966	.9967	.9968	.9969	.9970	.9971	.9972	.9973	.9974
2.8	.9974	.9975	.9976	.9977	.9977	.9978	.9979	.9979	.9980	.9981
2.9	.9981	.9982	.9982	.9983	.9984	.9984	.9985	.9985	.9986	.9987
3.0	.9987	.9987	.9987	.9988	.9988	.9989	.9989	.9989	.9990	.9990

As an alternative to a normal distribution table, several algorithms can be used to find the area under a curve that corresponds to a particular z value. These algorithms are useful in that they can easily be incorporated into spreadsheet software. We present one such algorithm here.

Let z' equal the absolute value of z. Let r equal

$$1 + z' \times (C_1 + z' \times [C_2 + z' \times (C_3 + z'$$
$$\times [C_4 + z' \times (C_5 + z' \times C_6)])])$$

where

$C_1 = .049867347$ $C_4 = .0000380036$
$C_2 = .0211410061$ $C_5 = .0000488906$
$C_3 = .0032776263$ $C_6 = .000005383$

Let P (probability that target return will equal or exceed expected return) equal $.5 \times e^{[\ln(r) \times (-16)]}$

$$\text{If } z \leq 0, P = 1 - P$$

To demonstrate this algorithm, suppose that $z = -.15$. If we substitute this value into our equation for r we find that r equals .9929845242.

$r = 1 + .15 \times (.049867347 + .15 \times [.0211410061 + .15 \times (.0032776263$
    $+ .15 \times [.0000380036 + .15 \times (.0000488906 + .15 \times [.000005383])])])$
    $= .9929845242$

If we substitute r into our equation for P we find that P equals .440383, since z is less than 0:

$$P = .5 \times e^{[\ln(.9929845242) \times (-16)]} = .559617$$
$$= 1 - .559617 = .440383$$

Note that the value corresponding to $-.15$ in the normal distribution table equals .4404.

HYPOTHESIS TESTS

One important application of probability distributions in financial analysis is *hypothesis tests.* You have gathered historical data on XYZ Corporation dating back nine years and have computed the sample mean and variance of return to be .10 and .0036, respectively. While the sample mean is positive, nine years of historical data is not very much information on which to be certain that the expected holding period return is positive looking forward into the coming year. Statisticians have traditionally addressed this issue through the mechanism of *hypothesis tests*.

The convention is to set up a straw man, identified as the *null hypothesis* (frequently abbreviated H_O), which we hope the data will refute. In the present instance the null hypothesis is that the mean return is zero. Under this hypothesis a sample mean return of positive 10 percent may be perfectly reasonable, given that equity returns are somewhat variable and that nine years is simply too short a time to get an adequate fix on the distribution of returns. The alternative, referred to as an *alternative hypothesis* (abbreviated as H_A), is that the mean return is in fact positive. In summary these statements read:

> Null hypothesis H_O: Mean return $= 0$.
>
> Alternative hypothesis H_A: Mean return > 0.

If the mean return is in fact zero and the variance of returns is .0036, then it is possible to infer whether the sample mean of 10 percent is higher than we would expect in the normal course of events. If the sample mean is higher than some defined *critical value*, then we say we reject the null hypothesis in favor of the alternative. To define this critical value we must determine the probability distribution of the sample mean.

The sample mean represents the cumulation of nine annual holding period returns. If these returns are very nearly independent, then the probability distribution of the sample mean will approximate a normal distribution. Under the null hypothesis the mean of this normal distribution will be zero, with variance equal to the variance of returns *divided by* the number of returns used to compute the sample mean, which in this case is nine. The square root of this variance is referred to as the *standard error* of the sample mean, to avoid confusing it with the standard deviation of the data. Clearly, as the number of returns increases, the sample mean becomes an increasingly precise estimate of the true mean, and the variance of the sample mean goes down to zero. We thus standardize the sample mean to obtain a *test statistic, t*.

Test statistic $t =$ (Sample mean $- 0.0$) $\div$ Standard error of the sample mean

$$= (.10 - 0.0) \div \sqrt{\left(\frac{.0036}{9}\right)}$$

$$= .10 \div .02 = 5.0$$

We can establish a critical value of this test statistic by referring to the tables for the normal distribution.[3] Suppose we establish as the bounds of reasonable variation that the critical value should be exceeded only 5 percent of the time. This number is referred to as the *significance level* of the test. From the tables we see that the critical value is 1.65 since

$$\text{Probability } (t > 1.65) = 1. - \text{Probability } (t \leq 1.65)$$
$$= 1. - N(1.65)$$
$$= .05$$

Since in the example $t = 5.0$, which is greater than the critical value, we say we *reject* the null hypothesis. In plain English, we accept the hypothesis that the true mean return is positive.

This formalism may appear a little excessive. Once we see that the value of the test statistic is very large it is obvious that we are going to reject the null hypothesis. This intuition is quite accurate. The importance of the formalism is to state in very precise language the hypothesis we wish to examine. For example, in a regression analysis setting we may be interested in the question of whether a particular factor has any influence whatsoever on a variable of interest. This influence is defined by a *regression coefficient*. In this case the null hypothesis is that the factor has no influence, against an alternative that it does:

Null hypothesis H_O: Regression coefficient $= 0$.

Alternative hypothesis H_A: Regression coefficient $\neq 0$.

This is referred to as a *two-tailed test,* as opposed to the *one-tailed test* introduced before. If the test statistic is distributed as approximately normal,[4] we can refer to the normal probability distribution tables to determine that

---

[3]Where we have to estimate the variance of the data along with the mean, the distribution of the test statistic will not be normal, but student-t instead. The normal distribution will be a reasonable approximation and almost exact for more than 30 observations. Because of this and other slight ambiguities in the definition of critical values it is interesting to note that the Supreme Court of the United States has stated (in the context of discrimination suits) that in statistical evidence presented to the federal courts, critical values should exceed "two or three standard deviations from the mean" (*Hazelwood School District* v. *United States* 433 U.S. 299 [1977]). This erring on the side of conservatism is very healthy and recognizes the fact that our statistical theory is at best an approximation to reality.

[4]See previous footnote.

$$\text{Probability } (t > 1.96 \text{ or } t \leq 1.96) = 2 \times \text{Probability } (t \leq -1.96)$$
$$= 2 \times N(-1.96)$$
$$= 2 \times .025 = .05$$

Thus, when the significance level of the test is .05 as before, we reject the null hypothesis that the factor has no influence when the *absolute value* of the test statistic exceeds 1.96.

Glossary

A

Alpha A measure of risk-adjusted return that represents that part of return typically attributed to investment skill. Mathematically, alpha equals (Portfolio return − Risk-free rate) − [Beta × (Market return − Risk-free rate)].

Alternative hypothesis A hypothesis that, if true, indicates that a result is statistically significant. For example, tests of market efficiency have as a null hypothesis that an investment strategy's alpha equals zero. The alternative hypothesis is that alpha is significantly different from zero.

American option The right to buy (call) or sell (put) an asset at a prespecified price for a prespecified period of time, as distinct from a European option, which can only be exercised at expiration.

Annuity An arrangement whereby the recipient receives a prespecified payment annually for a prespecified number of years.

Anomaly The notion that risk-adjusted returns are associated with attributes such as yield or size or with time periods such as the turn of the year or weekends.

Arbitrage A process whereby profits are earned by exchanging assets without incurring risk. For example, an arbitrageur would buy futures when they sell at a discount, and sell short the underlying asset. At expiration their prices would be equal so that the arbitrageur could realize the initial spread by receiving the cash for the futures contracts and with the proceeds cover his or her short position and still realize a profit.

B

Basis The difference in price between a futures contract and the underlying asset.

Basis risk The volatility of the basis as measured by its standard deviation.

Bayesian estimation The introduction of subjective probability concepts in decision rules that are used under conditions of uncertainty.

Beta A measure of an asset's sensitivity to an underlying index or factor. For example, an asset with a beta of 1.2 would be expected to return 12 percent if the market returned 10 percent and − 12 percent if the market returned − 10 percent. Beta is computed as an asset's correlation with the index times the ratio of the asset's standard deviation to the index's standard deviation. In certain applications, excess return (relative to the risk free rate) is used.

Bimodal A distribution of outcomes is bimodal if it has two modes. The mode is the value that occurs most often.

Binomial option pricing model (BOPM) A valuation model for options that assumes that changes in asset prices follow a binomial distribution in that prices can only increase or decrease by certain specified amounts, with certain probability. The value of the option is computed by beginning with the values at the end of the binomial tree and working backward to solve for the option's value at the beginning of the binomial tree. This model assumes that prices change discreetly rather than continuously and that an asset's value can only move up or down in the next period.

Black-Scholes option pricing model (BSOPM) A valuation model for options that assumes that asset prices change continuously and that investors cannot earn arbitrage profits. According to the Black-Scholes model the value of an option depends on the price of the underlying asset, the exercise price, the risk-free return, the time to expiration, and the standard deviation of the

underlying asset. Importantly, the expected return of the underlying asset is not relevant.

Boxplot A graph that shows the median, the interquartile range, 5th and 95th percentiles, and the outliers of a distribution. It is more descriptive than a histogram because it shows the skewness of a distribution.

Buy and hold A strategy whereby an asset mix is bought and left unchanged throughout the investment horizon. It is not rebalanced to the initial mix. Buy and hold strategies are represented by straight-line payoff functions.

C

Call option A contract that gives the owner the right but not the obligation to purchase an asset at a prespecified exercise price for a prespecified period of time.

Capital asset pricing model (CAPM) A model of asset pricing that assumes that the expected risk premium of an asset (expected return less the return on some riskless asset) is proportional to its systematic risk (beta). The model assumes that a capitalization-weighted index of all assets is the benchmark against which systematic risk is measured. A corollary of the CAPM is that asset-specific risk is uncompensated and should be diversified away.

Capitalization rate In real estate valuation the rate used to discount future cash flows to estimate a property's present value.

Central tendency In a distribution of data, that single value that is chosen to represent all of the data. It is usually represented by the mean value (average), the median value (value for which half the observations are above/below it), or the mode (value that occurs most frequently).

Closet indexing The practice by active investment managers of surreptitiously mimicking an index so as not to chance underperforming an index significantly. This deceptive practice assumes that clients typically keep mediocre managers for a long time and fire managers who, by incurring a lot of risk, underperform an index by a wide margin over a short measurement period.

Cluster analysis A method of grouping variables according to how closely they correlate in terms of important attributes. A major application in financial analysis is to determine economic or industry sectors on the basis of return correlations.

Coefficient of variation The ratio of standard deviation to sample mean, this quantity is a method for scaling the standard deviation to allow the analyst to compare different measures of dispersion. The reciprocal of the coefficient of variation of fund risk premiums is known as the *Sharpe measure*.

Concave payoff function A payoff that increases at a decreasing rate with the value of an underlying risky asset. Strategies that buy low and sell high, such as rebalancing strategies, produce concave payoff functions.

Continuously compounded return Refers to a rate of return calculation that assumes an investment's return is reinvested at the same rate at every point in time. The realized return in the limit is computed by raising the mathematical constant e (2.718) to the power of the simple return and subtracting 1. Also, $1 invested at an annual rate of 100 percent and compounded continuously will grow to $2.718 in one year.

Convex payoff function A payoff that increases at an increasing rate with the

value of an underlying risky asset. Strategies that buy high and sell low, such as portfolio insurance, produce convex payoff functions.

Convexity The second derivative of the price of a bond with respect to changes in interest rate. Duration is the first derivative and measures how a bond's price changes as interest rates change. However, this relationship is nonlinear since duration also changes as interest rates change. Convexity captures the change in duration with respect to changes in interest rates. The more dispersed a bond's cash flows, the more convex it is and the more its duration will change, given a change in interest rates.

Correlation coefficient A measure (ranging in value from 1.00 to -1.00) of the association between a dependent variable and one or more independent variables. A correlation coefficient is a measure not necessarily of causality but rather of the strength of a relationship. A correlation coefficient of 1.00 implies that the variables move perfectly in lockstep; a correlation coefficient of -1.00 implies that they move inversely in lockstep; and a correlationship of 0.00 implies that the variables as calibrated are uncorrelated.

Correlation matrix A matrix whose rows represent the same variables as its columns and whose elements represent the correlation coefficients for each pair of variables.

Covariance A measure of the extent to which a pair of variables moves together. It is computed as the average distance from the mean of one variable times the average distance from the mean of the other variable.

Cross-sectional regression A regression analysis where the observations are measured as of the same point in time or over the same time period but differ according to another dimension. For example an analyst may regress differences in stock returns measured in the same period for different companies with differences in the companies' yields for the same period.

D

Dedication   A fixed-income management strategy designed to insulate a portfolio from interest rate changes by matching the securities' cash flows to the cash flows associated with a stream of liabilities.

Degrees of freedom   In statistical inference the size of the sample from which the parameters are estimated minus the number of parameters estimated.

Derivative security   A security whose value is derived from the value of the underlying asset, such as an option or a futures contract. Derivative securities do not create wealth, but provide the crucial service of facilitating the transfer of risk from hedgers to speculators.

Discount bond   A bond whose price is below par value because interest rates for bonds of the same quality and duration are above the rate that prevailed when the discount bond was valued at par. The discount in the bond's price compensates for the fact that an investor can receive a higher coupon from a bond valued at par.

Discount rate   The rate of interest that is used to discount a stream of cash flows to a present value.

Discriminant function   A linear function that uses the observed correlation structure to determine into which of several possible classifications a particular item belongs. It can, for example, be used to determine whether a particular security falls into the classification of firms likely to be subject to financial distress.

Dispersion, measures of   Values that summarize the extent to which the observations of a sample differ from the sample's value of central tendency. The standard deviation, which is the square root of the average of the squared differences between the observations and average of all observations, is the most common measure of dispersion. For certain distributions, such as the normal distribution, the mean and standard deviation are sufficient to characterize the entire distribution.

Diversification   The practice of holding a large number of assets in a portfolio so as to reduce the portfolio's sensitivity to an individual asset's return. Diversification differs from hedging in that it reduces sensitivity to specific risk whereas hedging reduces sensitivity to systematic risk.

Dividend discount model   A valuation model for common stock that assumes that the present value of a stock is equal to the discounted value of its future stream of dividends. Since it is impossible to estimate each future dividend payment individually, the dividend discount model is often abbreviated such that a stock's present value is estimated as its current dividend divided by the difference between its required return and the growth rate of its dividends. Also called the dividend growth model.

Dollar-weighted rate of return   A portfolio's internal rate of return. This measure of portfolio return is considered deficient for purposes of performance measurement, because it is influenced by the timing and magnitude of contributions and disbursements that are beyond the control of the portfolio manager.

Dummy variable   In regression analysis a variable used to indicate whether or not an observation has a certain characteristic but nothing about the degree to which it has such a characteristic. For example the effect of industry membership can be tested by assigning a value of one to companies in a particular industry and zero to companies not in the industry.

Duration   The average time to receipt of cash flows weighted by their present values. It measures the sensitivity of a bond's price to a change in interest rates, and it is computed as the first derivative of bond price with respect to interest rates.

Durbin-Watson statistic   A measure of the extent to which the residuals from a regression analysis are correlated with each other. The value of the Durbin-Watson statistic ranges from zero to four, and a value of two indicates that there is no first-degree autocorrelation. If too much autocorrelation is present the regression is misspecified, and the results are specious. With economic and financial time series, it is often useful to transform the data to percent changes or first differences to reduce autocorrelation.

Dynamic hedging   An investment strategy that calls for a fund's mix between a risky and a riskless asset to be revised continually so as to ensure that the fund will not fall below a prespecified floor value if the risky asset declines and that it will participate to some extent in the risky asset's appreciation should it rise in value. A popular version of dynamic hedging is a strategy that replicates a protective put option strategy by following the hedge ratio implied by the option pricing formula.

E

e   The mathematical constant equal to 2.718282 that is the value of $1 compounded continuously for one year at a rate of 100 percent. *e* is used to compute a continuously compounded

return by raising its value to the power of the simple return and subtracting 1.

Efficient frontier   A continuum of portfolios plotted in expected return and standard deviation dimensions with the characteristic that no portfolio not part of the efficient frontier has a higher expected return for a given level of risk.

Estimation error   The difference between the parameters of a theoretical distribution and the values that are used as estimates of the parameters.

Estimation risk   The extent to which the uncertainty of a distribution increases by virtue of using estimates of the true values as opposed to the true parameter values (which obviously are not known). It is useful to adjust the results of statistical analysis to account for estimation risk.

European option   The right to buy (call) or sell (put) an asset at a prespecified price at a prespecified expiration date, as distinct from an American option, which can be exercised at any time up to its expiration date.

Exercise price   A prespecified price at which an asset can be bought (call) or sold (put) by the owner of an option. It is also referred to as the strike price.

Expected return   The geometric rate of return the holder of an asset expects to receive over a particular holding period. It is often estimated from the asset's historical rates of return.

F

Factor analysis   A statistical technique for uncovering common sources of variability in data. For example, factor analysis is often used to uncover the underlying factors in security returns. It is limited, however, in that the factors are statistical constructs and are not easily associated with economic or financial variables.

Factor loading The exposure of a security to a particular factor. The extent to which a security's return is conditioned on the value of a particular factor. The coefficient in an equation where a security's return equals a linear combination of one or more factors.

Factor sensitivity Factor loading.

Fitted values In regression analysis, values of the dependent variable as defined by the linear function estimated using regression analysis. They are used to provide forecasted values.

Forward rate The future interest rate implied by the current term structure of interest rates. For example, if a one-year instrument has a rate of 6 percent and a two-year instrument has a rate of 8 percent, an investor expects to be able to purchase a one-year instrument today and a one-year instrument one year from today such that his compound return over the two-year period would equal the current rate on the two-year instrument. Thus the forward rate on a one-year instrument equals $(1.08) \times (1.08)/(1.06) - 1 = 10.04$ percent.

Future value The value of an investment at a future date, computed by compounding forward its present value and interim cash flows at the prevailing rate of interest.

Futures contract A contract that has uniform terms concerning price, quantity, and expiration and that obligates the seller to pay the value of the contract to the buyer at a prespecified date.

F-value A measure of the significance of all of the coefficients in a regression analysis. A sufficiently large F-value, given the degrees of freedom, indicates that one can reject the hypothesis that all of the regression coefficients equal zero. In other words the coefficients collectively are significant.

G

Geometric rate of return A measure of return that, controlling for cash flows, reflects the actual change in an asset's value. For example, if an asset increases 100 percent and then decreases 50 percent, its geometric return equals $[(1 + 1.00) \times (1 - .50)] - 1 = 0$ percent. Thus if you started with $100 you would end up with $100. The arithmetic average return, however, is $(1.00 - .50) \div 2 = 25$ percent, which does not reflect the actual change in the asset's value.

H

Hedge ratio In dynamic hedging, the percentage of a fund that is allocated to the risky asset at a given point in time so as to ensure that the fund's value will not fall below a prespecified value. In option valuation the number of stocks that would have to be purchased to cover each call that is written, in order to be insulated from changes in the value of the stock.

Heteroscedasticity In regression analysis a situation where the value of the residuals changes from observation to observation systematically through time or as a function of values of the independent variables. Heteroscedasticity indicates that the regression equation is misspecified and that extrapolation is dangerous since the extrapolated values are more prone to error than the fitted values.

Histogram A graph in the form of a bar chart that shows the distribution of a sample of data points. Typically each bar represents a range of values for the data points, which is indicated by the horizontal axis. The vertical axis represents the frequency of data falling within the indicated range.

Hypothesis test In statistical inference a test that is used to determine whether or not a result is significant for a given level of confidence. For example an hypothesis test can be used to determine if an investment return is significantly different from the return of a performance benchmark, such as the Standard & Poor's 500 Index. The null hypothesis is that the relative return is zero; the alternative hypothesis is that it is significantly different from zero. The null hypothesis can be rejected and the alternative hypothesis accepted if the ratio of the relative return to the relative risk is sufficiently high, given the required level of confidence.

I

Idiosyncratic component of return   That part of an asset's return that cannot be explained by exposure to some pervasive factor. It is attributable to a factor or factors unique to a particular company. In a linear model of return, the error term. Also called *nonsystematic* component of return.

Immunization   A fixed-income investment strategy designed to insulate a portfolio from changes in interest rates by controlling its duration and/or cash flows. A portfolio is approximately immunized from interest rate changes for a given time period if its duration is set equal to the length of the time period. This strategy locks in the portfolio's yield to maturity at the beginning of the time period because, if interest rates rise, declines in price are offset by higher reinvestment rates and vice versa. A portfolio is also immunized relative to a stream of liabilities if its cash flows are matched (dedicated) to the liability stream.

Implied variance   The variance of an asset implied by the price at which an option on that asset trades. Since the value of an option depends on the price

of the underlying asset, the exercise price, the time to expiration, the risk-free return, and the variance of the underlying asset and since all of the values except variance are known values, the variance can be inferred from the price at which the option trades. The implied value for the variance is solved for iteratively.

Index fund   A passive investment strategy designed to mimic the performance of a particular index. This strategy provides efficient diversification at a low cost, since transactions occur only to invest dividends and cash flows and since management fees are minimal. Moreover the performance of index funds over most extended measurement periods is superior to the performance of the average actively managed fund.

Initial margin   Funds that must be deposited with a broker (as a form of insurance) to commence a futures transaction.

Internal rate of return (IRR)   The rate of return that discounts a stream of cash flows back to a present value. In performance measurement the dollar-weighted rate of return.

Interquartile range   A range, containing half the data, that is the difference between the value for which 25 percent of the data are smaller and the value for which 25 percent of the data are larger. This measure of dispersion has the advantage of being less sensitive to outliers in the data than are other measures of dispersion.

L

Logarithmic transformation   The conversion of values to their logarithms, usually so that equal percentage changes have equal status. For example, in regressions that attempt to explain differences in security returns by differences in capitalization, capitalization is usually converted to its logarithm.

M

Market model   A model of security returns introduced by William Sharpe that assumes that differences in security returns can be explained only by differences in their exposure to the market portfolio return. This model implies that idiosyncratic risk is uncompensated and should be diversified away.

Mean absolute deviation (MAD)   The average value of differences from the mean, where the differences are evaluated without regard to sign. The MAD is a measure of dispersion.

Mean reversion   The notion that asset values revert to an average value or to an equilibrium value. Thus if an asset's price is above its equilibrium value the presumption of mean reversion is that the asset's price will eventually decline to its equilibrium value, while if its price is below its equilibrium value the presumption is that the asset's price will eventually rise to its equilibrium value.

Median   The middle value of a set of data, where the data are ranked from smallest to largest. The median is a measure of central tendency: one number chosen to represent the entire distribution of the data.

Mode   The most common number in a range of data. The modal range is that equally spaced range of the data in which most observations occur. Like the sample mean and median the mode is a measure of central tendency.

Multicollinearity   The tendency of independent variables in regression analysis to be correlated with each other. While the presence of such correlation does not affect the interpretation of

estimated regression coefficients, it does affect the interpretation of hypothesis tests based on t-values of the estimated coefficients.

Multifactor models   Models of the return-generating process where returns of individual securities are related to each other only to the extent that they are all related to a greater or lesser degree to a finite set of (more than one) common factors.

Multiple regression analysis   Regression analysis that estimates the linear relationship between a dependent variable and more than one independent variable.

N

Naked option strategies   The writing or issuance of options not covered by offsetting positions in other options or the underlying security.

Net cost of carry   In valuing a financial futures contract, the interest cost associated with purchasing the underlying asset on margin less the income associated with the underlying asset.

Net operating income   In the context of real estate analysis, rental and nonrental income (gross potential income) less an allowance for vacancy and other losses for operating expenses such as payroll and real estate taxes, and is net of extraordinary items.

Net present value   The present value of cash inflows *less* the present value of cash outflows resulting from establishing a position in a particular security.

Nonparametric performance measurement   Measures of forecasting ability that depend not on the ability to predict the magnitude of market changes but on the direction of such changes.

Nonsystematic component of returns   That part of return that cannot be explained by the single- or multifactor model of returns. Such components of return can be diversified away in a sufficiently large and well-diversified portfolio. Also called *idiosyncratic* component of return.

Normal portfolio A portfolio that is used as a benchmark for the performance of a particular money manager and that matches the risk attributable to the manager's style. Such a comparison provides a measure of his or her discretionary investment decisions.

Null hypothesis The maintained hypothesis in statistical hypothesis testing against which the sample data are compared to determine whether the maintained hypothesis may be accepted or rejected.

O

One-sided (or -tailed) tests Hypothesis tests in which the alternative to the null hypothesis maintains that not only is the parameter of interest different from that specified by the null hypothesis, but also that this difference has a particular sign.

Optimal portfolio The portfolio choice that leads to the greatest expected utility (highest preference curve in mean-standard deviation space), given the initial wealth of the investor.

Options Contracts that give the holder the right (not obligation) to buy or sell a particular asset at a specified exercise price within a set time period.

Outliers Data values that are extreme relative to the other data. Many statistical procedures are sensitive to such values. They may represent errors in the data. For this reason many statisticians simply exclude them from consideration, either literally (trimmed means and standard deviations) or effectively, by considering medians and other measures that neglect

the magnitude of such numbers. On the other hand they may reflect excluded factors that need to be accounted for.

P

Payoff diagram A two-dimensional diagram in which the horizontal axis represents the terminal value of a risky asset and the vertical axis represents the terminal value of alternative strategies involving allocation between a risky asset and a riskless asset or alternative option strategies.

Payoff function Within the context of a payoff diagram, a line that relates the terminal value of a particular asset allocation strategy between a risky and a riskless asset or a particular option strategy to the terminal value of the risky asset.

Percentiles Measures of the distribution of the data (returns in the context of performance measurement) given by ranking the data from lowest to highest, where the percentile of a given number is the percentage of other numbers that are less than that number. For example the median is the 50th percentile since half the data are less than the median and half are greater than or equal to it. The interquartile range is the difference between the 25th and 75th percentile, a range that includes 50 percent of the data.

Perpetuity formula A simplification of the present value formula given by the cash flow divided by the relevant discount rate. This formula applies where the periodic cash flow will remain the same in perpetuity and the rate used to discount each cash flow is the same.

Portfolio The aggregation of all assets held by an investor.

Portfolio insurance A technique involving continual rebalancing of a portfolio between a risky component and a riskless component that is meant to insure that the terminal value of the portfolio will not fall below some prespecified target value.

Portfolio weights The percentage weights by value of each asset in a portfolio, measured at the start of a particular holding period.

Preference curve: In portfolio theory, the curve that represents the set of hypothetical combinations of expected return and risk measured by standard deviation, that the investor would be indifferent among. Given certain assumptions relating to the distribution of asset returns and investor preferences, an alternative that has a lower standard deviation for the same mean, or higher mean return for the same standard deviation, is said to lie on a higher preference curve. The optimal portfolio is that portfolio whose return and risk lie on the highest possible preference curve.

Present value The sum of all discounted cash flows resulting from a particular investment. It represents the quantity of money that would be required to *exactly* duplicate the cash flows of a particular investment when invested to yield the prevailing return on investments of similar risk. Each discount factor is given by the reciprocal of one plus the discount rate for that cash flow raised to the power given by the period of time the investor has to wait before receiving the cash flow.

Price-earnings ratio (P/E) model Used in equity valuation, a simple variant of the dividend discount model that relates the price-earnings ratio to the payout ratio (one minus the retention ratio of earnings) divided by the appropriate discount rate less the rate at which earnings are expected to grow. This is nothing more than the present value formula, where the cash flows (dividends

received by the investor) are assumed to grow at the rate of growth of earnings for the foreseeable future.

Principal components analysis A relatively simple and mechanical procedure for obtaining statistical measures of factors to use in a multifactor model of security returns. Available in many statistical software computer packages, it operates by constructing one factor that explains the greater part of historical return variability. It then defines a second factor, unrelated to the first, that explains the next greatest amount of variability. The third and successive factors are defined in an analogous fashion.

Probability mass A technical term that describes the probability of observing a return (or other variable) equal to a certain value. In the context of option analysis it is the probability of observing an option value equal to the exercise value. In other words it is the probability of exercise.

Protective put A put option purchased on a security already held by an investor. It represents an insurance policy that guarantees that the value of the investment will not fall below the exercise value of the option.

Put option The right (not obligation) to sell a given security or portfolio of securities at a specified exercise price within a fixed time period.

Put-call parity A condition that describes the essential relationship that must exist between put and call options. Since a protective put (put option plus stock) has the same cash flow consequences as a call option plus cash invested at the riskless rate to yield an amount equal to the exercise value of the put, the put option must be worth the call value *less* the stock value *plus* the present value of the exercise price.

R

Range The difference between the smallest and largest value observed in a given set of data.

Rate of return The increment of value plus income received on an investment over a particular holding period, expressed as a fraction of the value measured at the start of the holding period.

Real estate market index (REMI) An index or proxy that attempts to measure vacancy rates through time by geographic market area and by structure type.

Regression analysis A method of statistical analysis that attempts to explain observed variability in a quantity of interest (referred to as the dependent variable) as a linear function of other variables (referred to as independent variables) plus some zero mean error. The market model may be estimated by this form of analysis: the return on the asset is the dependent variable while the independent variable is the return on the market. In this example the linear coefficient estimated by regression analysis is the beta.

Regression line The linear relationship estimated by means of regression analysis.

Reinvestment risk The risk that arises in the context of fixed-income analysis because the rate of return at which future coupon payments may be invested is uncertain at the time the fixed-income security is acquired.

Residual errors Those errors not explained by the linear relationship estimated using regression analysis.

Reversion A synonym for future value, used in real estate analysis.

Risk premium The return over and above the riskless return investors expect as a compensation for the risk they bear in holding a particular investment.

Run In a time series, an uninterrupted sequence of positive values or negative values or an uninterrupted sequence of values above the mean or below the mean.

S

Sample mean The simple average given as the sum of a set of observations, divided by the number of observations.

Scatter plot A graph consisting of a sequence of points meant to show the relationship between one variable plotted on the vertical, or Y, axis and another variable given on the horizontal, or X, axis.

Scenario analysis The analysis of 'what if' scenarios and the probability associated with each, used to arrive at a multifactor model of security returns.

Second generation duration Used in fixed-income analysis, a measure of duration where the relevant cash flows are discounted not by the yield to maturity of the instrument in question, but rather by the yields associated with zero coupon bonds that mature simultaneously with each cash flow.

Security market line The linear relationship between the measure of beta risk and expected return predicted by the capital asset pricing model.

Serial correlation The association between the prior period's observation and the subsequent period's observation. Positive serial correlation indicates the presence of trends while negative serial correlation indicates the presence of reversals.

Single-factor models Models of the return-generating process where returns on individual securities are related to each other only to the extent that all are related to a common, or *market*, index.

Skewed probability distributions
Distributions of the data where extreme
values on either side of the median are
more extensive on one side of the median
than on the other. Examples where the
upper tail of the distribution (values in
excess of the median) is far more
extensive than the lower tail, such as
day-to-day stock returns, are said to be
skewed to the right, or positively skewed.
Examples where the reverse is true are
said to be skewed to the left or negatively
skewed.

Specific risk   That part of an asset's risk
that is unique to the asset and thus can be
diversified away by combining the asset
in a large portfolio.

Spline smoothing   In data analysis a
technique used to fit a smooth curve to an
otherwise irregular scatter plot of points
in a graph. The technique involves fitting
a polynomial function to ranges of the
data in such a way that the fitted curves
join going from one range to the next and
have the same slopes and second
derivatives at such points.

Spreading strategy   The activity of
trading call or put options with different
exercise prices or expiration dates.

Standard deviation   A measure of
variability or volatility given
mathematically as the square root of
variance (see below) and measured in the
same units as the variable of interest.

Standard error   The standard deviation
of an estimate relative to the true or
underlying parameter value. The standard
error of the sample mean is given by the
square root of the quantity given by the
variance of the data expressed as a
fraction of the number of observations.

Student-*t* distribution   The theoretical
distribution of sample means and
regression coefficients used in hypothesis
testing situations. Where the so-called
degrees of freedom (number of

observations less the number of
parameters to be estimated) exceed 30,
the distribution may be approximated by
the well-known normal distribution.

Synthetic call   A position in cash, put
options, and the underlying security that
has cash flows that exactly match that of
a call option. As a consequence the
synthetic call should, absent arbitrage,
cost the same to establish as the
equivalent call option.

Systematic factors   Factors of variation
in asset returns that may not be
diversified away simply by holding a
sufficiently large and diversified portfolio.

Systematic risk   The component of an
asset's risk that is caused by exposure to
sources of risk that are common to many
assets, such as sensitivity to interest rates
or energy prices. Systematic risk cannot
be diversified away, although it can be
eliminated through hedging.

T

Tactical asset allocation   A valuation-
based asset allocation strategy usually
based on the presumption of mean
reversion. Tactical asset allocation
attempts to add value to a fund by
shifting away from an asset that appears
overvalued and toward an asset that
appears undervalued, according to some
notion of equilibrium or fair value.

Theoretical distribution   The
distribution of parameter estimates that
could be expected purely by chance if the
null hypothesis were true. This is used in
the context of hypothesis testing, where
one seeks to examine whether a sample
estimate is extreme relative to the value
specified by the null hypothesis.

Time-weighted rate of return   The
geometric (compounded) return measured
on the basis of periodic market valuations
of assets. An alternative to the dollar-

weighted return measure, it abstracts from cash flows; however, in principle it requires the valuations to be made at each cash flow. Approximations to this measure can be obtained by prorating cash flows to successive valuation points or computing internal rates of return between valuation points.

Total return A measure of return that includes not only income yield but also possibly unrealized capital gain (loss) over a specified holding period.

Treasury bills Fixed-income obligations of the U.S. government issued at a discount for terms to maturity not greater than one year. These instruments offer no coupons.

Trimmed standard deviation The standard deviation computed in such a way as to exclude extreme values, or outliers.

Truncated distribution Typically arising in the context of option analysis, a distribution (in this case the terminal value of the option) that obtains when some underlying distribution (price of the underlying asset) is transformed in such a way that values beyond a particular point (the exercise price) are replaced by values that occur precisely at that point. In the case of a call option the lower tail of the distribution of price is replaced by a "spike" at the exercise price.

t-statistic (or -value) The parameter estimate expressed as a fraction of the standard error. Under most circumstances this value will be approximately distributed as normal.

Two-sided (or -tailed) tests Hypothesis tests where the alternative to the maintained or null hypothesis states simply that the parameter of interest is different in value from that specified under the null hypothesis. It is sometimes said to be "easier" to reject a particular null hypothesis if the test is not two-sided

but is instead "one-sided," since the critical value of the appropriate test statistic is lower. This follows because such a test incorporates the additional information that deviations from the null hypothesis parameter value can only occur in one direction. Of course the value of such a test depends on the extent to which such information is in fact correct.

U

Unbiased estimators Estimators of underlying parameters constructed in such a way that in repeated experiments the average or expected value of the estimator would equal the true or underlying parameter value.

Universe comparisons A comparison of rates of return of a particular money manager as measured over a sequence of holding periods, with those achieved by other money managers with whom the manager competes. The returns are ranked, and the percentile ranks are compared.

Unsystematic component of return The source of return variability that may be diversified away by holding a sufficiently large and well-diversified portfolio. Synonymous with *idiosyncratic* component of return.

V

Vacancy rate In real estate analysis a concept that measures the total rentable space (in square feet) of a property minus leased space, expressed as a percent of total rentable space.

Variance A measure of volatility or dispersion of a variable, given as the average squared deviation of that variable from its mean value.

Variance ratio The variance estimated from multiple-period intervals divided by the variance estimated from single-period intervals, normalized by dividing this ratio by the number of periods in the interval used to estimate the variance in the numerator. If the observations from which the variance ratio is computed are random the variance should be close to one. A variance ratio greater than one indicates positive serial correlation while a variance ratio less than one indicates negative serial correlation.

Variation margin   In a futures transaction, funds that must be deposited with a broker on a daily basis to cover variation in the price of the contract.

W

Warrant   A call option where, upon exercise, the holder has the right to call the security from the original issuer of the underlying security.

Y

Yield curve   A plot of the yield to maturity of fixed-income securities as a function of the time to maturity. The yields are computed on the basis of prices (typically the mean of bid-ask spreads) quoted at a point in time.

Yield to maturity   The single discount rate that sets the present value of all cash flows from a fixed-income security equal to the current price. It thus represents the internal rate of return of a particular fixed-income investment.

Yield spread   The difference in yield of fixed-income securities with different attributes.

Z

Zero coupon bonds   Fixed-income securities that yield a cash flow only at maturity. Since there is no other income component they are referred to as "zero coupon."

INDEX